knowledge management in organizations

knowledge management in organizations

A CRITICAL INTRODUCTION

DONALD HISLOP

OXFORD
UNIVERSITY PRESS

OXFORD
UNIVERSITY PRESS

Great Clarendon Street, Oxford OX2 6DP

Oxford University Press is a department of the University of Oxford.
It furthers the University's objective of excellence in research, scholarship,
and education by publishing worldwide in

Oxford New York

Auckland Bangkok Buenos Aires Cape Town Chennai
Dar es Salaam Delhi Hong Kong Istanbul Karachi Kolkata
Kuala Lumpur Madrid Melbourne Mexico City Mumbai Nairobi
São Paulo Shanghai Taipei Tokyo Toronto

Oxford is a registered trade mark of Oxford University Press
in the UK and in certain other countries

Published in the United States
by Oxford University Press Inc., New York

British Library Cataloguing in Publication Data

Data available

Library of Congress Cataloging in Publication Data

Data available

ISBN 0-19-926206-3

1 3 5 7 9 10 8 6 4 2

Typeset by Newgen Imaging Systems (P) Ltd., Chennai, India
Printed in Great Britain by
Antony Rowe, Chippenham, Wiltshire

In Memory of William Millar Thom Hislop

■ ACKNOWLEDGEMENTS

Thanks are due to Catriona, Lorna, and Kara, the women in my life, whose love and support has been truly invaluable during the writing of this book.

Thanks are also due to Sue Newell, Harry Scarbrough, and Jacky Swan, for their agreement to let me use the research data from the project that I worked with them on. This ESRC funded project, which looked at the role of knowledge and networks in the implementation of IT-based information management systems in a number of European companies, is drawn on heavily here. Thanks are also due to Carolyn Axtell and Cara Brown who I worked with on a project on mobile teleworking, from which two of the case examples are drawn (the Gas Appliance Service Engineers case in Chapter 5 and the Cheshire Consultants case in Chapter 14).

Publisher's Acknowledgements

Grateful acknowledgement is made to the following sources for permission to reproduce material in this book.

Figure 1.1 (Fig. 1 in H. Scarbrough, and J. Swan (2001), 'Explaining the Diffusion of Knowledge Management: The Role of Fashion', *British Journal of Management*, 12: 2–12). By permission of Blackwell Publishing.

Figure 1.3 (Table 4.8 in M. Castells (1995), *The Rise of Network Society*, London: Blackwell). By permission of Blackwell Publishing.

Figure 7.1 (Fig. 2 in H. Tsoukas (1994), 'What is Management? An Outline of A Metatheory', *British Journal of Management*, 5/2: 289–301). By permission of Blackwell Publishing.

Figure 7.4 (Fig. 2.2 from C. Hales (1993), *Managing Through Organization*, London: Routledge). By permission of Thomson Publishing.

Figure 10.1 (Fig. 1 in C. Zietsma, M. Winn, O. Branzei, and I. Vertinsky (2002), 'The War of the Woods: Facilitators and Impediments of Organizational Learning Processes', *British Journal of Management*, 13: S61–74). By Permission of Blackwell Publishing.

Figure 11.3 (Fig. 22.1 in I. Nonaka, R. Toyama, and P. Byosiere (2001), 'A Theory of Organizational Knowledge Creation: Understanding the Dynamic Process of Creating Knowledge', in M. Dierkes, A. Bertoin Antal, J. Child, and I. Nonaka (eds.), *Handbook of Organizational Learning and Knowledge*, Oxford: Oxford University Press, 491–517). By permission of Oxford University Press.

Figure 12.1 (Fig. 1 in D. Cravens, N. Piercey, and S. Shipp (1996), 'New Organizational Forms for Competing in Highly Dynamic Environments. The Network Paradigm', *British Journal of Management*, 7/2:203–218). By permission of Blackwell Publishing.

Figure 13.3 (Fig. 2 from J. Birkinshaw, R. Nobel, and J. Ridderstale (2002), 'Knowledge as a Contingency Variable: Do the Characteristics of Knowledge Predict Organizational Structure?', *Organization Science*, 13/3: 274–89). By permission of INFORMS (Institute for Operations Research and Management Sciences), and authors.

Figure 15.1 (Fig. 2 from M. Alvesson and D. Karreman (2001). 'Odd Couple: Making Sense of the Curious Concept of Knowledge Management', *Journal of Management Studies*, 38/7: 995–1018). By permission of Blackwell Publishing.

Figure 15.2 (Fig. 1 from R. Suddaby and R. Greenwood (2001), 'Colonizing Knowledge: Commodification as a Dynamic of Jurisdictional Expansion in Professional Service Firms', *Human Relations*, 54/7: 933–53). By permission of Sage Publishing.

■ CONTENTS

List of figures   xi
List of tables   xii
Abbreviations   xiv

1 Why the current interest in knowledge management?   1

   Introduction   1
   Knowledge society and post-industrial society   3
   A critique of the knowledge society   6
   Themes and perspectives   8

PART 1
Epistemologies of knowledge   13

2 The objectivist perspective on knowledge   15

   What is knowledge?   15
   Objectivist perspectives on knowledge   16
   Typologies of knowledge   18
   An objectivist perspective on the sharing and management of knowledge   21
   Conclusion   25

3 The practice-based perspective on knowledge   27

   What is knowledge?   27
   Practice-based perspectives on knowledge   28
   Implications for the nature of the organizational knowledge base   35
   A practice-based perspective on the management and sharing of knowledge   36
   Conclusion   39

PART 2
Social and cultural issues related to managing and sharing knowledge   41

4 *'Why should I share my knowledge?'* what motivates people to
   share knowledge   43

   Introduction   43
   The 'first generation' knowledge management literature: the neglect of
      socio-cultural factors   44
   People's motivation and willingness to share knowledge   45
   What motivates people to share/hoard their knowledge?   49
   Conclusion   54

5   Communities of practice   57

    Introduction   57
    Defining and characterizing communities of practice   58
    Communities of practice and intra-community knowledge processes   63
    Managing communities of practice   65
    Disadvantages of communities of practice for knowledge processes   67
    Conclusion   70

6   Intercommunity, boundary-spanning knowledge processes   73

    Introduction   73
    The significance of intercommunity knowledge processes   73
    Characterizing intercommunity knowledge processes   75
    Identity, knowledge, trust, and social relations   80
    Facilitating/managing knowledge between communities   81
    Conclusion   84

7   Power, conflict, and knowledge processes   87

    Introduction   87
    Knowledge processes: the relevance of power and conflict   88
    Power and knowledge processes: theorizing the relationship   93
    Conclusion   101

8   Information and communication technologies and knowledge management   105

    Introduction   105
    Characterizing ICT-supported knowledge management processes   106
    Implementing ICT-based knowledge management systems   117
    Conclusion   119

9   Organizational culture, HRM policies, and knowledge management   123

    Introduction   123
    Linking HRM, business, and knowledge strategies   124
    Organizational culture and knowledge management   127
    HRM policies and practices   130
    Conclusion   136

PART 3
Learning, innovation, and knowledge management   139

10 Learning and knowledge management   141

    Introduction   141
    Characterizing learning   142
    The dynamics of organizational learning   143

The learning organization: emancipation of exploitation?   146
Conclusion   155

11 Innovation dynamics and knowledge processes   157

Introduction   157
Characterizing innovation processes   158
Innovation processes: power, knowledge, and networks   173
Conclusion   173

PART 4
Organizational contexts   177

12 Knowledge processes in network/virtual organizations   179

Introduction   179
N-V organizations and the 'problem' of dispersed knowledge   183
The social dynamics of cross-boundary knowledge processes in N-V organizations   186
ICT-mediated knowledge processes in N-V forms of organizing   192
Conclusion   194

13 Knowledge processes in global multinationals   197

Introduction   197
The structuring of multinationals and knowledge processes   198
A contingency perspective on structure   202
Knowledge sharing across sociocultural boundaries and business systems   208
Conclusion   212

14 Knowledge-intensive firms and knowledge workers   215

Introduction   215
The rise of the knowledge worker   216
Defining and characterizing knowledge workers and knowledge-intensive firms   217
A critique and a reformulation: all work as knowledge work and the concept of
    'knowledge intensiveness'   219
Knowledge work and ambiguity   222
Knowledge and knowledge processes in knowledge-intensive firms   223
The willingness of knowledge workers to participate in knowledge
    processes: conflicting interests?   225
Managing knowledge workers: balancing autonomy and control   228
Knowledge workers and the problem of retention   228
HRM policies to motivate knowledge workers   230
Conclusion   232

15 Conclusion   235

Introduction   235
Reflections on the knowledge management literature   236
Knowledge management: viable organizational practice or a contradiction
   in terms?   238
Understanding the dynamics and agents in the diffusion of knowledge on
   knowledge management   241
Conclusion   247

Bibliography   249
Index   265

■ LIST OF FIGURES

1.1.	The growth in knowledge management publications (from Scarbrough and Swan 2001)	3
1.2.	Characteristics of post-industrial society	4
1.3.	The changing character of the economy of the USA in the 20th century (from Castells 1995, table 4.8, 296)	5
2.1.	The conduit model of knowledge-sharing	22
5.1.	How communities of practice underpin knowledge processes	65
7.1.	The structure of capitalist employment relations (from Tsoukas 2000)	90
7.2.	Linking power, politics, and conflict	92
7.3.	The cyclical relationship between knowledge management processes and power	94
7.4.	The perceived legitimacy of, and response to attempts to use different power resources (from Hales 1993)	97
8.1.	Objectivist perspective on ICT roles in knowledge processes	107
9.1.	Linking business, knowledge, and HRM strategies	124
9.2.	Linking the psychological contract, organizational commitment, and organizational behaviours	131
10.1.	The modified Crossan et al. model (from Zietsma et al. 2002)	144
10.2.	Linking power and politics to learning	152
11.1.	Typical components in stage model of innovation	159
11.2.	Key characteristics in contemporary conceptualization of innovation processes	160
11.3.	The three layers of knowledge creation (from Nonaka et al. 2001)	164
12.1.	Classification of network forms of organizing (from Cravens et al. 1996)	182
13.1.	A centralized, hierarchical structure for multinationals	200
13.2.	A network structure for multinationals	201
13.3.	A typology of organizational knowledge bases (from Birkinshaw et al. 2002)	203
13.4.	Typical social relations within networks of different size	205
14.1.	Framework for conceptualizing work (from Frenkel et al. 1995)	220
15.1.	A typology of knowledge management strategies (from Alvesson and Karreman 2001)	236
15.2.	Suddaby and Greenwood's cycle of knowledge production and consumption	243

■ LIST OF TABLES

1.1.	Themes in the knowledge society literature	2
1.2.	Chapters where personal case study examples are utilized	11
2.	Competing epistemologies	14
2.1.	The objectivist character of knowledge	17
2.2.	The characteristics of tacit and explicit knowledge	19
2.3.	Generic knowledge types (adapted from Spender 1996)	20
2.4.	An objectivist perspective on knowledge management	23
2.5.	Priorities of ongoing knowledge management projects (adapted from Chart 2, Ruggles 1998, 83)	24
3.1.	Objectivist and practice-based epistemologies of knowledge	27
3.2.	Theoretical perspective related to the practice-based perspective	28
3.3.	Practice-based characteristics of knowledge	29
3.4.	Challenging dichotomies	30
3.5.	A practice-based perspective on knowledge management	37
4.	Obstacles to the success of knowledge management initiatives	42
4.1.	Thematic focus of early knowledge management literature (adapted from Scarbrough and Swan 2001, Table 2, 8)	44
4.2.	Factors making human motivation important to organizational knowledge processes	45
4.3.	Factors affecting people's willingness to share knowledge	50
5.1.	Difference between a CoP and formal work groups	58
5.2.	Generic characteristics of communities of practice	60
5.3.	Knowledge-related benefits of CoPs	64
6.1.	Factors underpinning effective knowledge-sharing (adapted from Hansen 1999)	75
6.2.	Factors making intercommunity knowledge processes difficult	76
6.3.	Knowledge-related factors adversely affecting intercommunity knowledge processes	77
6.4.	Typologies of trust	81
7.1.	Weberian-based types of action/rationality	91
7.2.	Properties of knowledge that can make it a power resource	95
7.3.	Power resources and modes of influence (adapted from Hales 1993)	95
8.1.	ICT applications relevant to knowledge management roles	108
8.2.	Criticisms of the objectivist perspective on knowledge	110
8.3.	Characteristics of various communication mediums	113
8.4.	Trust facilitating behaviours and actions (adapted from 4, Jarvenpaa and Leidner 1999, 807)	117
9.1.	Attitudes and behaviours relevant to knowledge management initiatives	123
9.2.	Codification and personalization knowledge strategies (from Hansen et al. 1999)	125
9.3.	Hunter et al. (2002)'s four knowledge strategies	126

9.4. Linking knowledge management initiatives to organizational culture
(from McDermott and O'Dell 2001) 128

9.5. Corporate curriculum and knowledge productivity (Garvey and
Williamson 2002) 134

10.1. Typologies of learning 142

10.2. Characteristics of learning process in Crossan–Zietsma model 145

10.3. The learning company framework of Pedler et al. (1997) 148

10.4. Factors affecting learning in organizations 156

11.1. Nonaka et al.'s modes of knowledge creation and type of ba
(from Nonaka et al. 2001) 165

11.2. Forms of collaboration 168

11.3. Mechanisms for enhancing organizational absorptive capacity
(adapted from Leonard Barton 1995) 169

11.4. Orlikowski's boundary-spanning practices 172

12. The core knowledge issues related to organizational types 178

12.1. Character and articulated advantages of N-V organizational structures 181

12.2. Factors inhibiting the development of 'mutual knowledge' in
ICT-mediated dispersed work contexts (adapted from Cramton 2001) 184

12.3. Factors affecting knowledge-sharing/searching attitudes in virtual work
groups (adapted from Ardichvili et al. 2003) 187

12.4. Factors affecting the character of involvement between partners in a
collaborative network (adapted from Hardy et al. 2003) 189

13.1. Knowledge-related benefits and disadvantages of cohesive networks
and networks with structural holes 206

13.2. Key institutional dimensions shaping the character of business systems 211

14.1. Frenkel et al.'s three dimensional conceptualization of work (from
Frenkel et al. 1995) 219

14.2. The ambiguities inherent to knowledge work (from Alvesson 2001) 221

14.3. Types of knowledge used by knowledge workers (from Empson 2001) 224

14.4. Type of loyalty and strategies for developing them (based on Alvesson 2000) 229

15.1. Problems with conceptions of knowledge in the 'popular' knowledge
management literature (from Alvesson and Karreman 2001) 237

15.2. Outcomes and objectives of organizational knowledge processes 240

■ ABBREVIATIONS

CoP	Community of Practice
HRM	Human Resource Management
ICTs	Information and Communication Technologies
KM	Knowledge Management
N-V Organization	Network-Virtual Organization
R&D	Research and Development

1

Why the current interest in knowledge management?

Introduction

Knowledge is at the heart of much of today's global economy, and managing knowledge has become vital to companies' success. (Kluge et al. 2001, 4)

The knowledge economy is not as yet all-conquering, but it is well on the way to being so . . . it marks a major transition in the nature of economic activity. Information technology, plus communications technology, are the enabling media of the new economy, but its agents are knowledge workers. . . . The know how of such workers is the most valuable property firms have. (Giddens 2000, 69)

This transformation from a world largely dominated by physical resources, to a world dominated by knowledge, implies a shift in the locus of economic power as profound as that which occurred at the time of the industrial revolution. (Burton-Jones 1999, 3)

*The basic economic resource . . . is no longer capital, nor natural resources . . . , nor 'labour'. . . . **It is and will be knowledge**.* (Drucker 1993, 7 emphasis in original)

We are witnessing a change in the nature of jobs. Muscle jobs are disappearing; finger and brain jobs are growing or, to put it more formally, labour-based industries have been displaced by skill-based industries, and these in turn will have to be replaced by knowledge-based industries. (Handy 1984, 4)

*Knowledge is a poorly understood and thus undervalued **economic** resource.* (Burton-Jones 1999, 5 emphasis added)

The real question is how can a company systematically exploit all dimensions of knowledge and fully utilize them to improve revenues, profits and growth. (Kluge et al. 2001, 190)

How often have you read/heard statements like these in the last few years? Innumerable times, probably. These statements illustrate a number of key themes that have come to

Table 1.1. Themes in the knowledge society literature

Key Themes
Knowledge is of central importance to advanced economies
Knowledge is key to organizational performance
Organizations & work have become more knowledge intensive

prominence during the course of the 1990s (Table 1.1). Firstly, knowledge is now the most important and valuable resource in the advanced industrial economies. Secondly, knowledge represents the most important economic asset that business organizations possess, and that it is the prime determinant of their innovativeness and profitability. Finally, the nature of paid employment and business organizations is changing, with an enormous growth in the number of knowledge workers, and knowledge-intensive organizations. On the basis of such assumptions, the contemporary explosion of interest in knowledge management can be understood.

The sentiments embodied in the introductory statements have been so often repeated that they have almost taken on the status of canonical statements, unquestionable truths. A general, implicit assumption in the vast majority of articles and books that express these sentiments is that their validity is so obvious that providing empirical evidence to support them is not deemed necessary. Thus, for example, Burton-Jones (1999) in the introduction to his book *Knowledge Capitalism* provides only the scantiest of evidence to support the assertion that we now live in a knowledge-based society, and that knowledge is the most important economic asset.

However, what is the empirical substance to these claims? Are they really so unquestionably true? Can empirical evidence be mobilized which challenges them? This chapter takes a critical perspective to these assertions, and shows that, in a number of ways, these claims can be challenged. This reflects the general philosophy of the book, which examines knowledge issues from a critical perspective, examining assumptions that are typically unquestioned in the knowledge management literature.

The extent to which knowledge management has become a topic of interest can be easily illustrated. Firstly, surveys show that knowledge management is a topic that an enormous number of business organizations have engaged with. Secondly, the late 1990s witnessed an exponential increase in the number of academic articles and books that deal with knowledge management issues (see Figure 1.1). Finally, there is also evidence that government policy-makers have engaged with this topic. Thus, a key element of 'New' Labour's economic and social vision for the future of the UK draws on the idea of the information/knowledge society. Many other national governments also have social and educational policies that are similarly predicated in this future vision (Thompson et al. 2001, 924; MacKeogh 2001).

To answer the question raised by the title of the chapter, why knowledge and knowledge management are currently regarded as so important, it is necessary to briefly examine the way work and society have been evolving and the way these changes have been

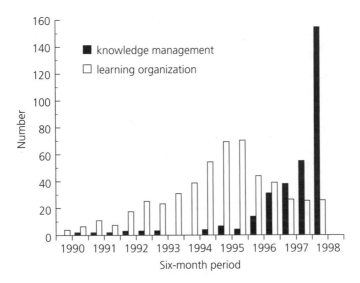

Fig. 1.1. The growth in knowledge management publications (from scarbrough and swan 2001)

theorized. This will involve elaborating (and then criticizing) Daniel Bell's early 1970s future vision of a 'post industrial society'. This is because either explicitly, or implicitly, this typically provides the theoretical foundation for much of the knowledge management literature.

This opening chapter has two primary functions. Firstly, it provides a general context to the growth of interest in knowledge management and, secondly, it provides an introduction to the themes examined in the book. The next section outlines the post-industrial society thesis, where the resonances with the contemporary knowledge management literature will become apparent. A critique of post-industrial society is then developed, where a number of its primary arguments are challenged. Finally, the chapter concludes by outlining the general aims of the book, drawing out the key themes that it will engage with, and the way they will be examined.

Knowledge society and post-industrial society

The knowledge management literature is typically based on an analysis which suggests that since approximately the mid-1970s, economies and society in general have become more information- and knowledge-intensive, with information/knowledge-intensive industries replacing manufacturing industry as the key wealth generators (see Neef 1999, for example). Arguably, the main source of inspiration for this vision was, and is, Daniel Bell's seminal book *The Coming of Post-Industrial Society*, which was first published in 1973. While earlier writers, notably Machlup (1962), developed a similar analysis, Bell's work has provided the main inspiration for contemporary writers in the area of knowledge management. As a consequence, Bell's post-industrial society and contemporary

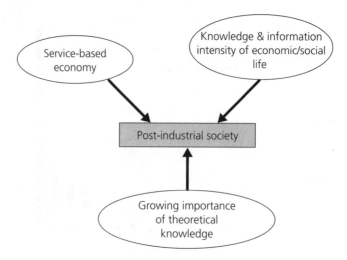

Fig. 1.2. Characteristics of post-industrial society

conceptualizations of knowledge society bear more than a passing resemblance to each other. Burton-Jones (1999, 4), for example, explicitly links his knowledge capitalism model to Bell's thesis. Further, Bell himself has, over time, used the terms knowledge and information societies interchangeably with the post-industrial society concept (Webster 1996).

Bell's analysis is based on a typology of societies characterized by their predominant mode of employment (Webster 1996). Thus, industrial society is characterized by an emphasis on manufacturing and fabrication: the building of things. In post-industrial societies, however, which are argued to evolve out of industrial societies, the service sector has replaced the manufacturing sector as the biggest source of employment. One crucial characteristic of Bell's post-industrial society is that knowledge and information play a much more significant role in economic and social life than during industrial society, as work in the service sector is argued to be significantly more information- and knowledge-intensive than industrial work. (see Fig. 1.2)

However, Bell suggests that not only has there been a quantitative increase in the role and importance of knowledge and information, but there has also been a qualitative change in the type of knowledge that is most important. In a post-industrial society, theoretical knowledge has become the most important type of knowledge. Theoretical knowledge represents abstract knowledge and principles, which can be codified, or at least embedded in systems of rules and frameworks for action. This is to a large extent because for Bell, in post-industrial societies professional service work is of central importance, and this type of work typically involves the development, use and application of abstract, theoretical knowledge more than manual work ever did. This relates not just to technical knowledge, such as may be used in R&D processes, but also encompasses a large and growing diversity of jobs which increasingly require the application and use of such knowledge—for example, formulation of government policy, architecture, medicine, software design, etc.

Post-industrial society

A society where service and knowledge-based goods/services have replaced industrial, manufactured goods as the main wealth generators.

An important element of Bell's analysis is that post-industrial societies represent an advancement on industrial societies, as in general more wealth will be generated, and workers individually will have better, more fulfilling jobs. In fact, there is a tendency towards utopianism in aspects of Bell's vision, as he argues that unpleasant, repetitive jobs will decline in number significantly; social inequality will reduce; (all) individuals will have increased amounts of disposable income to spend on personal services; society will be able to better plan for itself; and that social relations will become less individualistic and provide greater scope for community development and collective support.

What empirical evidence exists to support this characterization of contemporary society? Typically, statistical evidence is mobilized to show the increasing importance of service work, and the simultaneous decline of manufacturing employment. Thus, statistics on the US economy in the mid-1970s were argued to show that 46 per cent of it's economic output was from the information sector, and 47 per cent of the total workforce was employed in this sector (Kumar 1995). Castells (1995), in articulating his vision of a network/information society mobilized an impressive amount of evidence from a wide range of economies which showed the long-term, historical shift from industry to services, and from goods handling to information handling work (Figure 1.3).

Empirical evidence on the growing skill intensity of much work also supports Bell's thesis. Zuboff (1988) suggested that advances in computer technology had the potential to make work more knowledge- and skill-intensive, through the potential for problem solving, and abstraction these technologies provide workers. This perspective is supported by research conducted by Gallie et al. (1998) in the UK in the mid-1990s, where almost 65 per cent of workers surveyed reported experiencing an increase in the skill levels of their jobs. Further evidence also reinforces these conclusions (Felstead et al. 2000; NSTF 2000).

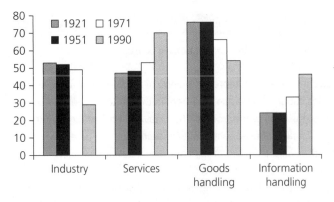

Fig. 1.3. The changing character of the economy of the USA in the 20th century (from Castells 1995, table 4.8, 296)

However, as will be seen in the following section, the extent of this trajectory of upskilling is questioned by a number of writers.

Overall therefore, aggregate statistical evidence appears to support the knowledge society/post-industrial society thesis, with Bell's analysis of the increasingly important role of information and knowledge in all aspects of social and economic life being apparently vindicated. Thus, one answer to the question, why is knowledge so important, is that there have been fundamental changes in the nature of economic and social life which have seen its importance grow significantly. However, Bell's thesis has been the subject of a sustained, and not insignificant critique, much of which has relevance to the knowledge society vision developed by contemporary writers on knowledge management. The following section changes focus to consider these criticisms.

A critique of the knowledge society

One of the main criticisms of the arguments made by knowledge society, or post-industrial society theorists, is that they typically conflate knowledge work with service sector jobs. Thus, as outlined, aggregate statistics on the size of service sector employment is usually used to indicate the transition to a knowledge society (see Figure 1.3). However, not all service sector work can be classified as knowledge work, as the service sector is a residual employment category for all types of work which are neither manufacturing nor agricultural. Thus the service sector encompasses an enormously heterogeneous range of job types, including consultants and cleaners, marketing executives and milkmen (and women), as well as scientists and security guards. Thus, the service sector does not represent a coherent and uniform category of employment. While some service sector work such as consultancy, research, etc. can be classified as being knowledge-intensive, other types of service work, such as security, office cleaning, fast food restaurant work is low skilled, repetitive, and routine (Thompson et al. 2001). Therefore to suggest that all service sector employment is knowledge-intensive work does not acknowledge the reality of much service sector work.

ILLUSTRATING THE ISSUES

The knowledgeability of call centre work

In the late 1990s call centre work represented one of the largest growing employment sectors in the UK. Predictions suggested that employment in the sector of the UK economy could account for 2.3 per cent of the total workforce by 2003. Taylor and Bain argue that call centre work is defined by the 'integration of telephone and VDU technologies', where workers receive inbound, or make outbound telephone calls. In their conclusion, Taylor and Bain summarize the character of the call centre labour process as follows.

'the typical call centre operator is young, female and works in a large, open plan office or fabricated building, which may well justify the white-collar factory description. Although probably full-time, she is increasingly likely to be a part-time permanent employee, working complex shift patterns which correspond to the peaks of customer demand. Promotion prospects and career advancement are limited so that the attraction of better pay and conditions in another call centre may prove irresistible. In all probability, work consists of an uninterrupted and endless sequence of similar conversations with customers she never meets. She has to concentrate hard on what is being said, jump from page to page on a screen, making sure that the details entered are accurate and that she has said the right things in a pleasant manner. The conversation ends and as she tidies up the loose ends there is another voice in her headset. The pressure is intense because she knows that her work is being measured, her speech monitored, and it often leaves her mentally, physically and emotionally exhausted.' (115)

Taylor and Bain (1999) ' "An Assembly Line in the Head": Work and Employment Relations in the call centre' *Industrial Relations Journal*, 30/2: 101–17.

Stop and think

Does the fact that call centre employment involves the use of computers, and a significant amount of customer interaction, mean that it is more knowledge-intensive than routine manufacturing work?

Secondly, empirical evidence for the claim that employment growth in knowledge-intensive occupations has occurred is at best ambiguous. For example, taking professional work as a proxy for knowledge work, Elias and Gregory (1994) show that there was a growth in professional occupational categories in the UK during the 1990s. However, this growth wasn't enormous, and further by 1990 professional occupations still only accounted for approximately 20 per cent of all employment (this figure is identical to the estimate made by Rifkin (2000, 174) for the USA in the mid-1990s). Thompson et al. (2001) also argue that employment growth has been equally significant in more routine, and low-skilled occupations. Thus, claims that there has been a massive expansion in knowledge work, and that knowledge work represents the largest area of employment can be questioned as being somewhat exaggerated.

Another aspect of the knowledge society thesis that has been criticized is the privileging of theoretical knowledge over other types of knowledge (typically, tacit knowledge and skills). An explicit example of this is Frenkel et al.'s analysis of knowledge work (1995). In their analysis the knowledge intensity of any job can be measured on three dimensions, one of which is the type of knowledge used. For Frenkel et al., theoretical knowledge is used as a measure of knowledge intensity, while what they call 'contextual' knowledge is not. However, this risks losing sight of the fact that, to some extent, all work is knowledgeable work (Knights et al. 1993, 976), involving the use of significant amounts of tacit knowledge (Manwaring and Wood 1985; Kusterer 1978). This therefore leads to disputes and difficulties in defining what constitutes knowledge work, which types of workers should be classified as knowledge workers, and leads to the knowledge required in routine, manual work being underestimated (see Chapter 14 for this debate).

Questions have also been raised regarding the way knowledge was conceptualized by Bell. His conception of theoretical knowledge as codifiable and objective draws on classical images of scientific knowledge. However, much contemporary analysis views knowledge as having substantially different characteristics, being partial, tacit, subjective, and context-dependent (see Chapters 2 and 3 for these debates).

While aspects of the analytical frameworks developed by post-industrial society and knowledge society theorists can be criticized and challenged, this does not mean that society and economies have remained unchanged, or that every aspect of these analyses is unfounded. Thus, it is undeniable that the last quarter of the twentieth century was a period of profound change. For the advanced, industrial economies there was not only a significant change in the type of products and services produced, and the nature of work itself, but the role of information and knowledge, in many aspects of social and economic life, also increased substantially. However, it is arguably going too far to suggest that these changes represent a fundamental rupture, witnessing the birth of a new type of society. This is because while much change has occurred, there have also been significant elements of continuity—organizations remain driven by the same imperatives of accumulation, and the general social relations of capitalism remains unchanged. Thus, Kumar (1995, p. 31) suggests, 'capitalist industrialism has not been transcended, but simply extended, deepened and perfected.'

Thus to challenge Bell's conceptualization of a post-industrial society as representing a fundamental rupture with existing social and economic structures is not to suggest that there has been no change. Equally, such critiques cannot be used to conclude that knowledge is not important to contemporary business organizations.

Themes and perspectives

This final section of the first chapter articulates the general philosophy of this book, as well as outlining the themes and issues examined in each chapter.

Critical perspectives

This is not intended to be a prescriptive book, providing a toolkit on how to manage knowledge for improved organizational performance. There are plenty of books already in existence that meet this need. The primary objective of the book is to provide a critical review and analysis of the key themes that underpin the subject of knowledge management in organizations. Thus, its primary purpose is to provide readers with a rich understanding of the debates and diversity of perspectives that exist through drilling down below the surface assumptions that go unquestioned in too much knowledge management literature. This will allow an in-depth exploration of the issues underlying the theme of knowledge management. Thus, it should make it easier for students to understand what knowledge in organizations is, as well as the complex dynamics of organizational knowledge processes.

While the critique just outlined undermined the general knowledge society thesis, this does not make studying the subject of knowledge in organizations redundant and irrelevant. In fact, it makes such a task even more important! This is because taking a critical stance involves going beyond the taken-for-granted assumptions that remain unexplored in the more prescriptive knowledge management literature. Undertaking such an analysis reveals fundamental, and important questions, which are likely to be of perennial interest, such as what is knowledge? Can it be controlled? Can it be codified? What are the difficulties involved in sharing it? The book therefore engages with the philosophical and theoretical academic literature on the subject of knowledge in organizations, and does justice to the complexity of the issues raised, by examining how they are likely to affect processes of knowledge use and development in organizations. A critical perspective also has the advantage of exploring issues which are ignored or downplayed by the more prescriptive literature, such as how conflict, power, and politics affect the way knowledge is used in organizations.

The importance of examining the subject from a critical perspective is made more important by the fact that critical perspectives have been drowned out in the enormous flood of literature on knowledge management that has been published since the mid-1990s. Swan and Scarbrough (2001), looking back on a special issue of the *Journal of Management Studies* from 1993 (Vol. 30, no. 6) on, 'Knowledge Workers and Contemporary Organizations' lament that too much writing has lost the criticality that embodied much of the early writing on the subject. This textbook attempts to deal with this by rediscovering these critical perspectives.

Key themes

The description and critique of the knowledge society thesis raises a number of important themes, which the book will explore. One of the fundamental questions of interest is obviously, what do we mean by the term 'knowledge'? This question will be explored in detail in Chapters 2 and 3. These chapters present two different and contrasting perspectives on what knowledge is, which reflects the status of the debate in the academic literature. As will be seen in subsequent chapters, these perspectives have quite different implications with regard to how knowledge is managed, produced, and shared.

Chapter 4 then moves on to the question of how knowledge processes in organizations are intimately linked to the topic of human motivation. The chapter challenges the assumption that people are likely to be willing to share their knowledge, and explores why this is the case. This chapter utilizes the now copious literature that argues for a greater sensitivity to human and social factors.

Chapters 5 and 6 look at the dynamics of knowledge-sharing and knowledge generation in two distinctive types of group situation. These chapters both illustrate different aspects of the collective and shared nature of much organizational knowledge. Chapter 5 uses the community of practice concept to consider the dynamics of knowledge sharing and knowledge production in a homogeneous group context, where the people working together have well-established social relations, a significant degree of common knowledge, and a sense of collective identity. Chapter 5 closes by examining the potential dark side of communities of practice, which has been relatively unexplored in the communities of practice literature. Chapter 6 considers knowledge processes in heterogeneous group contexts where there are limited social relations, a limited degree of common knowledge, and a limited sense of collective identity (for example in international project teams). This chapter shows how the dynamics of knowledge sharing and production in such a context are significantly different from those that are typical within communities of practice.

Chapter 7 builds from some of the issues touched on in Chapter 4: how knowledge processes are shaped by the conflict and politics that are an inherent part of organizational life. In general, the chapter considers how and why knowledge and power are inextricably linked, and specifically examines how conflicts in the development and use of knowledge can also be linked to the fundamental character of the employment relationship.

One of the most heated debates in the knowledge management literature relates to the role that information technology can play in processes of knowledge management, which range from perspectives which suggest that IT can play a crucial role, to diametrically opposed perspectives which argue that the nature of knowledge makes it impossible to share knowledge electronically. In examining this debate Chapter 8 links back to issues of epistemology, and definitions of what knowledge is, that are discussed in Chapters 2 and 3.

Chapter 9 links closely with the theme of human motivation, as it examines the way that organizations have, and can attempt to shape, the knowledge behaviours of their staff through developing specific HRM policies and practices, or culture management exercises.

Chapters 10 and 11 examine the subject of learning and knowledge acquisition. Chapter 10 examines the general concept of the learning organization, which became popularized through the 1990s. The chapter examines the contrasting viewpoints on the learning organization that have emerged, specifically engaging with the debate on whether the learning organization increases opportunities for self-development or simply represents a new method of control and exploitation. Chapter 11 examines learning and knowledge acquisition during formal processes of innovation and R&D. This chapter shows how these processes are shaped by the tacit and context-dependent nature of knowledge, as well as the role played by the broader institutional context.

Chapters 12, 13, and 14 shift from being thematically focused to examining the character and dynamics of knowledge sharing in three different types of organizational context: knowledge-intensive firms, global multinationals, and virtual/network organizations. The reasons for examining these organizational contexts are that they link closely to the themes and issues examined in the book, and also because they all represent important contemporary organizational forms. The book closes in Chapter 15 by engaging with the not insignificant question of whether knowledge management represents a passing management fad.

Throughout the book extensive use is made of case study examples to illustrate the issues discussed. These examples are dawn from two primary sources. Firstly, use is made of the vast body of writing on knowledge management, much of which contains empirical evidence on organizational experiences with knowledge management initiatives. Secondly, use is also made of empirical evidence on seven case study companies from a range of European countries that I was involved in researching (see Acknowledgements for the details of these projects). Most of these companies are utilized in more than one example. Thus, to provide an overview of where each company is used, this information is summarized in Table 1.2.

Table 1.2. Chapters where personal case study examples are utilized

Company name	Company type	Chapters where used
Swed-Truck	Swedish-based fork lift truck company	• Chapter 3: autonomous business units and the fragmented nature of the organizational knowledge base. • Chapter 3: an example of a successful knowledge management process based in a practice-based perspective.
Castco	UK-based casting and injection moulding company	• Chapter 2: stories as a form of collective knowledge. • Chapter 9: linking business and knowledge management strategies.
Pharma-co	Specialist, UK-based, international pharma-ceutical corporation	• Chapter 3: the contested nature of 'truth claims'. • Chapter 8: the dynamics of ICT mediated communication processes.
UK-Pension	UK pension and life assurance company	• Chapter 5: communities of practice and the structuring of work • Chapter 6: boundary objects facilitating inter-community interactions.
Diamond Pension	UK pension and life assurance company	• Chapter 11: network-based collaboration in system development work.
France-co	French-based company which designs and manufactures mechanical connectors	• Chapter 6: the difficulties of knowledge-sharing between communities of practice due to epistemic differences. • Chapter 7: knowledge-hoarding as a political strategy.
Globalbank	Dutch-based, international bank	• Chapter 2: an example of a successful knowledge management initiative which utilized and objectivist perspective on knowledge. • Chapter 6: the difficulties of inter-community knowledge-sharing due to identity differences. • Chapter 8: the problems with technologically centred knowledge management initiatives.

REVIEW QUESTIONS

1 Are you, or have you been a knowledge worker? Reflect on any work experience you have had. What type of knowledge was important (contextual, skill-based knowledge, or abstract, theoretical knowledge?). Could the jobs you have done be described as knowledge-intensive? Do they fit with the classical image of knowledge-intensive jobs? (such as consultancy, R&D work . . .).

2 What is your position on the knowledge society debate? Do the contemporary changes in economic and social life represent a fundamentally different society, deserving the 'post' prefix?

3 What uses are there for knowledge other than organizational profit? Draw up a list of uses to which knowledge in organizations could be put. For example, to protect or advance the

interests of a particular subgroup. How many examples can you think of? Having done this, reflect on the extent to which there is potential for the objectives of these uses to be in conflict with the organizational goal of using knowledge for the primary purpose of improving organizational performance.

FURTHER READING

- Alan Burton Jones (1999). *Knowledge Capitalism*. Oxford: Oxford University Press.
  This represents a good example of a text clearly arguing in favour of the knowledge society thesis and examining the implications of it for organizations and managers.

- J. Swan and H. Scarbrough (2001). 'Editorial: Knowledge Management: Concepts and Controversies', *Journal of Management Studies*, 38/7: 913–21.
  Provides an interesting analysis on how the knowledge management literature has evolved since the early 1990s.

- H. Scarbrough and J. Swan (2001). 'Explaining the Diffusion of Knowledge Management', *British Journal of Management*, 12: 3–12.
  Examines the growth of interest in knowledge management from the point of view of the Fads and Fashions literature.

- F. Webster (1996). *Theories of the Information Society* (particularly ch. 3). London: Routledge.
  Provides a comprehensive description and critique of Bell's post-industrial society thesis.

Epistemologies of knowledge

Chapter 1 has introduced the idea that increasingly knowledge is seen as representing the most important asset organizations possess, and that society has witnessed a significant increase in both the number of knowledge workers, and knowledge-intensive organizations. This begs the most fundamental of questions: what is knowledge? As you may expect, however, answering it is by no means simple. This is to a large extent because in the contemporary literature on knowledge there are an enormous diversity of definitions, and from the way knowledge is described by different writers it is obvious that it is conceptualized in hugely divergent ways.

This section of the book explores these competing conceptualizations, in an attempt to do justice to this debate. Rather than suggest that there is one single 'true' definition of what knowledge is, the book reflects the fragmented nature of the contemporary debate on this topic and presents the differing definitions and descriptions. As will be seen, the competing conceptualizations examined are based on fundamentally different epistemologies.

 Epistemology

Philosophy addressing the nature of knowledge. Concerned with questions such as: is knowledge objective and measurable? Can knowledge be acquired or is it experienced? What is regarded as valid knowledge, and why?

Just as Burrell and Morgan (1979) argued that there are two broad perspectives in the social sciences with regard to epistemology: the positivist and anti-positivist,[1] there are two broad epistemological camps in the contemporary debate on the nature of knowledge. These two (competing?) perspectives have been labelled in a range of ways by different authors (see Table 2). On the one side, there is what will be called the objectivist perspective, while on the other side, with a radically different viewpoint, is what will be called the practice-based perspective on knowledge. Chapters 2 and 3 examine these perspectives in turn, examining not only how they conceptualize knowledge, but also how the management and sharing of knowledge is characterized, based on their different assumptions about knowledge. Therefore, to best understand these

[1] For a definition of Positivism, see Ch. 2.

Table 2. Competing epistemologies

Author	Objectivist perspective	Practice-based perspective
Werr and Stjernberg (2003)	Knowledge as theory	Knowledge as practice
Empson (2001)	Knowledge as an asset	Knowing as a process
Cook and Brown (1999)	Epistemology of possession	Epistemology of practice
McAdam and McCreedy (2000)	'Knowledge as truth'	Knowledge as socially constructed
Scarbrough (1998)	'Content' theory of knowledge	'Relational' view of knowledge

competing perspectives, and to allow an effective comparison of their differences, it is useful to read these chapters in parallel, and consider them as being two halves of a debate.

While the practice-based perspective, as will be seen, is founded on a critique of the objectivist perspective, the objectivist perspective has by no means been abandoned. In terms of contemporary knowledge management practice and analysis there is evidence that both perspectives are still widely used. This therefore increases the utility of having an understanding of both perspectives, and is why the book has been structured to examine them separately.

These represent probably the most difficult chapters to read, as they are dealing with relatively abstract ideas. However, they provide a useful foundation to the issues addressed in the remainder of the book. Therefore a thorough grasp of these issues should facilitate a deeper understanding of what follows.

2

The objectivist perspective on knowledge

What is knowledge?

What is knowledge represents one of the most fundamental questions that humanity has grappled with, and has occupied the minds of philosophers for centuries. Thus while the contemporary explosion of interest in knowledge management has reignited interest in the topic, it is by no means a new or original question. Furthermore, even in contemporary times, interest in the topic of knowledge stems from more than the growth of interest in knowledge management. For example, post-modern philosophy has raised questions about the assumed objectivity of knowledge, and in the process has sparked an enormous debate.

More relevant to the purposes of this book than engaging with historical and philosophical analyses of how definitions of knowledge have changed and evolved, is to engage with and describe contemporary conceptualizations of knowledge with the objective of reflecting on their utility and value. Therefore, after quickly distinguishing between data, information, and knowledge, the rest of this chapter concentrates on examining the objectivist epistemology of knowledge, as it provides the basis to a substantial proportion of the contemporary knowledge management literature.

A useful way of arriving at a definition of what knowledge is can be achieved by differentiating it from what it is not. One of the most common distinctions in the contemporary knowledge literature is between knowledge, information, and data. *Data* can be defined as raw number, images, words, sounds which are derived from observation or measurement. For example, data could be the raw numbers, and replies from a marketing survey of a company's clients, aimed at establishing their changing preferences. *Information*, in comparison, represents data arranged in a meaningful pattern, data where some intellectual input has been added. For example, where the raw data from the marketing survey has been analysed using a specific statistical technique, to produce some structured results.

Finally, *knowledge* can be understood to emerge from the application, analysis, and productive use of data and/or information. In other words, knowledge can be seen as data or information with a further layer of intellectual analysis added, where it is interpreted, meaning is attached, and is structured and linked with existing systems of beliefs and bodies of knowledge. Knowledge therefore provides the means to analyse and understand data/information, provides beliefs about the causality of events/actions, and provides the basis to guide meaningful action/thought. Thus, for example, knowledge is used and developed when the analysis of the statistical results from the marketing survey are done. This may be where the results are compared and contrasted with previous surveys, where particular causal relations and systems of meaning are inferred (for example, maybe those between 18 and 25 years of age have quite specific attitudes towards consumption), and where the analysis of the results is used to justify a specific course of action (for example, focus the marketing of the product on the 18–25 age category).

 Data • Information • Knowledge

Data Raw images, numbers, words, sounds etc., which result from observation or measurement.

Information Data arranged or organized into a meaningful pattern

Knowledge Means to analyse/understand information/data, belief about causality of events/actions, and provides the basis to guide meaningful action and thought.

Following the above definitions, one common way that data, information, and knowledge are interrelated is in a hierarchical structure, where the relationship is primarily unidirectional, with data supporting the generation of information, which is in turn used to generate knowledge. However, the interrelationship between these elements is much more complicated than this. While data and information can provide the building blocks of knowledge, equally knowledge can be used to generate data and information, therefore the relationship between them is dynamic and interactive, rather than simply unidirectional. Further, the knowledge we possess shapes the type of information/data we collect, and the way it is analysed. Thus people with different knowledge bases may develop different interpretations of the significance of the same events/results. Examples of such situations include: competing political parties analysing, post-hoc, election results; differing interpretations of why a new product release did not generate anticipated revenue levels; different interpretations of the results of a marketing survey.

Stop and think

Try and think of an organizational situation you have been in where different people have developed divergent interpretations of specific events, actions, or circumstances? What was the basis of these differences? Can these differences be partly or wholly attributed to the different knowledge bases, and values of the relevant individuals?

Objectivist perspectives on knowledge

While the previous section established a broad, and general definition of knowledge, this definition said little about what knowledge is actually like, and what its characteristic properties are. To do this it is necessary to examine in detail different epistemological

Table 2.1. The objectivist character of knowledge

Character of knowledge from an objectivist epistemology

---

1. Knowledge is an entity/object
2. Based on a positivistic philosophy: knowledge regarded as objective 'facts'
3. Explicit knowledge (objective) privileged over tacit knowledge (subjective)
4. Knowledge is derived from an intellectual process

---

perspectives on knowledge. The rest of this chapter describes the objectivist epistemology of knowledge (see Table 2.1), outlining both the way it characterizes knowledge, and how it conceptualizes the sharing of knowledge. Cook and Brown (1999) refer to this perspective as the *'epistemology of possession'* as knowledge is regarded as an entity that people or groups possess.

The entitative character of knowledge represents its primary characteristic from the objectivist perspective. Knowledge is regarded as an entity/commodity that people possess, but which can exist independently of people in a codifiable form. Such knowledge can exist in a number of forms including documents, diagrams, computer systems, or be embedded in physical artefacts such as machinery or tools. Thus, for example, a text-based manual of computer-operating procedures, whether in the form of a document, CD, or web page, represents a form of explicit knowledge. From the objectivist perspective, the idea that explicit knowledge can exist in a textual form stems from a number of assumptions about the nature of language, including that language has fixed and objective meanings, and that there is a direct equivalence between words, and that which they denote.

A further assumption about the nature of knowledge is that it is regarded as objective. The assumption is that it is possible to develop a type of knowledge and understanding that is free from individual subjectivity. This represents what McAdam and McCreedy (2000) described as the 'knowledge is truth' perspective, where explicit knowledge is seen as equivalent to a canonical body of scientific facts and laws which are consistent across cultures and time. These ideas are deeply rooted in the philosophy of positivism, the idea that the social world can be studied 'scientifically', i.e. that social phenomena can be quantified and measured, that general laws and principles be established, and that objective knowledge is produced as a result.

 Positivism

While Comte, a nineteenth-century French philosopher, founded what is now called Positivism, Durkheim was arguably the first to translate these ideas into the realm of sociology. Durkheim was concerned to make sociology into a science, and advocated the use of positivistic philosophy. This philosophy assumes that cause and effect can be established between social phenomena through the use of observation and testing, and that general laws and principles can be established. These general laws and principles constitute objective knowledge.

The third key element of the objectivist epistemology is that it privileges explicit knowledge over tacit knowledge (see the following section for a definition and description of tacit and explicit knowledge). Primarily, explicit knowledge is regarded as equivalent to objective knowledge. Tacit knowledge on the other hand—knowledge which is difficult to articulate in an explicit form—is regarded as more informal, less rigorous, and highly subjective, being embedded within the cultural values and assumptions of those who possess and use it (Sayer 1992). Nonaka et al. (2000), for example, make this explicit by suggesting that, 'explicit knowledge can be expressed in formal and systematic language and shared in the form of data, scientific formulae. . . . In contrast, tacit knowledge is highly personal. . . . Subjective insights, intuitions and hunches fall into this category of knowledge.'

The final major assumption is that knowledge is regarded as primarily a cognitive, intellectual entity (but which is ultimately codifiable). As Cook and Brown (1999, 384) suggest, knowledge, 'is something that is held in the head'. From this perspective, the development and production of knowledge comes from a process of intellectual reflection (individual or collective), and is primarily a cognitive process.

One of the most well-known exemplars of this perspective in the contemporary knowledge literature is the body of work produced by Nonaka and his colleagues (Nonaka 1994; Nonaka and Takeuchi 1995; Nonaka et al. 2000). While Nonaka et al. view knowledge as dynamic rather than static, with new knowledge being continually created through a dialogue between tacit and explicit knowledge (through their four widely articulated methods of knowledge conversion), ultimately they conceptualize knowledge as an entity that individuals possess. More straightforward exemplars are economic based analyses of knowledge, such as Szulanski (1996) and Glazer (1998), both of whom base their analysis on the foundational assumption that knowledge represents a commodity/entity.

Glazer's article provides a number of indicators that it is based on a positivistic philosophy, and has an entitative view of knowledge. For example, this is reflected in the objective of the article, which is to facilitate efforts to 'develop reliable and valid **measures** of knowledge' (176, emphasis added). Further, it also locates itself in a tradition of '*scientific research*' (176), and talks about considering, 'knowledge as a "commodity" ' (176). Finally, it concludes in optimistic tones by challenging the pessimism that suggests that attempts to develop measures of knowledge are flawed and misguided, and that the difficulties in doing this are surmountable.

Typologies of knowledge

Based on these epistemological foundations, the vast majority of the contemporary knowledge literature then progresses by developing typologies that distinguish between fundamentally different types of knowledge. Two of the most common distinctions made, which are examined here are between tacit and explicit knowledge, and individual and collective knowledge.

Tacit and explicit knowledge

The tacit–explicit dichotomy is largely ubiquitous in analyses into the characteristics of organizational knowledge. Explicit knowledge, from an objectivist perspective, is

Table 2.2. The characteristics of tacit and explicit knowledge

Tacit knowledge	Explicit knowledge
Inexpressible in a codifiable form	codifiable
Subjective	objective
Personal	impersonal
Context specific	context independent
Difficult to share	easy to share

synonymous with objective knowledge, as outlined in Table 2.2. Therefore, it is unnecessary to restate in detail its characteristics. Suffice to say that explicit knowledge is regarded as objective, standing above and separate from both individual and social value systems and secondly that it can be codified into a tangible form.

Tacit knowledge on the other hand represents knowledge that people possess, but which is inexpressible. It incorporates both physical/cognitive skills (such as the ability to juggle, to do mental arithmetic, to weld, or to create a successful advertising slogan), and cognitive frameworks (such as the value systems that people possess). The main characteristics of tacit knowledge are therefore that it is personal, and is difficult, if not impossible to disembody and codify. This is because tacit knowledge may not only be difficult to articulate, it may even be subconscious (see Table 2.2).

This distinction between tacit and explicit knowledge is by no means unique to the objectivist epistemology of knowledge, but the specific way that the distinction is theorized within this perspective is quite particular. Importantly, as will be seen later in the chapter, some major implications flow from this depiction of the dichotomy in terms of the way knowledge-sharing processes are conceptualized. Within the objectivist epistemological framework there is an 'either/or' logic to the dichotomy, with knowledge typically being regarded as either tacit or explicit. This characterization of the dichotomy is explicit in the following quotation, '[t]here are two types of knowledge: explicit knowledge and tacit knowledge' (Nonaka et al. 2000). Thus from this perspective tacit and explicit knowledge do not represent the extremes of a spectrum, but instead represent two pure and separate forms of knowledge.

Typically, this polarized dichotomy is argued to be based on the work of Michael Polanyi (1958, 1983). Nonaka, for example, makes this reference explicit. However, as will be shown in Chapter 3, there is another, distinctly different interpretation of Polanyi's work, which questions this conceptualization of the tacit–explicit dichotomy.

Individual-group knowledge

While Nonaka argues that knowledge can only ever exist at the level of the individual, this idea is disputed by a range of other writers. These writers argue that while much knowledge does reside within individuals, there is a sense in which knowledge can reside in social groups. This insight is used as the basis for a further dichotomy of knowledge types: into individual and group/social level knowledge. One of the most well-known

Table 2.3. Generic knowledge types (adapted from Spender 1996)

	Individual	Social
Explicit	Conscious	Objectified
Tacit	Automatic	Collective

advocates of such a perspective is Spender (1996), who combined the tacit–explicit dichotomy, with the individual–group dichotomy to produce a two by two matrix with four generic types of knowledge (Table 2.3).

Examining social/group knowledge at the organizational level *objectified* knowledge represents explicit group knowledge, for example a documented system of rules, operating procedures, or formalized organizational routines. *Collective* knowledge on the other hand represents tacit group knowledge, knowledge possessed by a group that is not codified. Examples of this include informal organizational routines and ways of working, stories, and shared systems of understanding. For example, the value systems that people possess have a collective element, as they are related to values and ideas that circulate within the particular social milieu that people work within. The massive expansion of the culture management industry that has occurred since the mid-1980s, which attempts to inculcate specific value systems within organizations, suggests that there is an optimism amongst organizational management that such shared systems of values can be developed.

ILLUSTRATING THE ISSUES

Distrusting large consultancies: stories as a form of collective (tacit-group) knowledge

Castco is a relatively small UK-based company that produces specialist castings and injection mouldings for a range of industrial sectors. To improve the sharing of knowledge and information between divisions, it implemented a common, corporate-wide information management system. However, in the process of selecting a consulting company to help them with this project, all of the major, international consulting companies were explicitly, and deliberately excluded from the bidding process.

The same reasons for this exclusion were made by a number of the staff who were interviewed—there was a general mistrust/dislike of the 'big' consultants as they were argued to sell large-scale Business Process Re-engineering solutions, and were also extremely expensive. These attitudes and values were part of the prevailing organizational culture, as they were relatively independent of the direct, personal experiences of the project staff. These attitudes were espoused quite consistently by different project team members, even though none of them had personally worked with these large consulting firms. These cultural values appeared to circulate through Castco in the form of stories, which diffused through processes of socialization and communication. Stories were therefore a visible manifestation of the cultural values towards consultants. Thus stories can act as important repositories of knowledge, and represent a form of collective knowledge, which is widely shared, but relatively tacit in nature.

Stop and think

Is it appropriate to refer to stories as a form of collective knowledge? While stories have a collective element, being shared by a range of people, such knowledge is ultimately possessed by people, who may have quite different interpretations of the same story.

What scope do management in an organization have to shape, or change the stories that circulate within organizations?

However, the organizational context is by no means the only level at which group knowledge can exist. One specific, more microlevel type of collective knowledge that is increasingly being referred to is that possessed and held within communities of practice (see Chapter 5). At a more macrolevel, Lam (1997) also found that the national cultural context could play an important role in shaping the nature of organizational knowledge. She examined the sharing of knowledge between Japanese and UK divisions within a multinational corporation and found that what she referred to as the 'social embedded-ness of knowledge' made these processes complicated and extremely time-consuming. Primarily, significant differences existed between the Japanese and UK divisions involved in the joint venture in: the dominant type of knowledge; the degree of tacitness of this knowledge; the distribution of knowledge within the organization; and the knowledge-sharing mechanisms typically utilized. Lam attributed these significant differences to the different societal settings in which the two divisions operated.

Stop and think

Do you have any experiences of having to share knowledge with people of different nationalities? Was this process difficult/easy? Were there any noticeable differences in the nature of the knowledge, or the values underlying it between those involved in the process? If they existed, did these differences complicate the sharing of knowledge?

An objectivist perspective on the sharing and management of knowledge

Having examined both the fundamental character of knowledge, and the way knowledge can be categorized into different types, the final section of this chapter examines the implications of these ideas for the sharing and management of knowledge. This section begins by making explicit the general model of knowledge-sharing which flows from objectivist assumptions regarding knowledge, before concluding by outlining the way knowledge management processes are characterized.

Conduit model of knowledge-sharing

Based on the strict dichotomy on which the objectivist perspective is founded, where tacit and explicit knowledge are regarded as distinctive and separate types of knowledge with quite specific characteristics, the sharing of tacit and explicit knowledge is also regarded as being fundamentally different. From this perspective, while the sharing of tacit knowledge is acknowledged to be difficult, complex, and time-consuming, the sharing of explicit knowledge by contrast is regarded as relatively straightforward. The difficulties involved in sharing tacit knowledge, and the nature of such processes are not typically central to objectivist models of knowledge-sharing. These issues are therefore not examined here. Instead, they are considered in Chapter 3, as the sharing of tacit knowledge is a more fundamental element of the practice-based perspective on knowledge.

The privileging of explicit over tacit knowledge, which represents one of the distinguishing characteristics of the objectivist perspective, becomes apparent as the knowledge-sharing model underpinning the objectivist perspective focuses almost exclusively on explicit knowledge. From the objectivist perspective, the easy transferability of explicit knowledge represents one of its defining characteristics. For example, Grant (1996, 111) suggests that, 'explicit knowledge is revealed by its communication. This ease of communication is its fundamental property.'

This straightforward communicability of explicit knowledge is intimately related to the assumptions, outlined earlier concerning the nature of language, and the idea that explicit knowledge can be codified into a textual form.

The sharing of (explicit) knowledge represents what has been referred to as the conduit or transmitter/receiver model (see Figure 2.1). This model suggests that knowledge is shared by the transferral of explicit, codified knowledge (in the form of text, a diagram, or an electronic document, etc.) from an isolated sender, to a separate receiver. The metaphor of knowledge-sharing as being similar to the posting of a letter is thus appropriate. The idea behind this model is that the sender, in isolation from the receiver, can produce some wholly explicit knowledge, and then transfer it remotely to the receiver. The receiver then takes this knowledge and is able to understand it and use it without any other form of interaction with the sender. Further, it is assumed that no important aspects of this explicit knowledge are lost in the transfer process, and that both sender and receiver derive the same meaning from the knowledge.

Szulanski (1996) is a good example of an article based on such assumptions. It examines the importance and difficulty of sharing knowledge within organizations, let alone between organizations. Szulanski concludes that the 'internal stickiness' of organizational knowledge is *not* caused by a lack of motivation on the part of the sender or receiver, but is most typically due to the character of the knowledge being transferred and the context of the transfer. While it is acknowledged that most organizational knowledge has tacit components, and can be embedded in organizational routines, it is suggested that knowledge-sharing involves, 'the exchange of organizational knowledge between a source and a recipient' (1996, 28), which indicates its basis in the conduit model of knowledge-sharing.

Where the sharing and management of tacit knowledge is considered from the objectivist perspective, the focus is on *converting* tacit knowledge to explicit knowledge

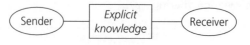

Fig. 2.1. The conduit model of knowledge-sharing

(what Nonaka et al. refer to as 'externalization'), rather than the direct sharing of tacit knowledge. Further, there is a generally optimistic assumption that much tacit knowledge can be, at least partially, converted into an explicit form. This means that the difficulties of sharing tacit knowledge can be ignored or downplayed, because once tacit knowledge has been made explicit it is regarded as being relatively straightforward to then share and manage it.

Knowledge management processes

Building from these assumptions regarding the sharing of knowledge, we can now examine the nature of knowledge management processes from an objectivist perspective (Table 2.4). The starting point is the processes of codifying relevant knowledge, converting tacit to explicit knowledge. From this perspective there is an acknowledgement that much organizational knowledge may be tacit. But this is accompanied by an optimism that it is possible to convert much of this knowledge to an explicit form. For example, while all the assembly instructions for putting together a car, or all the stages in a telesales customer interaction may not be totally explicit, with effort and work it is assumed to be possible to make all this knowledge explicit, and codify it into a complete set of instructions/body of knowledge. This can be achieved by getting relevant workers to articulate all their knowledge about such processes, making explicit all the assumptions, behaviours, and actions they utilize in accomplishing the task being examined. Thus, the first stage in any knowledge management initiative, from this perspective, is to identify what knowledge is important and then make it explicit.

Stop and think

Think about an example of tacit knowledge that you possess. To what extent could this knowledge be converted into an explicit form? Could it be codified such that someone else could utilize it? Further, how easy, and how time-consuming is this process likely to be?

The next stage in the knowledge management process involves collecting all the codified knowledge together into a central repository, and then structuring it in a systematic way to make it easily accessible to others. Thus, for example, the knowledge may be

Table 2.4. An objectivist perspective on knowledge management

Knowledge management: objectivist perspective

- Convert tacit to explicit knowledge
- Codification/capture of relevant knowledge
- Collect knowledge in central repository
- Structure/systematize knowledge (into discrete categories)
- Technology plays a key role

Table 2.5. Priorities of ongoing knowledge management projects (adapted from Chart 2, Ruggles 1998, 83.)

Knowledge management project priorities	% of respondents
Create an intranet	47
Data warehousing/Create knowledge repositories	33
Implementing decision-support tools	33
Implementing groupware	33

collected in a central database, where it is not only stored, but also categorized, indexed, and cross-referenced. The importance of doing this effectively is related to the final part of the knowledge management process: making this knowledge accessible to all people who may want to use it. One of the primary rationales for organizations managing their knowledge is to allow knowledge to be more widely and effectively shared within organizations (so that 'best practices' can be shared, etc.). This makes organizing knowledge, and making it accessible, equally as important as the codification/conversion stage.

Finally, technology typically plays a key role in knowledge management processes utilizing the objectivist perspective. For example, technology can play an important role in almost every element of the knowledge management process. First, it can provide a repository (for example databases). Secondly, it can play a role in the organizing of knowledge (for example with electronic cross-referencing systems). Finally, it can provide conduits and mechanisms through which knowledge can be transferred into, or extracted from, a central repository (for example through an intranet system or search engine). The role of technology in knowledge management processes is examined more fully in Chapter 8.

These characteristics are visible in the majority of the earliest knowledge management initiatives. For example, Ruggles (1998) reports the findings of a survey of 431 US and European companies. The emphasis of these initiatives was heavily technological (the top four reported priorities of these projects all had a significant technological element), conceptualizing knowledge as a codifiable asset, and focusing on the codification, storage, and making accessible this codified knowledge (see Table 2.5). *Management Review* (Management Review & AMA, 1999) reports on a survey of 1600 US managers conducted in 1998/9, and reached similar conclusions. In this survey the top priorities were: (1) identify useful information; (2) establish repositories and retrieval systems; (3) gather knowledge from customers; and (4) create and maintain employee talent.

 ILLUSTRATING THE ISSUES

Globalbank: an objectivist approach to knowledge management

Globalbank is a Dutch-based, globally dispersed bank. From the mid-1990s onwards it invested significantly in intranet technologies, as this was perceived as facilitating the sharing of knowledge across divisions. One specific intranet-based knowledge management system which was ultimately successful, was developed by the IT support function.

Globalbank's IT function was enormous, employing 1500 staff in Amsterdam, where it was centred, and approximately 5000 staff worldwide. There was felt to be a significant need for a knowledge management system, to support IT staff, as staff were typically widely dispersed, both geographically and divisionally, and were involved in doing similar tasks for different divisions. The objectivist assumptions regarding knowledge were apparent in a number of ways. Firstly, in terms of knowledge, the project team had an entitative conception of knowledge, which was apparent from the assumption that relevant knowledge could be codified. Secondly, there was a large technological emphasis to the project, with it being assumed that the knowledge which had been codified could be stored in databases linked to an intranet system. A significant part of the intranet project team's work was also concerned with categorizing this knowledge using an indexing system which made it easy for staff to find and access what they were looking for. Finally, with regards to knowledge-sharing, the project exemplified the transmitter–receiver logic of the objectivist perspective: knowledge-sharing happened through staff firstly codifying their knowledge, putting it in the database, where other staff would then be able to access and utilize it without a need to personally interact together.

Once the system had been developed and implemented it was deemed relatively successful, as staff in the IT support function made frequent use of the system, and found it to be helpful in their work.

Stop and think

With such systems what happens to any knowledge which cannot be codified?

The success of such intranet-based knowledge management systems is dependent upon people being willing to codify and store their knowledge. Are workers typically likely to be willing to do this? Secondly, what can management do to motivate workers to participate in such processes?

However, as the following chapters show, this characterization of knowledge management has been the subject of a growing critique, both in terms of the way knowledge is conceptualized (see Chapter 3), and also in terms of issues which are downplayed and neglected in knowledge management processes (see Chapters 4–9, the 'Issues' section of the book).

Chapter 3, for example, suggests that the objectivist framework underestimates the extent to which knowledge is embodied (tacit), embedded (context dependent), and subjective (value laden). Further, Chapters 4–9 consider how issues such as human motivation, politics, and personal identity require to be taken account of in attempting to manage knowledge. Therefore, as the book progresses, the somewhat simplistic model of knowledge management characterized here will be challenged.

Conclusion

This chapter has examined the objectivist perspective on knowledge and knowledge management. The key elements to this perspective can be summarized as follows:

- It is based on a positivistic philosophy.
- Knowledge is assumed to be codifiable and objective.

- Knowledge is regarded as a discrete entity—something we possess and can make explicit.
- Tacit and explicit knowledge are assumed to be separate and distinctive types of knowledge.
- Explicit knowledge (which is characterized as being objective) is privileged over tacit knowledge (which is characterized as being personal and subjective).
- Knowledge-sharing is based on a 'transmitter–receiver' model.
- Knowledge management initiatives emphasize the codification of knowledge.
- The role of technology in knowledge management initiatives is regarded as key.

This perspective represents one of the two dominant conceptualizations of knowledge, and knowledge management in the contemporary literature on the subject. Chapter 3 changes focus to examine the second, totally different perspective on knowledge, the practice-based perspective.

REVIEW QUESTIONS

1 Think about your experience of social/group knowledge in the workplace. Is it largely tacit or explicit? Did it exist in the form of systems of rules, routines, stories, etc.?

2 National culture and communities of practice have been discussed as two types of social context/setting where collective knowledge can be seen to exist. In what other social contexts, in your own experience, have you witnessed collective knowledge to exist—organization, family, geographic region, peer group, friendship network, profession?

3 Does the use of IT as part of a knowledge management system always indicate an objectivist perspective on knowledge? Have any of the organizations you have worked in developed IT-centred knowledge management systems? Did they embody objectivist assumptions regarding knowledge? How successful were these initiatives?

4 To what extent is knowledge in the social sciences objective? If knowledge in organizations is acknowledged as being somewhat subjective, does this mean objectivist-based knowledge management strategies have limited utility?

FURTHER READING

- I. Nonaka (1994). 'A Dynamic Theory of Organizational Knowledge Creation', *Organization Science*, 5 (1), 14–37.
  One of the most widely read and referenced papers on knowledge creation-conversion. Provides a good introduction to Nonaka's arguments.

- G. Szulanski (1996). 'Exploring Internal Stickiness: Impediments to the Transfer of Best Practice within the Firm', *Strategic Management Journal*, 17, Winter Special Issue, 27–43.
  A good examplar of an empirical study of knowledge-sharing based on the transmitter–receiver model.

- J-C. Spender (1996). 'Organizational Knowledge, Learning and Memory: Three Concepts in Search of a Theory', *Journal of Organizational Change Management*, 9 (1), 63–78.
  Articulates characteristics of and relations between four generic knowledge types.

3

The practice-based perspective on knowledge

What is knowledge?

Chapter 2 provided one specific answer to the question 'what is knowledge?' However, the objectivist perspective has been widely challenged, and for a number of different reasons. Arguably the most fundamental challenge and critique of it is that it is based on flawed epistemological assumptions. Chapter 3 therefore presents an alternative answer to the question 'what is knowledge?' This chapter is based on fundamentally different epistemological assumptions, and as will be seen, characterizes knowledge and knowledge management practices quite differently from the objectivist perspective (see Table 3.1).

The practice-based perspective conceptualizes knowledge not as a codifiable object/entity, but instead emphasizes the extent to which it is embedded within and inseparable from practice. Cook and Brown (1999) labelled this perspective an 'epistemology of practice' due to the centrality of human activity to its conception of knowledge. Further, Gherardi (2000, 218) argues that 'practice connects 'knowing' with 'doing''. Thus, the embeddedness of knowledge in human activity (practice) represents one of the central characteristics of this epistemological perspective.

Table 3.1. Objectivist and practice-based epistemologies of knowledge

Objectivist epistemology	Practice-based epistemology
Knowledge derived from an intellectual process	• knowledge is embedded in practice • knowing/doing inseparable
Knowledge is a disembodied entity/object	• knowledge is embodied in people • knowledge is socially constructed
Knowledge is objective 'facts'	• knowledge is culturally embedded • knowledge is contestable • knowledge is socially constructed
Explicit knowledge (objective) privileged over tacit knowledge (subjective)	• tacit and explicit knowledge are inseparable and mutually constituted
Distinct knowledge categories	• Knowledge is multidimensional

Table 3.2. Theoretical perspective related to the practice-based perspective

Writer	Theoretical perspective
Empsom (2001)	Interpretive
Blackler (1995)	*Activity Theory*
Tsoukas (1996)	*Ethnomethodology/interpretive philosophy*
Cook & Brown (1999)	*American Pragmatists*
Lave & Wenger (1991)	*Situated Learning Theory*
Sayer (1992)	*Critical Realism*
Suchman (2003)	*Actor Network Theory*

 Practice

Practice refers to purposeful human activity. It is based on the assumption that activity includes both physical and cognitive elements, and that these elements are inseparable. Knowledge use and development is therefore regarded as a fundamental aspect of activity.

While the objectivist perspective was closely aligned with a positivistic philosophy, the practice-based perspective is compatible with a number of different philosophical perspectives (Table 3.2). Another perspective that has much in common with the practice-based perspective, but has thus far not been utilized by knowledge management analysts is Critical Realism (with the exception of Mutch 2003).[2]

The chapter follows a similar structure to Chapter 2, and begins by firstly outlining the way knowledge is characterized within the practice-based perspective. Following this, the chapter then examines how knowledge management processes are conceptualized. As the chapter proceeds, the vast differences that exist between the practice-based, and the objectivist perspective on knowledge illustrated in Table 3.1, should become more apparent.

Practice-based perspectives on knowledge

The practice-based epistemology can be understood in terms of seven specific, but inter-related factors, each of which are now examined in turn (Table 3.3).

The embeddedness of knowledge in practice

Perhaps the most important difference between the objectivist and practice-based epistemologies of knowledge is that the practice-based perspective challenges the entitative conception of knowledge. From this perspective, knowledge isn't regarded as a discrete

---

[2] It is beyond the scope of this book to examine in detail the differences between these theoretical perspectives.

Table 3.3. Practice-based characteristics of knowledge

Characteristics of knowledge from practice-based epistemology
1. Knowledge is embedded in practice
2. Tacit and explicit knowledge are inseparable
3. Knowledge is embodied in people
4. Knowledge is socially constructed
5. Knowledge is culturally embedded
6. Knowledge is multidimensional
7. Knowledge is contestable

entity/object that can be codified and separated from people. Instead, knowledge, or as some of the writers from this perspective prefer, knowing, is inseparable from human activity. Thus all activity is to some extent knowledgeable, involving the use and/or development of knowledge. Conversely, all knowledge work, whether using it, sharing it, developing it, or creating it, will involve an element of activity. Blackler (1995, 1023) summed this up as follows, 'rather than regarding knowledge as something that people have, it is suggested that knowing is better regarded as something they do.'

As well as challenging the knowing–doing dichotomy, this perspective also challenges the mind–body dichotomy that is inherent to the objectivist perspective (see Table 3.4 later). As outlined, the objectivist perspective, drawing on the classical images of science, conceptualizes knowledge as being primarily derived from cognitive processes, some-thing involving the brain but not the body. The practice-based perspective instead views knowing and the development of knowledge as occurring on an ongoing basis through the routine activities that people undertake. Knowing thus can be seen as less of a purely cognitive process, and more of a holistic process involving the whole body (Gherardi 2000). Thus, from this perspective, thinking and doing are fused in knowledgeable activity, the development and use of embodied knowledge in undertaking specific activities/tasks.

These ideas can be illustrated through considering a number of examples. First, Orr's (1990) widely referenced study of photocopier engineers emphasizes how their knowl-edge developed through a process of dialogue and improvization, which involved the adaptation of existing knowledge to new and novel situations. Similarly, Patriotta (2003), in a study of a Fiat Auto plant in Italy, showed the embeddedness of knowledge in the nar-ratives possessed by workers, and how these narratives evolved in the resolution of 'dis-ruptive occurrences' (349). Thirdly, DeFillippi and Arthur (1998) in a study of film (i.e. movie) production, showed that for apprentice technicians processes of learning by watching were crucial. Knowledge in this context tended to develop through processes of socialization, observation, and practice. The final example, of the traditional craft skill of metalworking can be illustrated by a quotation:

When you have a bar of iron in front of you which has to be twisted and wrought into a certain shape. . . . then you learn to apply ideas to things. You become practical. *You cannot think the iron into the position and shape that is wanted, but you cannot do it without thought.* Your thoughts, if you are to succeed in your purpose, must be limited, circumscribed, bound down to the facts of the situation. McKinlay (1996, 86, emphasis added)

This quotation also reflects what a growing number of authors are arguing (see, for example, Alvesson 2000, 2001), that all work can be regarded as knowledge work, and that all workers, whether bus drivers, cleaners, accountants, management consultants, or research scientists, are, to some extent knowledge workers. However, this debate will be examined in more detail in Chapter 14.

Tacit and explicit knowledge are inseparable

Another point of departure between the objectivist and practice-based perspectives on knowledge is in the way that the relationship between tacit and explicit knowledge is conceptualized. The practice-based perspective suggests that rather than tacit and explicit knowledge representing separate and distinctive types of knowledge, they represent two aspects of knowledge and are in fact are inseparable, and are mutually constituted (Tsoukas 1996; Werr and Stjernberg 2003). One consequence of this is that there is no such thing as fully explicit knowledge, as all knowledge will have tacit dimensions. Clark (2000) uses the term 'explacit knowledge' to linguistically symbolizes their inseparability (Table 3.4). For example text, which is often referred to as a form of codified knowledge, has tacit components, without which no reader could make sense of it. Examples of these tacit elements include an understanding of the language in which they are written, or the grammar and syntax used to structure them. Polanyi (1969, 195) suggests that, 'The idea of a strictly explicit knowledge is indeed self-contradictory; deprived of their tacit coefficients, all spoken words, all formulae, all maps and graphs, are strictly meaningless.'

 ILLUSTRATING THE ISSUES

This book: partially explicit knowledge

This book represents a piece of partially explicit knowledge for two reasons. Firstly, as an author I have not been able to make fully explicit all the ideas, assumptions, theoretical frameworks and values which underpin what I have written. From the point of view of the reader it can also be considered partially explicit, as to read it you require to have a good grasp of the English language, and have some knowledge of other relevant academic topics.

Table 3.4. Challenging dichotomies

Challenging objectivist dichotomies
Explacit knowledge (tacit and explicit knowledge)
Knowledgeable activity (knowing and doing)
Sensual cognition (brain and body)

While, as outlined in Chapter 2, Polanyi's work is often used to justify the tacit–explicit dichotomy, a number of writers suggest that this misunderstands his analysis (Brown and Duguid 2001; Prichard 2000). These writers challenge this and suggest that his analysis is grounded more in the practice-based perspective.

Knowledge is embodied

The objectivist perspective on knowledge assumes that knowledge can exist in a fully explicit and codified form, that knowledge can exist independently of human beings. This position is fundamentally challenged by the practice-based perspective on knowledge, which assumes all knowledge or knowing is personal. The practice-based perspective therefore assumes that it is impossible to totally disembody knowledge from people into a fully explicit form. This assumption is therefore closely related to, and flows from, the previous two issues examined: that all knowledge has tacit dimensions, and that knowledge is embedded in, and inseparable from practice.

The practice-based nature of knowing/knowledge assumes that knowledge develops through practice: people's knowledge develops as they conduct activities and gain experience. Further, the inseparable and mutually constituted nature of tacit and explicit knowledge means that it is not possible to make such knowledge fully explicit. There will always be an element to which knowledge resides in the head/body of those who developed and possess it. Thus while it may be possible to partially convert tacit knowledge into an explicit form, in contradiction with the objectivist perspective, the practice-based perspective assumes that such processes can never be complete. For example, in terms of a situation most readers are likely to be familiar with from one context or another, consider the nature of knowledge sharing in 'master–apprentice' type relations, where someone experienced attempts to share their knowledge with a more inexperienced colleague. The practice-based perspective assumes that the practice-based nature of the knowledge and expertise the 'master' possesses means that this knowledge will be to some extent embodied, and cannot be fully articulated and made explicit. Further, the practice-based perspective assumes that for the apprentice to learn the knowledge of the master requires that they communicate, interact, and work together, typically over an extended period of time.

A further sense in which knowledge is embodied (and simultaneously embedded in practice) relates to what Tsoukas (1996) referred to as the 'indeterminacy of practice', where the essential distinctiveness of all situations that people act in requires them to continually make personal judgements. No matter how explicit and well defined the rules are that may guide action, there will always be some element of ambiguity or uncertainty that creates a need for actors to make inferences and judgements. For example, applying this insight to the perspective of the 'apprentice' just discussed, no matter how formalized, structured, and explicit the knowledge they have acquired, there will always be circumstances that emerge where an element of judgement will be required. Thus, knowledge/knowing involves the active agency of people making decisions in light of the specific circumstances in which they find themselves.

The socially constructed and culturally embedded nature of knowledge

Two factors that are closely interwoven are that knowledge is socially constructed and culturally embedded. It is therefore necessary to examine them simultaneously. In stark contrast to the 'knowledge is truth' assumption of the objectivist perspective on knowledge, where it is suggested that codified knowledge can exist in an objective form independent of social and cultural values, the epistemology of practice perspective argues that all knowledge is socially constructed in nature, which makes it somewhat subjective and open to interpretation. Thus, knowledge is never totally neutral and unbiased, and is, to some extent, inseparable from the values of those who produced it.

As with the objectivist perspective, this viewpoint is based on a particular understanding about the nature of language. The objectivist perspective assumes that language has fixed and objective meanings, and that there is a direct equivalence between words and that which they denote. Instead, the practice-based perspective suggests that language has no such fixed meanings, and that in fact the meaning of language is inherently ambiguous. This subjectivity, or interpretive flexibility in language, thus undermines any claims about the objective status of any knowledge, whether it is highly tacit and personal, or whether it is partially explicit and codified. However, the socially negotiated nature of language limits the scope individuals have to modify and interpret the meaning and use of language (Sayer 1992; Tsoukas 1996).

  Perspective making and taking

Perspective making is the process through which a community develops, strengthens, and sustains its knowledge and values. Perspective taking is the process through which people develop an understanding of the knowledge, values, and 'worldview' of others.

The socially constructed nature of knowledge applies to both its production and its interpretation. Polanyi (1969) referred to these two processes as sense-giving and sense-reading, while Boland and Tenkasi (1995) used the terms perspective making and perspective taking. Thus both the production of knowledge, and the reading/interpretation required to develop an understanding of it, involves an active process of meaning construction/inference. For example, a written report is a piece of partially explicit knowledge, whose meaning is constructed by its author/s. However, readers may infer a different meaning and analysis. This aspect of the practice-based perspective therefore has profound implications for the way knowledge is shared and managed, as the attractive simplicity of the transmitter–receiver model is questioned.

Stop and think

Can you think of an example from your organizational experience of where a range of people inferred different meanings from a report? Can these differences partly be explained by the fluidity of meaning in language?

Further, this process of meaning construction/inference is typically culturally embedded. The meanings people attach to language/events are shaped by the values and assumptions of the social and cultural context in which people live and work. One way in which pre-existing values and assumptions influence these processes of knowledge construction/ knowledge interpretation is through the filtering of data-information in deciding what is considered 'relevant'. A dramatic, and tragic example of such a filtering process was one of the contributory factors to the Challenger Space Shuttle accident (Baumard 1999; Starbuck and Milliken 1988). In this case NASA engineers neglected what turned out to be important information regarding O-ring erosion, as based on the assumptions they had, such a situation was regarded as presenting a minute risk. This cultural embeddedness results in much knowledge being context-specific and context-dependent, making its relevance, and trans-ferability between contexts not necessarily always straightforward.

The idea of knowledge being culturally embedded links to the concept of collective knowledge discussed in Chapter 2. Collective knowledge was shown to be culturally embedded in a number of different contexts, such as within communities of practice, or within the context of a national or regional culture. What distinguishes the cultural embedding of knowledge in the practice-based perspective from collective knowledge in the objectivist perspective, is that from the practice-based perspective *all* knowledge is to some extent culturally embedded. Thus from this perspective, none of the knowledge we possess is totally separate and independent from the social contexts that people operate in.

The simultaneous multidimensionality of knowledge

The use of taxonomies, as illustrated in the previous chapter, suggests that all knowledge can be classified into distinctive categories, i.e. that it is either tacit or explicit, or that it is tacit-collective, or explicit-individual, etc. This idea is questioned by a number of writers who suggest that while such an approach may have analytical benefits, it misrepresents the complexity of organizational knowledge. Tsoukas (1996), for example, suggests that dichotomies such as tacit–explicit and individual–group are unhelpful as they disguise the extent to which these elements are inseparable, and mutually defined. Blackler (1995, 1032) makes a similar point by suggesting that,

. . . it is a mistake to assume that embodied, embedded, embrained, encultured and encoded know-ledge can sensibly be conceived as separate from each other. Knowledge is multi-faceted and complex, being both situated and abstract, implicit and explicit, distributed and individual, physical and mental, developing and static, verbal and encoded.

Thus the practice-base perspective rejects the taxonomy-based approach to categoriz-ing knowledge. For example, consider the knowledge that an engineer uses to design a car's chassis, or that a craftsman(/person) uses to assemble and build it. In both cases this knowledge is simultaneously individual and collective; tacit and explicit; physical and mental; and abstract and situated.

Stop and think

Think of some specific organizational knowledge that you possess. Can it be classified into a neat category, such as tacit-collective, or does it have multiple dimensions simultaneously?

The contestible nature of knowledge

The final key aspect of the practice-based perspective is the acknowledgement that the subjective, socially constructed, and culturally embedded nature of knowledge, means that what constitutes knowledge is open to dispute. This therefore challenges and undermines the idea central to the objectivist perspective that it is possible to produce truly objective knowledge. Thus, competing conceptions of what constitutes 'legitimate' knowledge can occur where different groups/individuals develop incompatible and contradictory analyses of the same events, which may lead to conflict due to attempts by these groups to have their knowledge legitimated.

One of the main consequences which flow from this, therefore, is that issues of power, politics, and conflict become more important than are acknowledged by the objectivist perspective. Most fundamentally, Michel Foucault's conception of power/knowledge suggests that these concepts are inseparable (Foucault 1980; McKinlay 2000). Relatedly, Storey and Barnett (2000) suggest that all knowledge management initiatives require to be seen as highly political, and are likely to be accompanied by what they describe as *'turf wars'* by different organizational interest groups attempting to gain some control over these projects. The importance of acknowledging and taking account of the contested and political nature of knowledge is magnified by the fact that this aspect of knowledge, and knowledge management initiatives is typically either neglected or ignored by the majority of the knowledge management literature. These issues are examined more fully in Chapter 7.

ILLUSTRATING THE ISSUES

The politics of introducing change: competing 'truth claims'

Pharma-co is a UK pharmaceutical company. Until the early 1980s it had been a government-owned research laboratory, and by the mid-1990s there was still evidence in part of the company of the technically focused culture which had historically predominated. During the mid-1990s a decision was made to implement a new information management system. The dominant rhetoric used by the project team to justify the need for change was that the changing nature of their markets required significant changes to be made to improve the competitiveness of their production facilities. An important figure to Pharma-co's project was the World Manufacturing Director, who strongly championed it. When the project started he had been a relatively recent recruit to the organization. As part of Pharma-co's long-term strategy of adopting more commercial and cost-sensitive operating practices a need had been identified to introduce such attitudes to its senior management. The recruitment of the World Manufacturing Director was one of these appointments. Thus his 'commercial' knowledge from working outside of the company was highly regarded by senior management. However, resistance to the proposed changes emerged from middle managers within the production function. They suggested the proposed changes were fundamentally unnecessary, and that Pharma-co could remain competitive through staying focused on the development and production of technically innovative products. The traditional culture which had been historically predominant within Pharma-co was focused around production.

One of the main factors strengthening the argument of production management was their detailed knowledge of the company's internal manufacturing practices. Thus at the start of Pharma-co's change project there was a highly political conflict between those for and against change which centred on the validity of their knowledge and the way they used it to legitimate their different analyses of the extent to which change was needed.

Stop and think

In such situations, to what extent is it possible to objectively evaluate the competing arguments and decide on the 'correct' course of action?

What does the different perspectives of the interests group say about the cultural embeddedness of knowledge? To what extent are the viewpoints of those in conflict derived from the values and ideas of the organizational communities they are embedded in?

Implications for the nature of the organizational knowledge base

The above outlined characteristics of knowledge have profound implications with regard to the nature of organizational knowledge bases, as a growing number of writers recognize. The practice-based perspective on knowledge suggests that rather than being unitary and coherent, organizational knowledge bases are in fact fragmented and dispersed, being made up of specialized and specific knowledge communities, which have some degree of overlapping 'common knowledge' (Kogut and Zanger 1992). This led Brown and Duguid (1991, 53) to suggesting that organizations require to be conceptualized as a 'community-of-communities', and Blackler et al. (2000) as decentred and distributed knowledge systems. Finally, as will be seen in the following section, these insights have enormous implications for the sharing and management of knowledge in organizations.

The fragmentation of the organizational knowledge base relates closely to the idea that knowledge is embedded in practice. Typically, the practices undertaken by organizational staff, and hence the knowledge they possess, are localized and specific, being shaped by the particular demands of their context (local customers, market conditions, character of national/regional regulation and legislation, etc.). The degree of fragmentation and specialization will also be related to the culture of the organization, and the extent to which it encourages and supports autonomous or standardized working practices.

ILLUSTRATING THE ISSUES

Autonomous business units and specialized knowledge communities
....

In Swed-Truck, which sold, rented, and serviced fork lift trucks, work had historically been organized into small, discrete business units, which had responsibility for all business within specific geographic regions. Within this structure, there was little need for interaction between business units, and they operated as virtual stand-alone businesses. While each business unit in principle sold the same range of products and services, in reality they had significant autonomy over how they did this. This was because both the nature of the market and character of customers varied significantly for each business, and also that management in each business unit offered different levels of service and support. The autonomy of the business units was such that the evolution of their working practices, the upgrading of their IT systems etc., was done purely on the basis of local considerations. Thus, discrete and specific knowledge communities developed, with staff in each business unit possessing substantial amounts of specialized knowledge, relevant to their own localized working practices, and customer demands, which had limited transferability and relevance, in other business units.

Stop and think

Is the existence of such specialist communities, with their own knowledge bases and ways of working necessarily a problem for organizations?

To what extent is it possible in multidivisional corporations to balance the conflicting demands of providing divisions the autonomy to work independently and have some level of standardization across the corporation?

Not only can the knowledge of organizational communities be different (i.e. specialized and specific), but it may also be based on qualitatively different assumptions, values, and interpretative frameworks. Brown and Duguid (2001) referred to these as 'epistemic differences'. For example, the communication and interaction difficulties between staff from different functions of an organization (such as production and R&D, or finance and R&D), or between staff from different disciplinary backgrounds (such as in a multidisciplinary project team) can be to some extent explained by such differences. As will be seen in Chapter 6, where this issue is explored in detail, this significantly affects the dynamics of knowledge-sharing processes. Finally, these issues are again examined in Chapter 13 which examines knowledge-sharing within the context of global multinationals, where, what Becker (2001) referred to this as the problem of *large numbers'*, means that as organizational size increases, so do the problems in managing an increasingly fragmented organizational knowledge base.

Stop and think

Think about an organization you have worked in. Was its knowledge base fragmented? Further, what factors influenced the nature of the knowledge base more: the management culture or the diversity of local conditions?

A practice-based perspective on the management and sharing of knowledge

Having considered in detail how the practice-based epistemology conceptualizes knowledge it is now time to examine the implications of these ideas for understanding the character of organizational knowledge-sharing and knowledge management processes (see Table 3.5).

One of the central components of the practice-based perspective on knowledge management is that it eschews the idea that it is possible for organizations to collect knowledge

Table 3.5. A practice-based perspective on knowledge management

---

Knowledge management from a practice-based epistemology

---

1. Knowledge sharing/acquisition requires 'perspective making' and 'perspective taking'—developing an understanding of tacit assumptions

2. Knowledge sharing/acquisition through
    – 'rich' social interaction
    – immersion in practice—watching and/or doing

3. Management role to facilitate social interaction

---

together into a central repository, or for middle and senior managers to fully understand the knowledge of those who work for them (Goodall and Roberts 2003). Tsoukas (1996, 15), quoting Hayek, suggests that a belief in the ability to achieve such a state represents the 'synoptic delusion . . . that knowledge can be surveyed by a single mind.' Thus managerial understanding of organizational knowledge will always be fragmented and incomplete, and attempts to collect knowledge in a central location likely to be limited. The following quotation from Tsoukas (1996, 22) sums this up, and points towards the practice-based perspective's conceptualization of knowledge-sharing processes: 'the key to achieving coordinated action does not so much depend on those "higher up" collecting more and more knowledge, as on those "lower down" finding more and more ways to get connected and interrelating the knowledge each one has.'

The practice-based perspective further suggests that the transmitter–receiver model of knowledge-sharing is questionable because the sharing of knowledge does not involve the simple transferral of a fixed entity between two people. Instead, the sharing of knowledge involves two people actively inferring and constructing meaning. This perspective suggests that to be effective the sharing of knowledge requires individuals to develop an appreciation of (some of) the tacit assumptions and values on which the knowledge of others is based—the processes of 'perspective making' and 'perspective taking' outlined earlier by Boland and Tenkasi (1995). This challenges the assumption embedded in the transmitter–receiver model that the knowledge exchanged in such processes is unchanged. Bolisani and Scarso (2000) suggest the practice-based perspective on knowledge-sharing represents a 'language game', due to the importance of dialogue and language to such processes. Boland and Tenkasi (1995, 358) argue that effective knowledge-sharing involves, 'a process of mutual perspective taking where distinctive individual knowledge is exchanged, evaluated and integrated with that of others in the organization.'

The logic of the 'language game' model complicates the nature of knowledge-sharing processes, as the inherent ambiguity of language, combined with the fact that those involved in the knowledge-sharing process have different cognitive frameworks means that there is always scope for differing interpretations. Thus, as you read this book, the meaning you take from a piece of partially explicit knowledge may vary from the meaning I intend to convey.

These perspective-making, and perspective-taking processes typically require an extensive amount of social interaction and face-to-face communication, which is a conclusion reached by a number of empirical studies (see, for example, Lam 1997, 2000; Leonard-Barton 1995; Swan et al. 1999). The acquisition and sharing of knowledge typically occur through two distinct, but closely interrelated processes:

1. Immersion in practice—for example learning by doing, or learning by watching.
2. 'Rich' social interaction—for example, an interaction which allows people to develop some level of trust with each other, as well as develop some insights into the tacit knowledge, values, and assumptions of each other.

These processes are interrelated because learning by doing is likely *to* simultaneously involve an element of social interaction, and vice versa, the sort of 'discursive practice' referred to by Gherardi (2000, 221).

ILLUSTRATING THE ISSUES

Swed-truck: an example of practice-based knowledge management

In the late 1990s Swed-Truck (described earlier—see pages 35–6) decided to implement an organization-wide information management system, with the objective of introducing a greater level of coordination and standardization across its business units. To implement this it used a socially based model of knowledge-sharing, which made extensive use of intensive social inter-action. This can be considered by examining the system development phase only. The system being implemented involved the introduction of a common information system across a signific-ant number of different business units. As outlined earlier, their business units had operated quite autonomously from each other, and as a consequence had developed their own specialized knowledge bases. The project team decided that the development and implementation of a com-mon information management system required the utilization of this distributed knowledge, which was achieved through the creation of a project team bringing together staff from a range of their business units (who worked part time on the project). As a substantial amount of devel-opment work was necessary, this process lasted for a year. This interbusiness unit project team worked intensively with consultants to develop common systems that were compatible with the diverse needs of their different business units. While the project was not without its problems and delays, the project was deemed a success, and was implemented close to predicted time-scales.

Stop and think

To achieve rich social interactions is it necessary to get people together face-to-face?

How important to the success of knowledge-sharing processes is the existence of trust between participants to such processes?

From a practice-based perspective, the managerial role is therefore to encourage and facil-itate the type of communication and social interaction processes that will allow effective perspective making and taking to occur. This can be done through an enormously diverse range of ways including (to highlight just a few examples):

- develop a knowledge-sharing culture (through rewarding people for sharing);
- facilitating the development of organizational communities of practice;
- providing forums (electronic or face-to-face) which encourage and support knowledge-sharing;
- implement a formalized 'mentoring' system to pair experienced and inexperienced workers

These issues are examined in more detail in subsequent chapters, with Chapter 4 looking at general issues of motivation to share knowledge, Chapters 5 and 6 looking at the specific dynamics of knowledge-sharing within and between communities, Chapter 7 looking at the political nature of knowledge-sharing, while Chapter 9 considers the role that organizations can play through their human resource management policies and culture management practices. Finally, Chapter 8 considers the role that information systems may be able to play in facilitating perspective making and taking processes.

Conclusion

In conclusion, Chapters 2 and 3 have outlined two distinctive epistemological perspectives, which characterize knowledge in extremely different ways (see Table 3.1). These perspectives also conceptualized knowledge-sharing and knowledge management processes differently. They therefore have very different managerial implications with regard to how knowledge management efforts should be organized and structured:

- *Objectivist perspective*: focus on the codification and collection of knowledge, create mechanisms to allow this knowledge base to be searched and accessed, such as setting up a searchable database and encouraging staff to codify their knowledge and store it there.
- *Practice-based perspective*: facilitate interpersonal knowledge-sharing through diverse forms of interaction and communication, such as developing the levels of trust between the members of a new project team through allowing them to interact extensively face-to-face (perhaps in both work and social contexts) at the initial stages of the project.

REVIEW QUESTIONS

1 Think about an example of partially explicit knowledge you are familiar with, for example a set of instructions on how to conduct a certain task. What tacit knowledge is necessary for you to make sense of them? What does this say about the inseparability of tacit and explicit knowledge?

2 Can you think of an example from your own experience of where there has been dispute and conflict between competing knowledge claims? What political tactics and strategies did the conflicting parties utilize to justify their position? Did they use external 'expertise' as a way of rationalizing claims, etc?

3 Compare the two perspectives on knowledge outlined in Chapters 2 and 3. Which one more closely models the nature of knowledge in the organizations that you have worked in? If these organizations implemented knowledge management initiatives, which epistemological perspective were they based on? Did this affect the success of these initiatives?

FURTHER READING

- F. Blackler (1995). 'Knowledge, Knowledge Work and Organizations: An Overview and Interpretation', *Organization Studies*, 16/6: 1021–46.
  Widely referenced article that advocates adopting a practice/activity-based view of knowledge.

- S. Cook and J. Brown (1999). 'Bridging Epistemologies: The Generative Dance between Organizational Knowledge and Organizational Knowing', *Organization Science*, 10/4: 381–400.
  Links together the objectivist and practice-based perspectives into a unitary framework.

- H. Tsoukas (1996). 'The Firm as a Distributed Knowledge System: A Constructionist Approach', *Strategic Management Journal*, 17 (Winter Special Issue): 11–25.
  Argues that organizational knowledge bases are highly distributed.

- Special issue of *Organization* on 'Knowing in Practice' (2000), 7/2.
  A collection of theoretical and empirical papers all embedded in the practice-based perspective, but utilizing a diversity of theoretical frameworks.

Social and cultural issues related to managing and sharing knowledge

While enormous numbers of companies have implemented knowledge management projects, many of them have been either partial successes or outright failures. Surveys consistently reveal that the main obstacles to success in such initiatives are social and cultural factors (Table 4). A further conclusion that could be inferred from these results is that the organizations surveyed did not consistently take adequate account of these factors in their efforts to manage their knowledge. Thus, for those concerned with achieving an intellectual understanding of the dynamics of knowledge management initiatives, as well as those concerned with making specific knowledge management projects successful, appreciating the significance of social and cultural factors is vital. The six chapters in this section of the book all deal with this topic and thus arguably represent the core of the book.

Chapter 4, the opening chapter in this part, has two broad objectives. First, it examines the question of why social and cultural factors are so important by considering both why human motivation is essential to the sharing, codification, or search for knowledge, and further, why it can't be taken for granted that people will be willing to actively participate in such processes. The second objective of this chapter is to provide a brief overview of the diverse range of specific factors that affect the attitudes of workers to participate in knowledge management initiatives. Chapter 4 thus acts as a springboard into the remaining chapters in this section (Chapters 5–9), which each build from this overview, looking in depth at a range of social and cultural topics.

Chapter 5 examines the dynamics of knowledge-related processes within communities of practice. Chapter 6 builds from this by examining the dynamics of knowledge-sharing in a totally different context, where, unlike in communities of practice, people have limited common knowledge and only a weak sense of shared identity. This can include knowledge processes within multidisciplinary teams, or knowledge processes which span functional or organizational boundaries. Chapter 7 focuses on the topics of power and conflict, which, as will be seen, are under-researched areas in the knowledge management literature. Chapter 8 examines the impact and

Table 4. Obstacles to the success of knowledge management initiatives

Author	Survey details	Survey results
Ruggles (1998)	431 Respondents in USA and Europe. Conducted in 1997	• biggest problem in managing knowledge 'changing people's behaviour' (56% of respondents) • biggest impediment to knowledge transferal 'culture' (54% of respondents)
Management Review (1999)	1600 Respondents in the USA. Conducted 1998/9	Three most common problems: 1. 'getting people to seek best practice' 2. 'measuring results' 3. 'getting people to share their knowledge'
KPMG (2000)	423 large organizations from USA, UK, France and Germany	Two most important reasons for the failure of knowledge management initiatives to meet expectations: 1. 'lack of user uptake due to insufficient communication' (20% of respondents) 2. 'everyday use did not integrate into normal working day' (19% of respondents)
Pauleen and Mason (2002)	46 respondents in New Zealand from organizations (public and private)	The single largest barrier (identified by 45% of respondents) to knowledge management was culture.
Edwards et al. (2003)	25 Academics and practitioners involved in KM field	'People' and 'Culture' are the most important issues organizations should emphasize in their KM initiatives

role of technology in knowledge management initiatives. Finally, Chapter 9 considers the role that culture management and human resource management practices can have on knowledge management initiatives, and in shaping the attitudes of workers to participate in knowledge processes more generally.

4

'Why should I share my knowledge?' what motivates people to share knowledge

Introduction

As the topic of knowledge management has matured and evolved interest in human, cultural, and social questions has grown significantly. Thus, while the earliest literature (and organizational attempts to manage knowledge) typically assumed people would be willing to share their knowledge, and as a consequence neglected to look at factors that may influence knowledge-sharing attitudes, later literature illustrated how 'people'-related factors are key to knowledge management. This chapter provides an overview and an introduction to these issues through examining the interrelated questions of *why* human motivation is key to knowledge management initiatives, and *what* factors have been found to influence the knowledge-sharing attitudes and behaviours of workers.

The issues raised here connect to the two previous chapters on epistemologies of knowledge as, crudely, the early knowledge management literature, which typically neglected 'people'-related factors, was firmly embedded in the objectivist perspective on knowledge, while the growing realization of the importance of such factors owes much to insights developed from a practice-based perspective. Fundamentally, this is because its conceptualization of knowledge takes greater account of human agency, and views knowledge as being largely tacit and personal.

This chapter is structured into three main sections. The first outlines why the early knowledge management literature so conspicuously played down 'people'-related issues. The second and third sections then consider the questions of why human motivation is key to understanding the dynamics of knowledge management initiatives, and what personal and organizational factors influence people's attitudes to participating in knowledge management initiatives.

The 'first generation' knowledge management literature: the neglect of socio-cultural factors

Storey and Quintas suggest that crucial to the success of knowledge management initiatives is that *'employees are willing to share their knowledge and expertise'* (2001, 359). Today, such a statement appears commonsensical, a matter of stating the obvious. This is largely because such an assertion can be backed by a wide range of survey findings (see Table 1; Cranfield Business School 1998; Hauschild et al. 2001; Ribiere 2001), and case study evidence on knowledge management initiatives (see, Empson 2001; Flood et al. 2001; Kim and Mauborgne 1998; Morris 2001; Robertson and O'Malley Hammersley 2000). These reports show that human, social, and cultural factors are typically key determinants of the success or failure of knowledge management initiatives, for example, with evidence suggesting that a reluctance by workers to share, or even hoard their knowledge is not uncommon.

However, the importance of such issues has not always been recognized in the knowledge management literature. In much of the earliest writing on knowledge management, what Scarbrough and Carter (2000) refer to as the 'first generation' literature (very approximately all knowledge management literature before 1998), socio-cultural factors were not accorded this level of importance. Thus before looking in detail at why human and social factors are so important it is worth briefly looking at this early literature to help in understanding the assumptions it was based on and why 'people' questions were regarded as of secondary importance.

A good insight into the character and assumptions of the early knowledge management literature can be derived from a survey of it (Scarbrough et al. 1999; Scarbrough and Swan 2001). Literature up to and including 1998 was included in the survey, and was classified according to its primary thematic interests (see Table 4.1). This showed that almost 70 per cent of this literature was primarily focused on IT or information-systems-related issues, and that only 5 per cent (one in twenty articles) had a thematic emphasis on 'human resource' issues. Thus it is in no way inaccurate to suggest that this early literature focused primarily on technological issues, and neglected socio-cultural factors. The survey evidence reported earlier (see Table 2) indicates that the earliest knowledge management initiatives had a similar emphasis.

Table 4.1. Thematic focus of early knowledge management literature (adapted from Scarbrough and Swan 2001, Table 2, 8)

Thematic category	Number	%
Information Technology	73	40
Information Systems	51	28
Strategic Management	35	19
Human Resource	9	5
Consultancies	8	4
Other	8	4

This literature, and the earliest knowledge management initiatives, were typically based on a number of key assumptions:

- People will be willing to share knowledge.
- Knowledge is either codified, or is codifiable (tacit knowledge can be converted into an explicit form).
- Knowledge can be shared via IT systems.

The resonance between these assumptions and the objectivist perspective on knowledge outlined in Chapter 2 should be apparent, and the vast majority of this early, IT-based literature is fundamentally based on this epistemological perspective. As a consequence of these assumptions the emphasis of this literature (and KM initiatives) was on setting up mechanisms and a relevant (technological) infrastructure to support knowledge management efforts of codification, and electronic knowledge diffusion. Questions of whether people were willing to share their knowledge, or what could be done to motivate them to do so, were by and large ignored. But these assumptions have been undermined by empirical evidence and have been widely challenged as a consequence.

People's motivation and willingness to share knowledge

The title of this section contains the seeds of two important and interrelated questions, which over time gained greater and greater prominence in the knowledge management literature:

1. What is the role and significance of human motivation in knowledge-sharing processes?
2. How willing are people to share their knowledge?

The growing critique of the first-generation literature suggests that in answer to the first question, human motivation is of fundamental importance to knowledge-sharing processes, and that in answer to the second question, people's willingness to share their knowledge should *not* be taken for granted. These conclusions can be understood by looking at three specific issues (see Table 4.2), each of which are examined in turn.

Table 4.2. Factors making human motivation important to organizational knowledge processes

Why human motivation and willingness are important to knowledge management and sharing processes
Embodied/personal/tacit nature of (much) knowledge
Nature of the employment relationship
Embeddedness of (potential for) conflict in intra-organizational relations

The personal and embodied nature of knowledge

The first factor which helps to explain why human agency and motivation is important to knowledge-sharing processes relates to the character of organizational knowledge. As the previous two chapters have examined this topic in detail, relevant issues can be examined without having to restate a lot of detail. The characteristics of knowledge considered relevant here are drawn largely from the practice-based perspective on knowledge (see Chapter 3). This is because, in general terms, the critique of the objectivist-orientated 'first generation' knowledge management literature has been made using insights derived from this perspective.

Primarily much organizational knowledge, rather than being explicit in a disembodied form, is personal, tacit, and embodied in people. Thus, Kim and Mauborgne suggest, 'knowledge is a resource locked in the human mind' (1998, 323). As a consequence, the sharing and transmission of such knowledge occurs through interaction and communication between people. Thus, the sharing and communication of knowledge requires a willingness on the part of those who have it to participate in such processes. Or, as Flood et al. (2001, 1153) suggest, 'the tacit knowledge . . . employees possess may be exploited only if these workers decide to part with this knowledge on a voluntary basis.'

Further, challenging the tacit–explicit dichotomy of discrete knowledge types as well as acknowledging the socially and contextually embedded nature of knowledge, suggests there are limits to the extent to which knowledge can be made explicit. Thus no matter how willing workers may be to make their knowledge explicit, they will never be able to make explicit all the assumptions and values on which it is based (often because they may not even be aware of all of them). For example, an experienced worker who has built up his knowledge over time will only be partly able to explicitly articulate his knowledge. Further, other workers attempting to fully understand this knowledge will typically require to directly communicate and interact with the experienced worker to help understand aspects of the knowledge that could not be made explicit. Finally, and crucially, the success of this process of knowledge-sharing, is dependent on the willingness of both workers making the effort to actively engage in this process.

Thus, as much organizational knowledge is embodied and personal in nature, and where there are finite limits to the extent to which this knowledge can be codified, the importance of the active agency of people in knowledge-sharing becomes apparent. However, the character of knowledge provides only part of the explanation why human and social issues are key to knowledge management initiatives. Two other issues of equal importance are the nature of the employment relationship, and the nature of intra-organizational relations. These issues help to explain why Scarbrough and Carter (2000) suggest that it is problematic to assume that organizations represent a harmonious environment where people are willing and happy to share their knowledge.

The nature of the employment relationship

The quotations at the start of Chapter 1 (p.1) portray knowledge as an economic asset which is owned by organizations, and which they have the power to manage. However, the knowledge that workers have can also be conceptualized as belonging to them rather than the organization. From this perspective, while workers may apply, develop, and use their knowledge towards the achievement of organizationally directed goals and objectives, the knowledge is fundamentally the workers, to use as, when, where, how, and if they want. This highlights the potential tension between workers and the organizations they work for over who owns and controls their knowledge, and points towards an important factor which may inhibit the willingness of workers to share their knowledge. This tension is neatly summed up by Scarbrough, who suggests that, '*knowing* as an active, lived experience is in a constant state of tension *with knowledge* as a commodity within firms and markets' (1999, 6, emphasis in original).

Thus while the knowledge-related objectives of the organization (to utilize and develop knowledge into an economic asset, and to extract economic value from it), and workers (to sustain, develop, use, and apply their knowledge as appropriate, to derive a sense of importance from their knowledge, and to have a knowledge base which enhances or sustains their employability) *may* coincide, it is equally possible that they may not. Therefore, from a managerial perspective, the willingness of workers to use their knowledge for the achievement of organizational objectives should not be taken for granted.

Such tensions are not new or novel. In fact they represent one of the most fundamental conflicts affecting management–worker relations. Thus, for example one of the fundamental aims of Taylorism was to dispossess craft workers of their knowledge, and embody it in a system of explicit managerial principles (Jaffee 2001).

ILLUSTRATING THE ISSUES

Tensions over the ownership of knowledge

Morris (2001) examined a knowledge codification project undertaken by a management consultancy. He found the codification project was significantly dependent on the consultants taking an active and willing part in the codification process. Morris suggests that this project represented an attempt by the company to assert its 'property rights' over the knowledge of its workers, to establish a sense of organizational ownership over it. In this case the workers were willing to participate in the project, but this was because they considered the codification project to have significant limitations. Ultimately the workers perceived that any attempt to codify their knowledge was likely to be partial and that they could thus participate in the project while simultaneously retaining key aspects of their knowledge that sustained their power and importance in the organization.

Stop and think

If the workers had perceived that it may have been possible for the organization to codify significant and important elements of their knowledge, would their attitude to participating in the project have been different?

The negative effect that conflict in the employment relationship may have on workers attitudes to knowledge-related activities takes on added importance when recent changes in the nature of the employment relationship are taken account of. Since approximately the mid-1970s there has been a massive upheaval both in the structuring of organizations (with a shift away from hierarchical, bureaucratic structures towards more flexible structures) and in the nature of the employment relationship. In general terms workers are required to be more *flexible* in the hours they work and tasks they do, while simultaneously employment has become less secure, and with fewer internal promotion opportunities (the 'New Deal' Capelli 1999). Some commentators argue that this has witnessed the rise of a 'contract culture' (Guest 1998), where workers have a limited levels of commitment and loyalty to the organizations they work for (see for example, Gallie et al. 2001; Scase 2001; Smithson and Lewis 1999).[3] This therefore suggests that the potential for conflict between the objectives of the workers and their employers over how the workers' knowledge is utlilized may be significant.

Stop and think

Are factors such as job security and promotion opportunities likely to affect a workers level of organizational commitment, or willingness to share or codify their knowledge?

Intra-organizational relations: the potential for conflict

While issues of power and conflict are looked at more fully in Chapter 7, they require to be touched on here, as one way that they get 'played out' is through attitudes to knowledge-sharing and codification. Primarily, the actual or perceived differences of interest between individuals or groups in knowledge management projects may affect attitudes to participating in such projects. Therefore, intergroup, or interpersonal conflict is the final factor considered which helps explain why the willingness of workers to share knowledge is an important issue to consider in knowledge management projects.

The contemporary knowledge literature is full of examples of where organizational conflicts have affected attitudes to knowledge-sharing. Both Hayes and Walsham (2000) and Ciborra and Patriotta (1998) illustrate how concerns by workers over the visibility of what they said and did in electronic knowledge exchange forums affected their attitudes to participation. Further, Newell et al. (2000) and Empson (2001) illustrated how intergroup conflicts and rivalries created a reluctance for intergroup knowledge-sharing. Further, Willman et al. (2001) and Morris (2001) show how concerns about 'giving away' specialist knowledge shaped attitudes towards knowledge codification projects. Such acts, as will be discussed in Chapter 7, represent expressions of power, which are all the more significant if the knowledge in question is scarce or regarded as valuable.

Stop and think

Can you think of an example from your own experience where there was interpersonal, or intergroup conflict with regards to the sharing and utilization of some knowledge? What was the basis of the conflict?

---

[3] There is an extensive debate in the human resource management literature over this topic, particularly over questions such as the degree to which managements believe in high commitment management practices, and the level of loyalty that workers have for their organizations.

Hayes and Walsham (2000) also show how the 'politicality' of the social context (such as to whom knowledge/information is visible, and real, potential, or perceived sanctions from knowledge-sharing behaviours) can vary significantly and affect knowledge-sharing attitudes and behaviours. They also acknowledged that the potential for surveillance and monitoring of such behaviours was greater in electronic forums, where a permanent record of contributions and interactions was available. These issues are discussed more fully in Chapters 7 and 8.

Thus the potentially conflictual nature of organizational life combined with the fact that knowledge represents an important power resource means that it may not necessarily be straightforward to get people to share their knowledge with colleagues.

What motivates people to share/hoard their knowledge?

The previous section looked in detail at the question of *why* it is important to take account of human attitudes to knowledge-sharing, which touched on how the social and cultural context in which knowledge management initiatives occur shapes their dynamics. This leads to questions of *what* specific aspects of the social and cultural context influences people's attitudes to knowledge-sharing. An enormous number of surveys and case studies of knowledge management initiatives have now been conducted, which have shed light on this question. In broad terms a wide range of extremely diverse factors have been found to be relevant (Table 4.3). The managerial implications from these insights, discussed more fully in the following five chapters, are as profound as they are straightforward: the success of knowledge management initiatives is crucially affected by the social and cultural context, and as a consequence these issues require to be properly accounted for in the planning and implementation of knowledge management initiatives. Ignoring them thus has potentially negative implications for the likely success of any initiative, as countless analyses illustrate (see Table 4.3). The rest of this section provides a brief overview of how each of these factors can affect knowledge-sharing attitudes and behaviours, and points towards subsequent chapters where these issues are examined more fully.

Inter-group and inter-personal conflict

As outlined above, the potential for conflicting interests in organizations is an important factor that can significantly influence the attitudes of workers to share their knowledge. The importance of knowledge as a significant power resource amplifies the potential for conflict that exists (Storey and Barnett 2000). Such conflicts can be over a wide range of issues (historical antagonisms and rivalries, concerns over reward and recognition, promotion opportunities, disputes over the legitimacy of knowledge claims, concerns over changes in status, and attempts to control knowledge management initiatives). The dynamics of intra- and inter-group-knowledge-sharing processes are examined more fully in Chapters 5 and 6, while issues of power, politics, and conflict are examined in Chapter 7.

Table 4.3. Factors affecting people's willingness to share knowledge

Factors affecting people's willingness to share knowledge	Case study examples
Intergroup/Personal Conflict	De Long & Fahey 2000; Empson 2001; Newell et al. 2000; Storey & Barnett 2000; Ward 2000
Concerns over whether status/expertise affected	Morris 2001; Willman et al. 2001; Andrews & Delahaye 2001
Sense of equity/fairness in organizational processes	Kim & Mauborgne 1998
Interpersonal trust	Andrews & Delahaye 2001; Morris & Empson 1998; Roberts 2000
Organizational commitment?	Storey & Quintas 2001; Guest & Patch 2000; Byrne 2001
General organizational culture	De Long & Fahey 2000; McDermott & O'Dell 2001; Pan & Scarbrough 1999; Ribiere 2001; Robertson & O'Malley Hammersley 2000; Robertson & Swan 2003
HRM Practices (reward/recognition)	Beaumont & Hunter 2002; Hansen et al. 1999; Hunter et al. 2002; Jarvenpaa & Staples 2000; Robertson & O'Malley Hammersley 2000; Swart & Kinnie 2003
Visibility of knowledge, attitudes, and values to senior level of organizational hierarchy	Ciborra and Patriotta 1998; Hayes & Walsham 2000

Empson (2001) provides a vivid example of such a conflict, and how it impacted on knowledge-sharing processes. She studied attempts to integrate the knowledge bases of companies following mergers and acquisitions (in accounting and consultancy companies). This study found wide-ranging resistance to the knowledge sharing/integration process between staff from the consulting companies being merged, based on perceived differences in the quality and character of their knowledge bases (such as the degree of tacitness), conflicting images of the companies being merged, and fears related to the potential negative consequences from participating in the process.

Equity and fairness

Kim and Mauborgne (1998), based on a study of senior managers from a small number of case-study organizations, suggest that the willingness of workers to share their knowledge can be related to whether they perceived a sense of *'procedural justice'* to exist in their organization. Procedural justice represents the extent to which organizational decision-making processes are fair, with fairness being related to how much people are involved in decision-making, the clarity of communication regarding why decisions are made, as well as a clarity of expectations. They suggest that when all these factors are in place workers will feel valued for their intellectual capabilities and skills. Kim and Mauborgne argue that making workers feel valued can impact on attitudes towards knowledge-sharing, 'when they felt that their ideas and person were recognized through fair process, they were willing to share their knowledge and give their all' (1998, 332). Conversely, they argue that when workers do not believe procedural justice exists, workers are likely to hoard their knowledge, and be less willing to participate in team-based cooperative work. This study suggests that organizations can significantly influence such attitudes through the way they manage their decision-making processes. The way in which organizational culture, and the use of specific human resource management policies can affect attitudes to knowledge-sharing are explored in Chapter 9.

Stop and think

What level of equity do workers expect from the organizations they work in? For example, with regards to involvement in decision-making, what type of decisions, and what levels of involvement do workers regard as fair?

Interpersonal trust

There is currently an enormous interest, and quantity of writing on the topic trust, with much of the contemporary literature considering how trust underpins effective group working, and interpersonal interaction (Jarvenpaa and Leidner 1999; Maznevski and Chudoba 2000; Meyerson et al. 1996; Nandhakumar 1999; Newell and Swan 2000). The crucial role of trust in facilitating knowledge-related processes is also being recognized (Andrews and Delahaye 2001; Davenport and Prusak 1998; McInerney and LeFevre 2000; Roberts 2000). Fundamentally, a lack of trust between individuals is likely to inhibit the extent to which people are willing to share knowledge with each other. This is because a lack of trust creates uncertainty and risk (or the perception of a risk) that all parties may not participate, or benefit equally, and that due to opportunistic behaviour, someone may lose out from sharing their knowledge (for example, by getting nothing in return).

For example, Andrews and Delahaye (2000) in a study of attitudes to knowledge-sharing by scientists found that perceptions of trustworthiness were crucially important in shaping who the scientists examined were willing to share their knowledge with. They provide a quotation from one of their interviewees who illustrated this by saying,

'If you haven't got trust and confidence then it doesn't matter what else you've put in place, or what other structures you put in place to try and encourage cooperation, it's not going to happen' (804).

 Trust

Trust refers to the belief people have about the likely behaviour of others, and the assumption that they will honour their obligations (not acting opportunistically). A trusting relationship is based on an expectation of reciprocity or mutual benefit.

The issue of trust highlights how the character of interpersonal relations crucially affects knowledge-sharing attitudes and behaviours. From a managerial point of view, sensitivity to the character of existing social relations, combined with attempting to facilitate trust-based relations may have a crucial impact on knowledge management initiatives. Finally, an issue explored further in Chapter 8 is how social relations and the development and maintenance of trust are affected when they are electronically mediated, through information and communication technologies.

Level of organizational commitment

A number of articles suggest that the level of commitment workers feel for the organizations they work in may affect both their knowledge sharing attitudes and behaviours as well as their level of loyalty (Byrne 2001; Guest and Patch 2000; Storey and Quintas 2001; Scarbrough and Carter 2000). While there is some empirical evidence that shows that loyalty levels are affected by organizational commitment (Buck and Watson 2002; Chen and Francesco 2000; Sturges and Guest 2001), there is no empirical evidence which shows how knowledge-sharing attitudes and behaviours are connected to commitment levels. Thus, the relationship between knowledge-sharing attitudes and organizational commitment is, at this point in time, somewhat theoretical and tentative.

Organizational commitment also connects with the issue trust. The degree to which the trust placed in organizations by their workers is fulfilled represents one of the main factors underpinning their level of organizational commitment (Guest and Conway 1999) The topic of organizational commitment will be revisited in Chapter 9, where it will be seen that developing commitment can be seen as part of an organization's knowledge management strategy as it can prevent the loss of valuable knowledge through increasing staff retention levels.

 Organizational commitment

The sense of emotional attachment that people feel to the organizations they work for, which may be reflected in value alignment and common goals.

Human resource management and culture management practices

An extensive amount of the knowledge management literature has shown how the culture of an organization, as well as the human resource management practices it utilizes (such as systems of pay and recognition, training, character of working conditions) can crucially impact on knowledge management initiatives (Hansen et al. 1999; Hislop 1999; Hunter and Beaumont 2002; McDermott and O'Dell 2001; Pan and Scarbrough 1999; Robertson and O'Malley Hammersley 2000). Two impacts these factors have is that not only can they affect the attitudes and behaviour of workers to knowledge management initiatives, but they can also affect staff retention levels. These issues are illustrated in the example below, and are examined more fully in Chapter 9.

ILLUSTRATING THE ISSUES

The role of culture management and HRM policies in facilitating knowledge-sharing

Robertson and O'Malley Hammersley (2000) considered how the HRM and culture management practices of Expert Consulting, a specialist UK consulting company, shaped the attitudes of their consultants to share their knowledge. The study found that Expert Consulting used a wide range of HRM practices to achieve this, including recruitment and selection (where workers were chosen for how well they fitted with the knowledge-sharing culture); training and development (where workers had a lot of autonomy to decide on their own training and development requirements); job design (where the workers were granted significant autonomy over how they worked); and the development of a culture of informality and openness to knowledge-sharing. The study concluded that Expert Consulting was successful in its endeavours, which was visible from the fact that not only were its workers willing to proactively share their knowledge, but that its retention rates were significantly higher than the industry average.

Concerns over the visibility of interactions

Both Hayes and Walsham (2000) and Ciborra and Patriotta (1998) showed how concern by workers over the visibility of their opinions to senior management inhibited their participation in electronic knowledge exchange forums. These concerns were related to how this information/knowledge might be used, or interpreted by senior managers. For example, Ciborra and Patriotta (1998, 50) showed that in one of the groupware systems they studied contribution levels changed dramatically following comments put on the system by a *'very senior manager'*. Their research showed that '[t]his 'intrusion'... provoked a panic reaction amongst employees and contributed to a freeze in the use of the system for some months.' Primarily in both studies, workers were loath to express opinions which might be seen as not complying with managerial perspectives in forums which were transparent and widely used. This theme connects closely with the issue of power, which is explored more fully in Chapter 7.

Stop and think

How typical are the findings of Hayes and Walsham, and Ciborra and Patriotta? If workers are aware that their knowledge and values will be visible to senior management, are they likely to censor, or modify how they act, and what they say?

Concerns about power/status/expertise

The final issue considered in this chapter which has been found to influence people's knowledge-sharing attitudes and behaviour is the extent to which people's power, status, and expertise is affected, or the extent to which they *perceive* it will be affected, by participating in knowledge-sharing processes. These perceptions and concerns can have positive or negative effects on knowledge-sharing behaviour, dependent upon how workers perceive their power, status, and expertise will be affected. On the positive side, the Morris example outlined earlier in the chapter (see p. 47) showed how consultants had a positive attitude to an organizational knowledge codification project, as they perceived that participating in the project would not jeopardize crucial elements of their specialist knowledge and expertise, and the status and power which they derived from having it. Willman et al. (2001) outline a more negative example, where traders in London's financial markets occasionally refrained from codifying elements of their tacit knowledge, due to the financial benefits, and status they believed they could derive from personally retaining, or 'hoarding' it. This issue connects closely to the topic of trust discussed above, as the degree of trust people have in their colleagues and employers will affect the risks and rewards they perceive to exist from participating in knowledge management initiatives.

These anxieties highlight a dilemma for workers related to participating in knowledge management initiatives: whether to share or hoard knowledge. Sharing knowledge has the potential benefits of improving a person's status as well as creating opportunities for the development of new knowledge, but has the risk that it involves workers 'giving away' the source of their expertise, status, and power. However, the opposite strategy of hoarding has its own risks and advantages. The advantage of hoarding is that it may protect an individual's expertise, but runs the risk of the importance of their knowledge not being recognized and rewarded. These issues will be explored more fully in Chapter 7.

Conclusion

The chapter has outlined the limitations of the first-generation knowledge management literature, which so conspicuously played down socio-cultural issues. The critique of this perspective has revealed the substantial limitations of much of this early literature, and has shown that:

1. Human, social, and cultural factors are fundamental to understanding both the attitudes of workers to knowledge management initiatives and the dynamics of knowledge management processes.
2. It is problematic to assume that people will be willing to actively participate in knowledge management initiatives.

These conclusions stem from three factors. Firstly, that much organizational knowledge is personal and embodied, requiring the willingness of its possessor for it to be shared, codified, etc. Secondly, the nature of the employment relationship means that in relation to knowledge management initiatives the interests of workers, and their employers may not always be compatible. Finally, the typically conflictual nature of intra-organizational relations means that control over knowledge and knowledge management initiatives in organizations are likely to be contested. The chapter also illustrated the wide range of specific factors which can influence people's willingness to share knowledge.

Finally, the most important managerial implication flowing from the issues addressed in this chapter are that attention requires to be paid to the character of the socio-cultural context, and that a lack of sensitivity to it is likely to jeopardize the success of any knowledge management initiative.

REVIEW QUESTIONS

1 Based on your own experience, what has been the attitudes of work colleagues to sharing their knowledge? Have you found them to be willing to share, or has hoarding been more typical? What are the most important factors which explain this behaviour?

2 How compatible have your and your employing organization's interests been with regard to how you have used your knowledge? Have the organization's goals and your own always been harmonious, or have there been any conflict and tensions over how you use your knowledge?

3 Have you found trust to be an important factor underpinning attitudes to knowledge-sharing? Have you had any experiences where a lack of trust has inhibited knowledge-sharing, or where the existence of trust has facilitated it?

FURTHER READING

- J. Storey, and E. Barnett (2000). 'Knowledge Management Initiatives: Learning from Failure', *Journal of Knowledge Management*, 4/2:145–56.

  Case study of a failed knowledge management initiative, which reveals the internal politics and conflicts that can affect knowledge management initiatives.

- H. Scarbrough (1999). 'Knowledge as Work: Conflicts in the Management of Knowledge Workers', *Technology Analysis and Strategic Management*, 11/1: 5–16.

  Considers the issues and dilemmas involved in organizations attempting to motivate knowledge workers to share their knowledge

- L. Hunter, P. Beaumont, and M. Lee (2002). 'Knowledge Management Practice in Scottish Law Firms', *Human Resource Management Journal*, 12/2: 4–21.

  Presents case study evidence of the type of knowledge management strategies utilized by some Scottish Law firms, and considers the implications for the HRM function.

- L. Empson (2001). 'Fear of Exploitation and Fear of Contamination: Impediments to Knowledge Transfer in Mergers between Professional Service Firms', *Human Relations*, 54/7: 839–62.

  Detailed case study examining reluctance of workers to share knowledge with new colleagues following a merger.

5

Communities of practice

Introduction

In the vast literature on knowledge management that has been produced, the concept of 'communities of practice' has been one of the most popular. Thus Edwards et al. (2003), in a survey of KM academics and practitioners, found that they represented the second most important concept developed in this literature. Unsurprisingly, therefore, an enormous number of articles have used it to understand the dynamics of organizational knowledge processes (for example, Baumard 1999; Brown and Duguid 2001; DeFillippi and Arthur 1998; Pan and Scarbrough 1999). More prescriptively, a growing number of writers suggest that developing communities of practice can be key to the success of knowledge management initiatives (for example Bate and Roberts 2002; Ward 2000; Wenger 1998; Wenger et al. 2002).

Communities of practice are informal groups of people who have some work-related activity in common. As will be seen, the communities of practice literature is most closely associated with the practice-based perspective on knowledge, as it assumes that the knowledge people have is embedded in, and inseparable from, the (collectively based) activities that people carry out. The informality of these communities stems from the fact that they emerge from the social interactions that are a necessary part of the work activities that people undertake. Further, while most of the literature on communities of practice focuses on organizationally specific communities, communities can span organizational boundaries (Brown and Duguid 2001). For example, Gittelman and Kogut (2003) analyse the researchers involved in the Unites States' biotechnology industry as constituting a community of practice.

While communities of practice may appear to be a totally new concept, discovered and developed within the knowledge management literature, this is not the case. For example, in the area of industrial sociology there has been an interest in the closely related concept of 'occupational communities', which significantly predates the emergence of knowledge management (Salaman 1974; van Maanen and Barley 1984). The invisibility of this literature stems from the fact that almost without exception it is ignored by knowledge management writers.

This chapter has a very specific focus, discussing and analysing the *internal dynamics* of communities of practice. The character and dynamics of inter-community knowledge processes are explored in Chapter 6. Chapters 5 and 6 can therefore can be read together, as they both examine the dynamics of group-based knowledge processes. The reason for doing this in two rather than one chapter is that, as will be discussed more fully in Chapter 6, the character and dynamics of intra- and inter-community knowledge processes are qualitatively different. Further, the dynamics of knowledge processes within 'virtual' communities are discussed in Chapters 8 and 12.

Defining and characterizing communities of practice

Communities of practice are groups of individuals and workers[4] who have some form of practice in common, for example, an informal group of IT staff within an organization which has responsibility for designing and maintaining similar IT systems. These groups are typically informal, and ad hoc in nature, developing out of the communication and interaction which is a necessary part of most work activities. Unlike formalized workgroups, and teams, they do not represent a part of the formal organizational structure and therefore typically do not appear on organization charts (see Table 5.1).

Table 5.1. Difference between a CoP and formal work groups

	Community of practice	**Organizational work group or team**
Objective	Evolving Shaped by common values Internally negotiated	Clear, formally defined Externally determined
Focus of efforts	Collective practice/knowledge	Provide specific service and/or product
Membership	Voluntary	Typically formalized and delegated (though occasionally voluntary)
Government of Internal structure	Consensually negotiated Non-hierarchical	Formalized division of labour Hierarchical structure Individualized roles & responsibilities
External system of management & control	Self-managing Informal, interpersonal relations	Formalized relations defined by organizational hierarchy Performance monitoring against specific targets goals
Time frame	Indefinite, internally negotiated	Permanent, or with finite time-frame/objective

[4] Communities of practice do not exist solely within business organizations. For example, one of the examples of a community provided by Lave and Wenger (1991) was of non-drinking, recovering alcoholics. However, in this chapter, the focus is narrowly on communities of practice within a workplace context.

ILLUSTRATING THE ISSUES

Gas appliance service engineers: a community of practice

In Gas-co, the UK's largest gas supply and service company, service engineers are home-based workers, who have no formal office space. The training of new engineers occurs through attendance at a number of formal, classroom-based training courses, as well as more informally, through a 'buddy system'. The buddy system operates for 26 weeks, and involves new engineers working along beside experienced engineers, and constitutes a form of on-the-job training. The individualized nature of the work, combined with the lack of an office base makes communication and interaction between engineers difficult. However, a strong sense of group identity is maintained through regular phone contacts with colleagues, and frequent formal and informal face-to-face group meetings. For example, if engineers find situations where they are unsure what to do, typically they phone up colleagues. Further, to ensure regular face-to-face contact many engineers arrange to go to the parts depot simultaneously, and use this opportunity to have coffee with each other, socialize, and share stories regarding their work.

Stop and think

Given the individualized nature of the work, and the informal nature of much of the interpersonal interactions, is there a risk that particularly shy people, or people who are not liked by their colleagues will not be fully integrated into the community, and may not benefit from the knowledge and information shared by others? Is this a potential negative side of all communities, where membership is affected by personality-related factors, which can lead to exclusion or the weak integration of some people?

Such groups have traditionally been treated with hostility by senior management, who may be concerned about how these groups may undermine formal structures and systems (Brown and Duguid 1991). However, more and more, as part of knowledge management initiatives, organizations are attempting to deliberately support and develop communities of practice due to their perceived benefits in relation to knowledge processes (see below). By their very nature, however, communities of practice are not easily amenable to deliberate management and control. The contradictions of attempting to formalize such inherently informal interactions are not insignificant, and will be discussed later.

 Community of practice

A group of people who have a particular activity in common, and as a consequence have some common knowledge, a sense of community identity, and some element of overlapping values

Premisses

The community of practice concept is based on two central premisses: the practice-based perspective on knowledge, and the group based-character of organizational activity. The primary relevance of the practice-based perspective on knowledge stems from the assumption in the communities of practice literature that knowing and doing are inseparable, as undertaking specific tasks requires the use and development of embodied knowledge. Thus, Brown and Duguid (1991, 43) argue that 'learning-in-working is an occupational necessity' and that carrying out work activities also involves the 'situated production of understanding' (1991, 44).[5]

The second major premiss is that organizational activities are typically collective, involving the coordinated interaction of groups of workers (see for example, Barnes 1977; Brown and Duguid 1998; Gherardi et al. 1998; McDermott 1999). Thus, one common feature of virtually every type of work imaginable, from office cleaning to management consulting, is that they involve an element of coordination and interaction with co-workers, subordinates and/or supervisors.

Therefore, while the knowledge that members of a community of practice have and develop is highly personal, there is an extent to which much of this knowledge is simultaneously shared within a community. From an objectivist perspective on knowledge, the common knowledge shared by the workers in a community of practice is collective/group knowledge (with both tacit and explicit elements—see Table 2.4).

Lave and Wenger (1991), who are typically acknowledged as being instrumental in the development and elaboration of the community of practice concept, define them as a community of practitioners within which situational learning develops, which results in the community developing, 'a set of relations among persons, activity and the world' (98). Extrapolating from this definition communities of practice can be seen to have three defining characteristics, all of which flow from the community members' involvement in some shared activities (Table 5.2). Firstly, participants in a community possess and develop a stock of common, shared knowledge. Secondly, communities typically also develop shared values and attitudes, a common 'world-view'. Boland and Tenkasi (1995) referred to the process of developing and communicating such views, 'perspective making' (see Chapter 3). Finally, and equally importantly, members of communities also possess a sense of communal identity (Brown and Duguid 2001). These elements of a community develop not only through the physical activities involved in collectively carrying out the communities tasks, but also through language and communication. Thus, for example, stories, or specialist jargon can be regarded as a part of the collective knowledge of the group, whose use by group members contributes to their sense of collective identity and shared values.

Table 5.2. Generic characteristics of communities of practice

Characteristics of CoPs
1. Body of common knowledge/practice
2. Sense of shared identity
3. Some common or overlapping values

---

[5] Brown and Duguid take this quotation from Orr (1990).

A useful way to illustrate these characteristics is through an example. Trowler and Turner (2002) illustrate how the Deaf Studies group of an English University constitutes a community of practice. This group consists of three hearing academics (who are fluent in sign language) and three deaf academics. The shared practice of this community constitutes both the teaching of the Deaf Studies curriculum, as well as research conducted by the group on a range of issues affecting deaf people. This group has a strong sense of collective identity, as well as a belief in a common goal (contributing to the education of deaf people and their integration in society, raising awareness of the social issues affecting deaf people, and furthering knowledge on the issues which affect deaf people through carrying out research). While the group communicates both internally and externally in both sign language and English, the shared language of the group is arguably sign language. The study also showed how the use of English language, and the English language protocols embedded in certain formal meetings and group forums, represented a form of power that significantly disadvantaged the deaf members of the working group.

Stop and think

Are you or have you ever been a member of a community of practice? What role, if any, did language in the form of specialist jargon and shared stories play in the development and reinforcement of the community?

Communities of practice are highly dynamic, evolving as new members become absorbed into a community, as existing members leave, and as the knowledge and practices of the community evolves with changing circumstances. Learning and knowledge evolution are therefore inherent and fundamental aspects of the dynamics of communities of practice, which helps explain why one of the main contexts in which the community of practice concept originated and developed was in the organizational learning literature.

Lave and Wenger (1991) used the term 'legitimate peripheral participation' to characterize the process by which people learn and become socialized into being a member of a community. This process is based on 'triadic' group relations involving masters (or 'old timers'), young masters (or 'journeymen'), and apprentices (or 'newcomers'). Apprentices learn from watching and communicating with the master and other members of the community, and start as peripheral members, participating initially in relatively straightforward tasks. However, over time, as the apprentices become competent with these basic skills, they gradually become introduced to more complex tasks. Legitimate peripheral participation is thus the process by which newcomers to a community acquire the knowledge required to be a community member, through gradually increasing levels of *participation* in community activities, during which time they simultaneously move from being *peripheral* members of the community to become more central and *legitimate* members of it. Informal learning from other group members is a key element of this process, or as Trowler and Turner (2002, 242) suggest, 'learning to become an organizational member is far more a question of socialization than of formal learning.'

ILLUSTRATING THE ISSUES

Legitimate peripheral participation: naval quartermasters

Hutchins (1993) describes the process of learning and socialization that apprentice naval quartermasters undergo (this study is also described and analysed by Fox 2000). Naval quartermasters are responsible for maintaining a continuous log of a ship's position. While much of this work is relatively solitary, key aspects (such as entering and leaving port) require a team of quartermasters to work together. Learning to be a quartermaster typically takes about one year. The preferred way that established quartermasters like to train new ones is through on the job learning. Over the year that it takes to learn to be a quartermaster, newcomers begin by doing relatively routine and straightforward tasks (such as taking bearings). Once such skills have been mastered, apprentices gradually become allowed to do more complex tasks, such as integrating all the different readings together, and interpreting the information. By the end of the year they will have become more central, experienced, and established members of their community, and will be in a position to train other new apprentices.

Stop and think

What is the potential for conflict between the established quartermasters and the apprentices? Is it possible that the established quartermasters may feel resentful towards and threatened by the apprentices, whom they may regard as providing a potential challenge to their status and authority? Further, can such tensions be managed and minimized?

Communities of practice and the organizational knowledge base

The communities of practice literature, building from insights developed using the practice-based perspective on knowledge (see Chapter 3), suggests that the knowledge base of organizations can be conceptualized as a 'community-of-communities' (Brown and Duguid 1991), or more poetically, a 'constellation of communities' (Gherardi and Nicolini 2002; Ward 2001). Thus, rather than the organizational knowledge base being a coherent and unitary body of knowledge, it can more accurately be conceptualized as fragmented, being constituted by a diverse range of localized bodies of specialist knowledge possessed by specific communities. While the knowledge base of these communities is overlapping and interdependent, with an element of common knowledge existing (Kogut and Zander 1992), much of the knowledge contained within these organizational communities is localized and specialized in nature, having limited relevance beyond its specific context of application.

However, the character and structure of organizational knowledge bases varies significantly between organizations (see for example Empson 2001; Lam 1997). This is because, as Brown and Duguid suggest (1998, 98), 'the distribution of knowledge in an organization . . . as a whole, reflects the social division of labour.' Thus the way in which work activities are structured within organizations will affect the character of the organizational knowledge base. For example, compare the case of the pension company described immediately below, where business units are structured by product, to the example described in Chapter 3 (see p. 35–6) where business units were structured into geographic regions. While the knowledge base in both cases is fragmented, the character of the knowledge bases reflects the different ways in which work is structured.

ILLUSTRATING THE ISSUES

Communities of practice and the structuring of work

Business in UK-Pension, one of the UK's largest and most recognizable pensions companies had traditionally been structured around their two main product areas, pensions and life assurance. These divisions were run as separate businesses, with their own, distinct management structures, staff, business processes, IT systems, and customer bases. Further, there had historically been little interaction between them. Communication only occurred within the divisions, and never between them. This resulted in the development of two separate and specialized knowledge communities, which only had knowledge of their own customers, IT systems, and working practices.

One illustration of the extent of this was in the fact that there was no sharing of customer information. Neither division had any straightforward way of finding out whether any of their customers had business in the other division, and it was impossible for customers with products in both divisions to get a single, summarized statement of their total portfolio. Further, the autonomy of these divisions was such that the evolution and development of their working practices, the upgrading of their IT systems etc., was done purely on the basis of intra-divisional considerations. For example, each division had its own separate IT systems and working practices for using them. These systems and working procedures were so different that administrative staff in the pensions division would not have been able to use the IT systems in the life assurance division without substantial training, and vice versa.

Chapters 12–14 examine the character of the knowledge base in three generic organizational contexts (virtual organizations, global multinationals, and knowledge-intensive organizations), which consider how these affect and are affected by organizational knowledge management initiatives.

Communities of practice and intra-community knowledge processes

Almost universally, the communities of practice literature considers communities of practice to be advantageous for both individuals and organizations. Thus they provide workers with a sense of collective identity, and a social context in which they can effectively develop and utilize their knowledge. For organizations, they can provide a vital source of innovation. The knowledge management literature, which has utilized the communities of practice concept, strongly argues that they can facilitate organizational knowledge processes (Table 5.3). The rest of this section considers the potential benefits in terms of knowledge processes that communities of practice can provide.

Table 5.3. Knowledge-related benefits of CoPs

Benefits of CoPs in terms of organizational knowledge processes	Case study examples
Underpin organizational innovativeness (through the creation, development and application of knowledge)	Amidon 1998; Brown & Duguid 1991; Dougherty 2001; Liedtka 1999; Mitsuru 1999; Wenger 1998; Wenger & Snyder 2000
Facilitate knowledge-sharing and support and encourage individual and group learning	Bate & Roberts 2002; Brown & Duguid 1998; DeFillippi & Arthur 1998; Gittelman & Kogut 2003; Hildreth et al 2000; Iles 1994; Lave & Wenger 1991; McDermott 1999; Raelin 1997; Ward 2000

In terms of knowledge processes, communities of practice have the potential to provide benefits in two broad areas. Firstly, communities of practice can underpin levels of organizational innovativeness through supporting and encouraging the creation, development, and use of knowledge. Thus, Orr (1990) showed how the community of practice that existed amongst Xerox's photocopy repair engineers allowed these workers to develop their knowledge and understanding through solving problems that could not be corrected by simply following the knowledge encoded in instruction manuals. Secondly, the common knowledge possessed by members of a community of practice, combined with their sense of collective identity, and system of shared values means they have the potential to facilitate individual and group learning, and the sharing of knowledge within the community.

ILLUSTRATING THE ISSUES

Knowledge-sharing within a community of practice

Hildreth et al. (2000) examined an internationally distributed community of practice within the IT support function of the research department in a 'major international company'. The group of IT support managers studied, while being internationally distributed (primarily in the UK, and the USA), had a common sense of purpose, a shared sense of identity, and its own specialist language and terminology. While the main form of interaction between group members in the UK and American sites was through e-mail, voice mail, and a telephone-based video link, the twice yearly face-to-face meetings the group had also played a key role. These face-to-face meetings, much more than the electronically mediated interactions, helped in the development of a sense of community identity and strengthened the interpersonal relations between community members. During the research undertaken, the group were observed, while working on a collaborative task, the development of a common planning document. This task, which involved communication and interaction between staff in the UK and the USA, was made possible by the shared sense of identity and common knowledge that these workers had. Further, the process of producing the document itself helped sustain and reinforce the sense of community that existed between these workers.

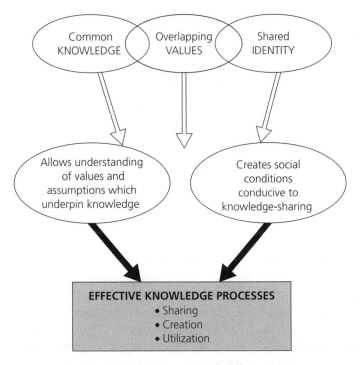

Fig. 5.1. How communities of practice underpin knowledge processes

Stop and think

How important is face-to-face contact in helping to sustain communities of practice? Is it possible for communities to develop and survive without any face-to-face contact at all between members?

The advantages of communities of practice in enabling such knowledge processes are closely related to the elements that members of a community share. As outlined earlier, members of a community of practice, not only have a stock of common knowledge, but also have a shared sense of identity, and some overlapping, common values. The simultaneous existence of these elements enables knowledge processes, as they simplify the communication of knowledge that is inherently sticky: tacit knowledge. This is for two reasons. Firstly, the existence of these three elements make appreciating the taken-for-granted assumptions, and values which underpin tacit knowledge easier to understand. Secondly, the existence of these elements is likely to produce and sustain trust-based relations, creating social conditions that are conducive to knowledge-sharing (see Figure 5.1).

Managing communities of practice

In discussing the topic of how to explicitly manage communities of practice, the difficulties, contradictions, and risks of (attempting to) do this require to be highlighted. The contradictions and difficulties related to managing communities of practice stem from their fundamentally informal, emergent, and somewhat ad hoc nature (see Table 5.1). These characteristics mean that communities of practice are not easily amenable to top-down control. Communities of practice are autonomous, self-managing systems, which can exist and flourish without the need for any senior management support (Baumard 1999). Managerial attempts to control and influence communities of practice may there-fore conflict with a community's system of self-management. Thus, the risk, in attempting to explicitly manage communities of practice is that such attempts may in fact have adverse effects on the community, and the very knowledge processes that such efforts are intended to support and develop. For example, one specific risk may be that attempts to formalize a community may introduce rigidities which inhibit its innovativeness or adaptability.

However, despite these difficulties and potential problems, more and more organiza-tions are attempting to develop and support communities of practice as part of their knowledge management initiatives. This section considers the ways in which this can be done. Due to the narrow focus of this chapter, only issues related to managing and sup-porting individual communities and intracommunity knowledge processes are exam-ined. The managerial implications of coordinating intercommunity relations and knowledge processes are discussed separately, in Chapter 6.

In general terms, the knowledge management literature advocates two main ways in which communities of practice could, or should be managed. Firstly, it is argued that their management should be done with a 'light touch'. Secondly, all management interven-tions should reinforce the essential attributes of communities that make them so effective at facilitating knowledge processes.

Two advocates of the 'light touch' approach to managing communities of practice are McDermott (1999), and Ward (2000). Thus, McDermott suggests that organizations should, 'develop natural knowledge communities without formalizing them' (110). Ward, utilizing a garden metaphor, argues that communities of practice require to be, 'tended and nurtured rather than commanded and controlled' (4). The gardening metaphor, suggesting the communities of practice have organic qualities and are contin-ually adapting and evolving, usefully captures the informal and emergent aspect of com-munities of practice. However, the limitation of this managerial advice is that it is somewhat vague and lacking in detail. Thus, the analyses that advocate such an approach typically fail to provide specific details on what the 'light touch' management approach looks like, or consists of.

More concrete is the second type of advice, to reinforce the best attributes of commun-ities of practice. This advice covers a range of issues including:

- Emphasize practice-based, peer-supported learning methods rather than formalized, classroom-based methods as this reinforces the existing ways that communities learn and share knowledge (Brown and Duguid 1991; Stamps 2000).

- Avoid privileging formal objectified knowledge, as this leads to a neglect of the 'non-canonical' tacit, practice-based knowledge developed by communities (Brown and Duguid 1991).

- Due to the significant length of time required for communities of practice to develop (to allow the creation of a common perspective, and a stock of common knowledge, as well as a sense of collective identity) continuity is important (Baumard 1999). Overly discontinuous social relations are thus likely to hamper their development.

- Find, nurture, and support existing communities (McDermott 1999). McDermott suggests that the best way to do this is reinforce each communities systems of self-management, for example strengthening their existing mechanisms for social interaction, and providing them with adequate autonomy to allow them to decide and control both what knowledge is important, as well as how it should be organized and shared.

Therefore, a significant amount of advice exists on how communities of practice can best be supported. However, ironically, much of this advice suggests that the best way to manage communities is to provide them the autonomy to manage themselves.

Stop and think

In your work experience, what has management attitudes to communities of practice been? Were they aware of them? Were they hostile to them? Were they given autonomy to be self-managing? Or, were attempts made to facilitate and manage them? Further, did these attitudes and behaviours facilitate or inhibit the operation of these communities?

Disadvantages of communities of practice for knowledge processes

As outlined earlier, much of the communities of practice literature presents communities in a very positive light, suggesting that in relation to knowledge processes they are largely or exclusively beneficial for organizations. However, the limitation of this idealistic characterization of communities is that it creates a blindness to the range of potential ways in which they may inhibit organizational knowledge processes. Thus, while communities of practice may facilitate processes of knowledge-sharing, they also have the potential to inhibit them. Arguably much of the communities literature has thus provided a somewhat one-sided, and unbalanced analysis of communities of practice. To avoid the same problem it is necessary to consider the potential dark side of communities of practice. Two specific issues are examined here: first, how power and conflict can shape the internal dynamics of communities; and secondly, the way communities may develop 'blinkers' which can inhibit innovations and intercommunity interaction. The issue of knowledge 'hoarding' within a community is discussed in Chapter 6, as this is related to intercommunity relations. The issues considered here relate primarily to intracommunity dynamics.

Power, conflict, and the internal dynamics of communities

As will be seen in Chapter 7, one of the major criticisms of the majority of the mainstream knowledge management literature is the neglect of issues of power and conflict. The communities of practice literature is no exception to this, and thus, generally, issues of power and conflict within communities are either typically downplayed or ignored. In *Situated Learning* (1991) Lave and Wenger, as will be seen below, do discuss these issues.

But their appeal for future analyses to take greater account of, 'unequal relations of power' (42) within communities has typically been neglected by subsequent writers (the most notable exception being Fox 2000). Further, these issues have also been downplayed in some of their own later work, such as Wenger (1998), where, as Fox makes clear, issues of power and conflict are largely relegated to footnotes. Further, while Wenger et al. (2002) devote a whole chapter to the 'downside of communities' issues of power are ignored.

Fundamentally, communities of practice have inherent tensions built into them which unavoidably results in them possessing an, 'unequal distribution of power' (Lave and Wenger 1991, 42), and where what Fox (2000) described as 'power conflicts' are likely. The uneven distribution of power results from the, by definition, greater amount of community knowledge masters have compared to newcomers. Thus while communities of practice do not have a formal hierarchical structure, this does not mean that all members of the community are equal. This uneven distribution of knowledge creates potential conflicts in processes of legitimate peripheral participation. For example, Lave and Wenger (1991, 57) argue that, 'There is a fundamental contradiction in the meaning to newcomers and old-timers of increasing participation by the former; for the centripetal development of full participants . . . implies the replacement of old timers.'

Legitimate peripheral participation thus requires the 'old-timers' helping to develop the knowledge of the 'newcomers' who will, over time, take their place. Further, the contradictions inherent in such a process are fundamental, and unavoidable (see Lave and Wenger, 1991, 113–17). Another source of conflict within communities of practice relates to the 'contradictory nature of collective social practice' (Lave and Wenger 1991, 58). This contradiction relates to the fact that while the members of a community work together collectively and cooperate, they are also simultaneously, to some extent, competing with each other inside their organizations, for example for promotion opportunities.

The power conflicts that are an inherent aspect of communities take on greater importance when communities are faced with change, which, over time they inevitably do. Change that requires a community's practices/knowledge to adapt, threatens the status quo (the reproduction of existing knowledge/practices), and can have contradictory implications for different members of a community of practice (Fox 2000). Thus old-timers may see such change as a threat to their status, power, and knowledge, whereas other members of a community may see it as an opportunity to develop and increase their own power, knowledge, and status. These insights have two implications with regard to how communities of practice respond to change, which are both neglected by the mainstream literature. Firstly, communities of practice are as likely to resist as support change, and secondly, it can't be assumed that all the members of a community will respond in the same way to change.

ILLUSTRATING THE ISSUES

A scientific community resisting culture change

Breu and Hemingway (2002) studied a large European scientific research organization, Alpha, which had recently been privatized. Following this privatization the scientists had been highly resistant to the introduction of a new, commercially focused business culture. The scientists in

Alpha constituted a community of practice as they had the three constituent elements of a community. Firstly, there was a shared, common practice (conducting 'blue sky' research in specialist disciplinary teams). Secondly, the scientists had a common set of values (a belief in the value of scientific research driven by scientific inquiry and the advancement of knowledge). Finally, the scientists in Alpha also had a collective sense of identity (as being professional scientists who were members of both a local and global research community).

The resistance by the scientists in Alpha had a number of sources. One factor was the particular change implementation strategy adopted (introducing large-scale change rapidly with only limited consultation). However, a large part of the scientists' resistance stemmed from the fact that they interpreted the values of the new economic culture (pursuing research driven by economic goals) as being antithetical to the values of their research community. Further, the scientists refused to change their values, and were able to quite effectively resist the changes through a range of strategies including continuing to pursue work driven by scientific values, recruiting new scientists in ways which perpetuated the existing culture, and developing independent and informal networks for the resourcing of research projects.

Stop and think

Gittelman and Kogut (2003) identified similar tensions in the United States biotechnology industry, between producing knowledge for scientific purposes and knowledge for economic gain. Does this mean that there are inevitable and unavoidable tensions between the commercialization of knowledge for profit and the development of knowledge for more abstract, scientific purposes?

Blinkered and inward-looking communities

While the collective sense of identity and values that exist between members of a community can create a bond that may facilitate the development of trust, and knowledge-sharing, there are potential negative consequences if such bonds are too strong. For example, where too strong a sense of community identity exists this may provide a basis for exclusion, where those not part of the 'community' are ignored, and their knowledge not considered to be relevant or important to the community (Alvesson 2000; Baumard 1999). This can cause communities to become inward-looking, and unreceptive to ideas generated outside the community. In such circumstances a communities' search processes may be limited rather than extensive, with consequent negative implications for the communities' innovativeness (Leonard and Sensiper 1998). See, for example, the Starbuck and Milliken (1998) example of the Challenger Space Shuttle disaster, outlined earlier (p. 33).

Such communities may not only neglect external ideas, but also people. Communities with a strong sense of identity may become exclusive clubs or 'cliques' (Wenger et al. 2002), where membership is tightly controlled, and the factors that define a community's identity used to exclude entry to others. Just as with the neglect of external ideas, such practices can result in communities becoming poor at absorbing new, external knowledge and ideas.

Stop and think

Have you worked as part of a team, or community where there has been a hostility or blindness to ideas generated outside of it? If so, did this have any effect on group or organizational performance?

Conclusion

Communities of Practice have been defined as informal groups that have some work activities in common. As a consequence, these communities develop: (1) a shared body of common knowledge; (2) a shared of collective identity; and (3) some overlapping values.

The mainstream knowledge management literature portrays communities of practice as being effective vehicles for knowledge-sharing and knowledge creation. Consequently, the existence of effectively operating communities of practice is typically argued to underpin individual and organizational-level learning processes, as well as supporting high levels of organizational innovativeness. The effectiveness of communities of practice in this respect is because:

- The existence of common knowledge and a shared system of values makes sharing tacit knowledge easier, as group members have insights into the implicit assumptions and values embedded in each other's knowledge.

- The shared knowledge, values, and identity which exist also facilitate the development and maintenance of trust-based relations, which, as outlined in Chapter 4, create social conditions conducive to knowledge-sharing.

However, the chapter also concluded that the mainstream literature on communities of practice portrays an overly optimistic image of them. To understand why communities of practice have the potential to inhibit as much as facilitate knowledge processes, account needs to be taken of issues of power and conflict within communities, as well as the way that too strong a sense of community identity may inhibit intercommunity processes of knowledge-sharing. This final conclusion points towards the dynamics of intercommunity interaction, which is the topic dealt with in Chapter 6.

REVIEW QUESTIONS

1   If you are, or have been a member of a community of practice, how were you socialized? How did you develop the knowledge, values, and identity that characterize membership? Did your socialization closely resemble the process of legitimate peripheral participation described by Lave and Wenger?

2   How relevant and accurate is the 'community of communities' metaphor for describing the knowledge base of any organizations you have worked in? Does this downplay the amount of common knowledge which is typically shared by workers in business organizations?

3   Based on any organizational experience you have had, what effect have communities of practice had on organizational knowledge processes? Have they been largely or purely positive and beneficial? Has there been any negative aspects to them such as knowledge hoarding, or an unwillingness to accept ideas from outside the community?

FURTHER READING

- J. Lave and E. Wenger (1991). *Situated Learning: Legitimate Peripheral Participation*. Cambridge: Cambridge University Press.

  A short, and highly accessible introduction to the concepts of situated learning, communities of practice, and legitimate peripheral participation.

- J. Brown and P. Duguid (1991). 'Organization Learning and Communities of Practice: Towards a Unified View of Working, Learning and Innovation', *Organization Science*, 2/1: 40–57.

  Applies the community of practice concept to work organizations, and discusses the nature of organizational learning.

- S. Fox (2000). 'Practice, Foucault and Actor-Network Theory', *Journal of Management Studies*, 37/6: 853–68.

  Contains a good discussion of why power and conflict need to be accounted for when considering communities of practice.

6

Intercommunity, boundary-spanning knowledge processes

Introduction

This chapter is premissed on the idea that knowledge processes within and between communities of practice are quite different and distinctive. This is primarily because while members of a community of practice have much common knowledge and a strong shared sense of identity, people who are not members of the same community typically do not. While Chapter 5 examined the characteristics of intracommunity knowledge processes, the focus of this chapter is exclusively on intercommunity knowledge processes. Further, this chapter will show that intercommunity knowledge processes are typically more complex and difficult to make successful. Why this is the case will be fully explored as the chapter progresses.

Intercommunity knowledge processes encapsulate an enormous variety of contexts and can involve knowledge processes which span community, occupational, organizational, functional, national, or project boundaries. This chapter builds on issues raised in Chapter 3, such as the nature of the organizational knowledge base, and is primarily founded in a practice-based perspective on knowledge. This will become apparent as the chapter progresses, as various terms and concepts are (re)introduced.

The chapter begins in the following section by considering why intercommunity knowledge processes are so important. After this, the main section of the chapter examines the character of intercommunity knowledge processes, and presents a number of examples to illustrate the points made. Finally, the chapter closes by considering the way that intercommunity knowledge processes can be facilitated and managed.

The significance of intercommunity knowledge processes

Consider the following situations:

- A joint technology development project involving close collaboration between UK and Japanese electronics companies (Lam 1997).

- The consolidation of the knowledge base in some accounting and consultancy companies following mergers and acquisitions (Empson 2001).

- Collaboration between indigenous Maori groups with the New Zealand government in negotiation over land treaties (Pauleen and Yoong 2001).

- Attempts by project-based companies involved in the design of complex products to share knowledge between projects (Prencipe and Tell 2001).

- A large-scale interuniversity research project involving staff from three UK universities whose disciplinary backgrounds encompass engineering, operation management, organizational behaviour, and marketing (Newell and Swan 2000).

- Interorganizational product development efforts in the biotechnology sector (Powell et al. 1996).

- Cross-occupational collaboration that occurs as part of the concurrent engineering work at a semiconductor equipment factory in the USA (Bechky 2003).

All these situations, while being diverse in character, have one thing in common: they involve the sharing, or joint utilization and development of knowledge among people who do not typically work together, and who have substantially different knowledge bases. One of the reasons why examining the dynamics of intercommunity knowledge processes is so important is that the type of working practices outlined in these examples is becoming more and more common. Thus evidence suggests that the use of project-based working methods and the utilization of interpersonal and interorganizational networks has become widespread (for example, see Castells 1996; Cravens et al. 1996; Davies and Brady 2000; Powell 1990). For example, all three of the organizational contexts examined later, in Chapters 12–14, i.e. knowledge-intensive firms, global multinationals, and network/virtual organizations, involve the utilization of intercommunity knowledge processes.

Another factor that signals the importance of intercommunity knowledge processes is the growing acknowledgement that the knowledge bases of all organizations are to some extent fragmented into separate, specialized knowledge communities. As outlined in Chapter 3, this led Brown and Duguid (1991, 53), to refer to organizations as being comparable to a 'community-of-communities'. Thus, the knowledge base of all organizations can be considered as being made up from a diversity of localized communities which have some overlapping knowledge in common, but which also possess much specialized and specific knowledge. As this perspective is closely associated with the practice-based perspective on knowledge, the specialized and localized nature of much organizational knowledge is related to the particular tasks and activities that different groups of workers undertake.

From this perspective, one of the general tasks of management is to coordinate these diverse internal communities, integrating, diffusing, and combining fragmented internal knowledge as necessary (Blackler et al. 2000; Brown and Duguid 2001; Grant 1996; Tsoukas 1996). Thus, if the knowledge base of all organizations is constituted by a diverse collection of specialized knowledge communities, managing intercommunity knowledge processes will be a day-to-day activity for most organizations.

Stop and think

Is the level of fragmentation in an organization's knowledge base likely to be proportional to organizational size? Further, if so, are the difficulties of managing such a fragmented knowledge base likely to be greatest for large, global multinationals?

Thus, the importance of intercommunity knowledge processes stems both from the fact that the contemporary restructuring of organizations is placing a greater emphasis on intercommunity and interorganizational working than has been traditional, and also because intra-organizational coordination can be conceptualized as involving intercommunity interaction.

Characterizing intercommunity knowledge processes

Intercommunity knowledge processes involve collaboration between individuals who are likely to have a limited amount knowledge in common, and who may have a limited, or weak sense of shared identity. As will be seen, in terms of knowledge processes, the consequences of this are significant.

As illustrated by Figure 5.1 in the previous chapter, knowledge processes within communities of practice are facilitated by the high degree of common knowledge, overlapping values, and shared sense of identity that community members typically possess. This is because in such circumstances it is likely that the tacit assumptions underpinning people's knowledge, which are key to effective knowledge-sharing, are likely to be well understood, or commonly shared. Also, the level of trust and mutual understanding between people in this context is also likely to be conducive to effective knowledge-sharing. Hansen (1999), in the context of product innovation and development processes, argues that effective knowledge-sharing requires two key elements to exist (Table 6.1). First, people must be willing to share their knowledge, and secondly, people must have the ability to share knowledge. Both these elements typically exist within communities of practice as due to the shared knowledge and values, there is enough mutual understanding to make the sharing of knowledge possible, while the sense of shared identity and values makes it probable that people will be willing to share their knowledge.

However, in intercommunity knowledge processes the situation is somewhat different (see Table 6.2). In these circumstances people will have much less shared, common knowledge, they may only have a weak sense of shared identity, or may even have distinctive and separate identities, and, finally, may have fundamentally different value

Table 6.1. Factors underpinning effective knowledge-sharing (adapted from Hansen 1999)

Willingness

Ability (adequate mutual understanding)

Table 6.2. Factors making intercommunity knowledge processes difficult

Limited common knowledge

Weak shared identity or different sense of identity

Values/assumptions potentially different

systems. Thus, the social relations between people who are not members of the same group/community are much less conducive to effective knowledge-sharing. For example, Hansen (1999) found that when weak ties existed between people this was likely to impede the transfer of complex knowledge (knowledge which was highly tacit, and which had a high level of interdependence with other knowledge).

The following two subsections consider how the lack of a shared identity, and/or a limited degree of common knowledge can inhibit knowledge processes, illustrating the issues examined with examples.

Identity

People from different groups or communities who work together may have either a weak sense of common identity, or may have distinctive and separate identities. For example, consider the situation described by Lam (1997), outlined above, and elaborated more fully later. In the electronics corporation examined, the Japanese and UK staff who required to collaborate had a weak sense of shared identity as being members of the same organization. Instead, their identity was more closely linked to the divisions they had historically worked within. More negatively, Empson (2001) found post-merger attempts at consolidating the organizational knowledge base in one of the consulting companies she examined to have been significantly inhibited by the strength of identity that staff retained for their pre-merger organizations, and the typically disdainful view that they had regarding the knowledge and experience of workers in the company they had been merged with.

This potentially weak sense of common identity arguably complicates knowledge processes through the potential for conflict this creates, as people with differing senses of identity may perceive differences of interest to exist between themselves and others. The issue of conflicting interests, and how this can inhibit knowledge-sharing was touched on earlier in Chapter 4 and is examined again more fully in Chapter 7.

 ILLUSTRATING THE ISSUES

Globalbank: conflicting identities inhibiting knowledge-sharing

Globalbank is a Dutch bank that grew aggressively by acquisition. By the late 1990s it had divisions in over 70 countries worldwide. At this point corporate management decided it was necessary to improve levels of coordination and knowledge-sharing between divisions. A key element of this strategy was the development of a global intranet, a project developed and managed by corporate IT staff. However, Globalbank had a strong historical culture of divisional autonomy, with divisions having typically operated completely independently from each other. Thus each division had controlled how it was organized, with the consequence that each division had its own working practices, IT systems, etc. For example, each division had its own intranet site, with its own specific style, level of functionality, etc.

Staff thus typically had a strong sense of identity with their division, and possessed specialist knowledge related to their division's particular customers, products, market conditions, and internal ways of working. The global intranet project experienced significant problems however, as management staff from most divisions were hostile to the idea, primarily because they perceived the objectives of the project to be incompatible with their desire to retain divisional autonomy. Thus one of the main obstacles to the project's progress was the stronger sense of identity that key divisional management staff typically had for their specific division rather than the corporate group as a whole.

Stop and think

What can be done to overcome the narrow sense of divisional identity that staff had, which was acting as a brake on the progress of the global intranet project?

Knowledge

The difficulties of knowledge-sharing between communities are however related to more than just the sense of identities that individuals possess. Another, equally important factor complicating such processes, outlined above, is the nature of the knowledge possessed by people in these situations. These difficulties stem from three interrelated factors (Table 6.3). Firstly, the degree of common knowledge shared by people may be quite limited, with different people possessing specialist knowledge related to the specific activities they each undertake. Secondly, the knowledge possessed by people may also be 'sticky' and difficult to share as it may be context-specific, tacit, and highly localized in nature (Brown and Duguid 1998; Lam 1997). Thirdly, and finally, there may be significant epistemological differences in the knowledge people possess (i.e. their knowledge is based on different underpinning assumptions and values). Thus, for example, Newell and Swan (2000) found that the difficulty of knowledge-sharing between different members of the research project they examined were related to epistemological differences in their knowledge, which stemmed from the different disciplinary backgrounds they came from.

Table 6.3. Knowledge-related factors adversely affecting intercommunity knowledge processes

Limited amount of common knowledge

Knowledge possessed by people is 'sticky' and difficult to share
(highly tacit and context-specific)

Epistemic differences
(people's knowledge based on different assumptions, values)

ILLUSTRATING THE ISSUES

The difficulties of sharing socially embedded knowledge

Lam (1997) examined a joint technology development between a Japanese and a UK electronics company. While the companies were competitors the Japanese company had a majority share-holding in the UK company. However, this collaborative relationship proved problematic, with staff frequently referring to, 'problems of poor communication, misinterpretation of specifications, and the clash between their approaches to product development', with these difficulties being primarily attributed to, 'differences in the organization of knowledge and work between the part-ner firms' (989). Lam found the knowledge of all relevant staff to be deeply embedded in the social and organizational context, and that further, the knowledge base and organizational context of both divisions were significantly different. While in the UK company there was an emphasis on form-alized knowledge, developed through education, in the Japanese company tacit knowledge accu-mulated through experience was more important. Secondly, in the UK company there was a clear demarcation of job boundaries, limited use of job rotation, and a tendency for people to develop narrowly specialized knowledge bases. In the Japanese company by contrast due to the emphasis on team-working the demarcation between jobs was blurred, and due to the use of job rotation, people's knowledge bases were typically broad. Finally, there were also significant differences in the way knowledge was shared and developed throughout the product cycle. In the UK division, product design, and the development of detailed specifications was principally the domain of design staff. In the Japanese company by contrast production and design staff both had an important role in the development of product specifications, with this 'interactive' way of working requiring a significant level of 'knowledge-sharing between upstream and downstream staff' (990). These differences therefore made the process of knowledge-sharing, and joint technology development extremely complicated.

Stop and think

This suggests that the sharing of knowledge between people with cultures which are quite different is likely to be difficult. From a management point of view, what can be done to address such problems?

The issue of epistemological differences is worth elaborating on, as such differences can have a profound effect on attempts to share or collectively utilize knowledge. Brown and Duguid (2001, 207) argue that while the advantage of communities of practice is that 'common . . . practice . . . creates social-epistemic bonds', conversely, '[p]eople with different practices have different assumptions, different outlooks, different interpretations of the world around them, and different ways of making sense of their encounters.' Thus, people from different communities of practice, or work groups, may not only have limited amounts of common, shared knowledge, but the knowledge they possess may be based on a fundamentally different system of values and assumptions.

Such issues may arise in multidisciplinary work (Newell and Swan 2000), where staff from different organizational subunits require to collaborate (Hansen 1999), in international collaborations involving people with significantly different cultures working together (Pauleen and Yoong 2001), where people from different occupational communities require to share knowledge (Bechky 2003), or where different organizational functions require to collaborate (see France-co example below). The complexity of knowledge-sharing in such circumstances stems from the fact that epistemological differences between people or groups can inhibit the development of even a fundamental understanding of the basic pre-misses, and values that the knowledge of others is based on. For example, the feeling of 'culture clash' that people can experience when visiting a country with very different cultural values stems from difficulties in understanding the basic values underlying 'other' cultures. Newell and Swan (2000) suggest that the greater the epistemological difference between collaborating parties, the less chance there is that such collaborations will be successful, and the more likely that they will not be able to effectively integrate their different perspectives and knowledge bases.

ILLUSTRATING THE ISSUES

France-Co: epistemic differences in cross-functional collaboration

France-Co produces specialist components for military and civil aircraft. As part of the company's attempts to introduce new management practices following the end of the Cold War it decided to implement an Enterprise Resource Planning (ERP) system, which was intended to improve levels of interfunctional knowledge-sharing. This project represented an enormous challenge for France-Co, as two of the most important functions for this project, sales and production, had historically shared little information. These functional groups possessed their own specialist bodies of knowledge and staff typically had a strong sense of identity for the function they worked in. Further, the knowledge possessed by staff in these groups was highly tacit, and was typically developed through practice, over time. Finally, relations between these functional communities had historically been antagonistic.

As France-Co's ERP project developed it became apparent that the lack of knowledge-sharing between these communities was proving detrimental to the project. Thus, initial attempts to implement the new system proved disastrous and had to be stopped. The main reason for this failure was that staff in both the sales and production functions were not sharing the type of knowledge and information that was necessary for the success of the project. While this reluctance to share knowledge was partly related to the historical antagonism between these functions, it was also related to the specialized nature of the knowledge they each possessed. This, combined with the extensive lack of interaction that had been typical, meant that they had a very poor understanding of how each other worked, or what their constraints and requirements were. Thus, even when staff from these communities were willing to share knowledge with each other, effectively doing so proved difficult, as each had an extremely limited understanding of what knowledge was relevant, important, or useful to the other.

When such significant epistemological differences exist it is necessary for the parties involved to develop an improved level of mutual understanding before any knowledge can be effectively shared, or collectively utilized (Bechky 2003). From a practice-based perspective, developing such an understanding involves the sort of perspective making and taking processes outlined in Chapter 3. While the practice-based perspective on knowledge assumes that processes of perspective making and taking are necessary for the sharing and communication of knowledge in *all* circumstances, the lack of common knowledge in intercommunity contexts raises the importance of such processes. These perspective making and taking processes do not result in the integration of the different knowledge bases into a coherent whole, but should instead involve a process of dialogue, where 'each community maintains its own voice while listening to the voice of the other' (Gherardi and Nicolini 2002, 421). Thus, perspective making and taking occurs through a process of talking, listening, acknowledging, and being tolerant to any differences identified.

In conclusion, intercommunity knowledge processes are inhibited by the differences in the knowledge possessed by the people involved in such processes. In general terms, the greater the degree of common knowledge that exists, the more straightforward knowledge processes are likely to be. Further, the character of knowledge processes in such circumstances are also affected by the degree of epistemological difference in the assumptions and values underpinning the knowledge bases involved, with a high level of epistemological difference likely to significantly increase the difficulty and complexity of such knowledge processes.

Identity, knowledge, trust, and social relations

One of the major conclusions to emerge from the previous section was that where the common knowledge base is limited, or where people have a limited sense of shared identity this means that the social relationship between parties is unlikely to be strong, and that the foundations for the existence of trust are relatively weak. Thus in such circumstances not only is the existence of strong trust unlikely, but the development of trust will typically be complicated and difficult. Fundamentally, the level of trust and mutual understanding between people who do not normally work together and who are not members of the same work group or community of practice is likely to inhibit the sharing and collective utilization of knowledge, as was discussed in Chapter 4.

The importance of trust in these social contexts, combined with the complexity of the concept of trust, means that it is worth elaborating more on the topic. Analyses of trust show it to be a theoretically complex concept which has multiple dimensions (Lane 1998; Newell and Swan 2000; Zucher 1996). Thus, most analyses of trust outline a number of different types of trust (see Table 6.4). Further, this work shows that these types of trust are distinctive in character, are developed in quite different ways, and have a complex, mutually interdependent relationship.

The limited basis for trust which exists in intergroup contexts, and particularly for newly formed intercommunity project groups can be seen from any of the three typologies of trust described. Thus the nature of the social relationship between people in a newly formed intercommunity work context precludes the existence of what Zucker (1996) referred to as process-based, and characteristic-based trust, what Lane (1998)

Table 6.4. Typologies of trust

Author/s	Type of trust	Description of trust
Zucker (1986)	Process based	Based on experience, and built up over time
	Characteristic based	Based on social similarities and cultural congruence
	Institutional based	Trust based on institutional or professional reputation, NOT interpersonal familiarity
Lane (1998)	Calculative	Trust based on some form of calculation regarding costs/benefits
	Norm/value based	Trust based on common social values
	Cognitive/expectation based	Trust based on common expectations about future events, and/or patterns of behaviour
Newell and Swan (2000)	Companion	Trust based on judgements of goodwill of friendship, built up over time
	Competence	Trust based on perception of others competence to carry out relevant tasks
	Commitment	Trust stemming from contractual obligations

referred to as value- or expectation-based trust, and what Newell and Swan (2000) referred to as companion- and competence-based trust. Thus in such circumstances, the only basis for trust is the most impersonal, and arguably weakest types of trust (institutional-based in Zucker's terms, calculative in Lane's terms, and commitment-based in Newell and Swan's terms). Thus, as will be discussed in the following section, one of the main ways to facilitate the development of knowledge processes in intercommunity work contexts is through the development of trust based on better mutual understanding and stronger social relations.

Stop and think

Reflect on the relationship you have with a range of people. To what extent are these relationships based on different types of trust? Further, how does the level and type of trust you have in different people affect the amount and type of knowledge and information you share with them?

Facilitating/managing knowledge between communities

Up to this point the chapter has emphasized the not insignificant difficulties in the effective, collective utilization of knowledge in intercommunity work groups. However, these difficulties are not insurmountable. Thus, there is much that can be done to address them, and increase the chance of intergroup work processes effectively making collective use of their knowledge. In general terms, this involves improving the level of mutual understanding and developing the social relationship between relevant people. Current writing suggests two broad ways in which this can be achieved. First, work can be invested in managing the social relationship between people, and secondly, developing the existing areas of overlap between people.

Relationship management

Relationship management involves attempting to develop the social relationship between the people involved in an intercommunity work group to become less based on the most impersonal, and relatively weak forms of trust outlined above. In Newell and Swan's terms, this involves moving away from a relationship based on commitment trust, to one where competence and companion types of trust are developed. However, successfully achieving such a transition is by no means straightforward. Primarily, the development of these more personal types of trust involves group members developing a greater level of sensitivity to and understanding of the knowledge, values, and assumptions held by other members of the same work group. This requires the processes of perspective making and taking outlined earlier in the chapter, which requires all parties to both talk and listen to each other. However, the more limited the amount of shared, common knowledge, and the greater the level of epistemological difference in the values and assumptions, the more time-consuming and complicated this process is likely to be. Further, to be effective such processes may well require a certain level of face-to-face interaction (Bechky 2003). This is because, as Lam (1997, 992) suggests effective collaboration in this context requires the development of, 'direct and intimate social relations . . . [as] . . . learners will need to become "insiders" of the social community in order to acquire its particular viewpoint.'

Brown and Duguid (1998) identified two roles that key individuals could take in the development of intercommunity social relations: brokers and translators. The brokering role is relevant where there is some pre-existing overlap in the knowledge of the communities/people involved. A broker is someone who inhabits both communities, and uses their knowledge and understanding of both to facilitate the development of mutual understanding between other members of the communities. Gherardi and Nicolini (2002) argue that a broker is someone who has the ability to, 'transfer and translate certain elements of one practice to another'. The role of translator is relevant where there is no overlapping common knowledge between communities/people. This requires the translator to have a detailed knowledge of both communities, and further, the translator requires to be trusted by the members of both communities as they play such a key role in interacting between them. Such roles are acknowledged to be extremely complex and difficult to successfully manage.

Stop and think

How important is face-to-face interaction for the development of trust and an effective working relationship between people from significantly different cultures? Can cross-cultural working relations be developed without any face-to-face interaction?

Boundary objects

The third and final method discussed by Brown and Duiguid (1998) to facilitate intercommunity knowledge-sharing involves the development and utilization of boundary objects. Boundary objects are entities that are common to a number of communities and can be either physical or linguistic/symbolic in character. Boundary objects provide a focus for negotiation, discussion, or even shared activity between people from different communities, and thus can be utilized to help develop and improve the working relationship between people, and the mutual understanding they have of each other. One of the most common type of boundary objects mentioned by Brown and Duguid are contracts, which typically provide a focus for intercommunity negotiation, and which can help provide an initial stimulus to a process of perspective making and taking at an early stage in the working relationship of an intercommunity work group.

Gherardi and Nicolini (2002) examined a building site, focusing on how safety issues were jointly negotiated by the three communities of practice with some responsibility for and involvement in safety issues. These three communities were engineers, site foremen, and main contractors. Boundary objects in this context included the physical site that everyone worked on, the building under construction, as well as the assorted range of raw materials that were used, and which were dotted around the building site. However, there were some equally important linguistic boundary objects, such as the term 'safety' itself. One of the main ways that relations between these three communities were developed, and negotiations of how safety was managed on site occurred was through discussion and negotiation over these boundary objects, which provided a common focus which brought the communities together.

ILLUSTRATING THE ISSUES

UK-Pension: boundary objects and brokers

As outlined in Chapter 5 (see p. 63), UK-Pension had traditionally been structured into two discrete divisions that operated with such significant levels of autonomy that they constituted separate and distinct communities of practice. As part of a major restructuring process which began in the mid-1990s UK-Pension attempted to move towards a more integrated structure, with greater links between their two main business areas: life assurance and pensions. One key way this was done was through setting up a cross-business call centre. This was a single call centre that would handle work from both business areas. Initially, the call centre was staffed by people from both divisions, with the leader of the call centre implementation project having the role of persuading staff to work in the centre. The project manager therefore was in the role of broker, and the call centre represented a (new) boundary object. While the call centre was a boundary object common to both communities, and which would provide a physical site where staff from both divisions would work together, staff were unfamiliar with it. Further, it represented a radical change in working practices for UK-Pension, not only because it required staff from both divisions to work together, but because it was the first large-scale use of a call centre within the company. Therefore, the brokering role played by the call centre project manager in communicating the purpose of the call centre to staff, and persuading some of them to work in it was key. In the end, the project manager was successful in his brokering role, as he was able to persuade an adequate number of staff to change jobs and work in the call centre.

Conclusion

This chapter narrowly focused on cross-community, boundary-spanning knowledge processes. Arguably, the relevance and importance of cross-community knowledge processes has increased due the changes in working practices that have emerged from the contemporary restructuring of work organizations. The difference between intra- and inter-community knowledge processes relates to the sense of shared identity and typically high level of common knowledge which exists within communities (see Chapter 5), but which is relatively absent from intercommunity contexts. Further, it may also be the case that not only are there limited amounts of common, shared knowledge between parties, but that there may be epistemic differences in the knowledge of the people and communities involved, where their knowledge is based on fundamentally different assumptions and values.

Typically, as illustrated by a number of examples, intercommunity knowledge processes are likely to be more complex and difficult to make successful than intracommunity processes. This is due to both the differences in identity, which may induce intercommunity conflict, and the lack of common knowledge. Somewhat simplistically, the less common knowledge that exists, and the greater the level of epistemic difference, the more complicated and difficult the knowledge-sharing process will typically be.

Knowledge-sharing across communities was shown to require two primary, and closely interrelated elements, both of which are developed through a process of social interaction and communication. First, an adequate level of trust requires to be developed between the individuals from both communities, ideally with the strongest forms of personal trust being developed. This type of trust has been variously labelled as process-based (Zucker), cognitive (Lane), and companion trust (Newell and Swan). Secondly, people from both communities require to develop a basic understanding of the values, assumptions, and viewpoints which underpin each other's knowledge base. This process of perspective making and taking, which was also examined in Chapter 3, requires not a merging of these different knowledge bases, but an appreciation of, sensitivity to, and tolerance of the differences in perspective which emerge.

Finally, the chapter examined the ways in which intercommunity knowledge processes can be facilitated, through brokers/translators attempting to bridge communities and develop relations between them, and through the use of boundary objects that are common to all relevant communities.

REVIEW QUESTIONS

1 The prevalence of interorganizational networking can be gauged by a simple piece of research. Examine the business section from any serious daily newspaper and you are likely to find relevant examples. However, is this type of working practice likely to be more common in some business sectors more than others? What factors affect the extent to which interorganizational networks are developed and utilized?

2 Theory suggests that more impersonal forms of trust, such as commitment-based trust or institutionally based trust are typically weaker and more fragile than trust developed through an ongoing social relationship, such as process-based trust. Does this reflect your own experience?

3 Reflect on any work experience that you have had. To what, if anything did you and your work colleagues most strongly feel a sense of identity as being part of: your immediate work group, the function you worked in, the division you worked for, or the overall corporate group? Are these senses of identity likely to inhibit the development of an effective working relationship, and the sharing of knowledge with people from different parts of the organization?

FURTHER READING

- J. Brown and P. Duguid (2001). 'Knowledge and Organization: A Social Practice Perspective', *Organization Science*, 12/2: 198–213.
  A largely theoretical, but well written and accessible paper which reflects on the what makes intercommunity knowledge-sharing difficult.

- A. Lam (1997). 'Embedded Firms, Embedded Knowledge: Problems in Collaboration and Knowledge Transfer in Global Cooperative Ventures', *Organization Studies*, 18/6: 973–96.
  A theoretically grounded case study which examines the difficulties of knowledge sharing within an international project team.

- S. Newell and J. Swan (2000). 'Trust and Inter-Organizational Networking', *Human Relations*, 53/10: 1287–1328.
  An empirically rich and theoretically innovate case study on the role of trust in shaping the dynamics of a multi-disciplinary project team.

- S. Gherardi and D. Nicolini (2002). 'Learning in a Constellation of Interconnected Practices: Canon or Dissonance?' *Journal of Management Studies*, 39/4: 419–36.
  Examines the role of boundary objects and brokers in facilitating intercommunity sense-making and working.

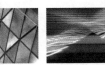

Power, conflict, and knowledge processes

Introduction

One of the defining characteristics of the vast majority of the writing on knowledge management is that any discussion of power is typically absent, and as a consequence it can only be assumed that this literature doesn't regard issues of power as being important in shaping and understanding organizational knowledge processes. This is not exclusively the case, because, as will be seen, a number of writers do take such issues seriously (for example Contu and Willmott 2003; Goodall and Roberts 2003). Such an omission is puzzling, as a cursory glance outside the narrow confines of the knowledge management literature reveals both the need to understand issues of power in explaining organizational dynamics, as well as the close relationship between knowledge and power. Thus, understanding the relationship between power and organizational knowledge processes is of fundamental importance, and the task of doing so is magnified by the general absence of such an analysis.

While power has not been adequately dealt with in the knowledge management literature there has been a growing acknowledgement that not only can people's attitudes to participate in knowledge activities be highly variable, but that interpersonal or intergroup conflict in knowledge processes is not uncommon. These issues are raised again here, but are explicitly linked to power. Arguably, a missing link in the knowledge management literature that does address such issues is that it does not address the fundamental causes of such conflicts. To do so requires power to be accounted for, which reveals not only the inherent potential for conflict that exists in organizations, but how power is structurally embedded in the employment relationship.

In the analysis presented, power and knowledge will be seen to be extremely closely interrelated, which is another reason why issues of power require to be accounted for in attempting to understand the dynamics of organizational knowledge processes. However, there isn't a consensus around either how power should be defined, or how its relationship to knowledge should be conceptualized. This is accounted for by examining two of the most influential perspectives, and considering their implications for knowledge processes.

The chapter is structured into three major subsections. The first subsection re-engages with the topics of the employment relationship and conflict, but suggests that a full understanding of their dynamics requires power to be accounted for. The following two subsections then separately examine the two perspectives on power considered. The first examines the 'power as a resource' perspective, while the second examines the work of Michel Foucault. However, what is common to both perspectives is the closeness of the relationship between power and knowledge.

Knowledge processes: the relevance of power and conflict

The objective of this section is to outline why issues of power and conflict are important, and require to be taken into consideration when examining knowledge processes. To do this involves returning to, and elaborating on two issues discussed in Chapter 4: the employment relationship and the inherent potential for conflict that exists within organizations. This section shows how locating these issues within their socio-economic context requires that power and politics be taken into account, and that it is fundamentally impossible to fully understand either the employment relationship or organizational conflict without reference to these issues.

Power and the employment relationship

The fundamental character of organizations is an issue which has, thus far, not been addressed in detail. As with so many other subjects of analysis in organization studies, there is little consensus on the topic. However, limitations of space preclude an examination of the different perspectives that exist. Instead, the perspective utilized here will simply be outlined, and all further analysis built from these assumptions. The model of organizations utilized here is neatly summed up by McKinlay and Starkey (1998, 2), who suggest that 'behind the façade of efficiency, equity, or humanity which surrounds formal organizations of all kinds lie distinct concentrations of power/knowledge'. From this perspective there are thus fundamental inequalities in the distribution of power and knowledge (or power-knowledge) in organizations, which can be (partly) explained by examining the nature of the employment relationship in detail.

Stop and think

What does your own experience say about the nature of organizations? Is conflict inevitable? Are power imbalances inherent?

As outlined in Chapter 4 there are contradictory tensions between workers and their employing organization over the ownership and control of workers' knowledge (Contu and Willmott 2003). On the one hand, their interests may be compatible, through the potential mutual benefits that workers and their employers may derive from the employer supporting and facilitating the workers' knowledge activities. On the other hand, simultaneously, the requirement of organizations to appropriate economic value from their workers' knowledge may conflict with their workers' individual objectives in this respect. For example, while there are economic benefits to organizations from having their workers share or codify their knowledge, workers may be unwilling to do so if they feel such a process may dilute and diminish their expertise. Such tensions are amplified by the (potential) fragility of the employment relationship resulting from the ability of both parties to easily terminate the relationship, the worker through leaving, or the employer through making workers redundant.

A concrete example of such a conflict was examined in Chapter 5 (see p. 68–9) where members of a scientific community of practice resisted the implementation of a 'commercial' culture as they believed that its economic focus, where the emphasis was on making profits from scientific research, was not compatible with the basic ethos of research driven by the more abstract objective of advancing knowledge (Breu and Hemingway 2002). The extent to which these objectives are generally compatible is discussed in Chapter 15.

However, only when the employment relationship is located within the socio-economic context of capitalist relations of production does a structurally embedded power relationship become visible (see Figure 7.1). This conceptualization of context is based on a realist perspective on social structure where social action is embedded in what Reed (2000, 52, 55) referred to as the 'recurring matrices of social structure', where such structures are assumed to, 'pre-date the social actions which reproduce and transform them'. More specifically, Tsoukas (2000), developing a realist conception of the employment relationship (see Figure 7.1) referred to the 'structural basis of managers' power' (34), which places workers in a typically subordinate relationship to managers/superiors. With this framework management are the mediating agents of capital owners and shareholders, where organizations are shaped by demands to make profit, and accumulate capital, and which requires managers/superiors to control and simultaneously achieve the cooperation (self-regulation) of workers in order to turn their labour power into actual, productive work effort (Contu and Willmott 2003).

 Realism

Realism is a philosophy that assumes that while social structures are produced (and reproduced) through social action, there are enduring social structures which exist independently of the social actors who produce them

At this point, a significant caveat is required when considering the situation of knowledge workers. The power of management over workers is contingent upon the specific characteristics of the organizational context, and the power of management can be diminished or enhanced by shifts in societal power relations (Tsoukas 2000). For knowledge workers two factors imbuing them with power are first, the typical importance of their knowledge to the organizations they work for, and secondly, the general scarcity of their skills in labour markets, which makes many knowledge workers highly sought after (Beaumont and Hunter 2002; Flood et al. 2001). These factors are thus likely to provide knowledge workers with significant amounts of power (this issue is returned to in

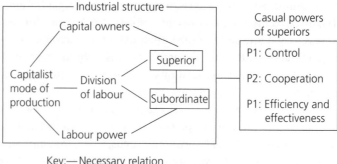

Fig. 7.1. The structure of capitalist employment relations (from Tsoukas 2000)

Chapter 14). However, the tensions and conflicts in the employment relationship out-lined above still apply. Thus, while the basic structure of the employment relationship is the same for all workers, the specific balance of power between management and workers can vary enormously. But a constant issue for managers in business organizations, whether referring to low-skilled routine workers, or highly skilled knowledge workers is the necessity to ensure that the labour power of these workers is converted into actual productive effort. What is likely to vary, depending on the balance of power in the employment relationship, is the extent to which strategies of control and/or cooperation are utilized (Figure 7.1).

Stop and think

How unique is the situation of knowledge workers? Are they the only type of workers whose knowledge is important and valued? Can you think of other types of workers who have important knowledge that provides them with a source of power?

In conclusion, the embeddedness of power, and the potential for conflict in capitalist employment relations means that power has to be accounted for when attempting to understand the dynamics of knowledge processes.

Conflict, power, and politics

The potential for conflict in organizations emanates from more than just the nature of the employment relationship. This potential flows from the different interests which exist within organizations between both individuals and groups. Marshall and Brady (2001, 103), for example, refer to the, 'frequent organizational reality of divergent interests, political struggles and power relations'. This divergence of interests may come from indi-viduals/groups competing over scarce organizational resources, or through clashes between the personal objectives and strategies that individual employees may pursue in order to sustain and develop their careers, such as receiving recognition for particular efforts/knowledge, receiving financial rewards, or gaining promotions. Using a Weberian

Table 7.1. Weberian-based types of action/rationality

Type of action	Underlying rationale	Knowledge-related examples
Traditional	Automatic, habitual action, borderline rational	Willing, unquestioning knowledge-sharing with colleagues within a long-established community of practice.
Affective	Shaped by emotion, borderline rational	Unwillingness to participate in knowledge process with individual/group due to (emotionally based) negative opinion regarding abilities and knowledge of others—Empson 2001.
Value Rational	Action oriented to values. Values believed not rationally based, but action in pursuit is.	Participate in knowledge process, such as R&D activities or innovation process, due to belief in social values and benefits of knowledge advancement—Fuller 2002 (knowledge production for its own sake).
Calculative	Instrumental rationality. Most rational action of all, based on means/end calculations.	Willing participation in knowledge process due to calculation that, on balance, benefits (recognition, financial reward) outweigh risks (loss of expertise)—Morris 2001.

framework, human action can also be classified into different categories, based on different types and degree of rationality (Craib 1997) (see Table 7.1). Thus the potential for conflict within organizations is due to the interest-laden nature of human behaviour, the diversity of interests that individuals/groups can pursue, and the competing rationalities that underpin their actions.

Empirical evidence suggests that the implementation of knowledge management initiatives, or participation in knowledge processes, is a common battleground where such conflicts are played out, as a growing body of case study evidence suggests that such interpersonal and intergroup tensions and conflicts are common in organizational knowledge processes (Empson 2001; Marshall and Brady 2001; Newell et al. 2000; Ward 2000; Willman et al. 2001).

However, to understand how conflicts evolve, and to explain the attitudes and behaviours of people in situations of conflict requires power and politics to be introduced, and demands an understanding of the relationship between these elements (see Figure 7.2). This complex relationship can usefully be explained by making reference to a specific example. Figure 7.2 can be understood as a cycle within a cycle, with the inner cycle of the political process being shaped by the broader cycle encompassing the relationship between this process, conflicts of interests, and power. Storey and Barnett (2000) analyse a single company case study of a failed knowledge management project. One of the main reasons for the failure of the project was that there was a lot of interfunctional conflict over the ownership of the project, with different functional groups attempting to use the knowledge management project as a political tool to pursue a broader agenda related to shaping the future of the company's IT infrastructure. These attempts were resisted and challenged by other individuals and groups within the organization producing 'micro-political

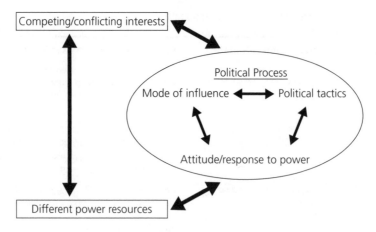

Fig. 7.2. Linking power, politics, and conflict

battles', where each interest group utilized particular political tactics and modes of influence, drawing upon the different power resources that they had. Thus, not only was the knowledge management initiative itself shaped by, and subject to, power struggles, political battles, and conflict, but ownership of the initiative itself was used as a political tactic to pursue a broader agenda. This model will be returned to, and elaborated upon in the following section, when the Hales model of power is described.

ILLUSTRATING THE ISSUES

France-Co: knowledge hoarding and cross-functional antagonisms
....

In the France-Co example discussed in Chapter 6, the unwillingness of Sales and Production staff to share knowledge with each other was seen to undermine their change project. As outlined, this was partly as a result of the epistemic differences in their knowledge bases.

However, equally important in explaining the reluctance of staff to share knowledge across functions were a number of other factors. Firstly, a deep-seated and historically embedded attitude of mutual suspicion, mistrust, and antagonism existed between these functions. Thus the requirement of the change project for staff in these functions to share knowledge with each other challenged this. Secondly, there was a concern by staff in both functions that by participating in the change programme and sharing their knowledge that somehow they would lose power and status through 'giving away' their expert knowledge. For example, the knowledge and experience of sales staff was typically tacit, and developed over time, through experience. These workers were concerned that the requirement of the change programme to codify this knowledge meant that they would lose either their autonomy, their expert knowledge, or both. For these reasons, sales staff were therefore quite reluctant to actively participate in the knowledge codification element of the change project. This behaviour could also be interpreted as political in nature as it was shaped by a particular agenda—attempting to either stop the change programme, or to shape it in ways deemed more acceptable and/or advantageous to the sales function. Finally, the reluctance of sales staff to participate in the codification process could be regarded as a political tactic involving the use of one of their sources of power—the knowledge they possessed.

Stop and think

Using the Weberian framework outlined in Table 7.1, what type (or types) of action/rationale underpins the behaviour of sales staff in France-co's change project?

In conclusion, this section has shown that not only does the diversity of interests and rationales which underpin action make intra-organizational conflict likely, but that to understand the dynamics of these conflicts requires issues of power and politics to be accounted for.

Power and knowledge processes: theorizing the relationship

Up until now, power is a term that has been used, but not defined. The following two subsections each provide separate and quite distinctive definitions of power. This is done deliberately to illustrate two of the dominant perspectives in the debate on what power is, and how it should be conceptualized. As well as defining power, the following two subsections also look at the consequences of these conceptualizations for the relationship between power and knowledge. As will be seen, what is common to both perspectives is that power and knowledge are closely interrelated, which provides further support to the arguments already examined that power requires to be accounted for when considering organizational knowledge processes.

The neglect of power in the knowledge management literature means that it has been necessary to draw on work from outside of it to provide one of the conceptualizations of power used. Thus, what can be defined as the 'power as resource' perspective is based on the work Colin Hales (1993) who developed his framework to understand the nature of managerial work. The second perspective examined is based on the work of Foucault, which as will be seen has been utilized and adapted by a number of writers to understand organizational knowledge processes.

Before proceeding to examine these two perspectives on power, and the implications they have for organizational knowledge processes, it is necessary to make one final observation. When considering the relationship between power and knowledge processes, the relationship requires to be understood as being cyclical in nature (see Figure 7.3). Thus, not only does the possession and use of power affect knowledge processes (as illustrated by the Storey and Barnett example just considered), knowledge processes themselves are likely to impact on the character, distribution, and use of power in organizations. Thus for example, Gray (2001) suggests that the use of ICT-based knowledge repositories is likely to change the balance of power in organizations. While he suggests this may result in a reduction of the power of workers (as repositories may make workers more easily substituted, and that they may reduce the analytical content of work), he argues that the effect of such technologies on the organizational balance of power will be mediated by the choices and strategies that organizational management pursue.

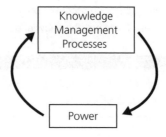

Fig. 7.3. The cyclical relationship between knowledge management processes and power

Power as a resource

As outlined, the subsection develops a conceptualization of power drawn from the work of Hales (1993). However, for the purposes of this book, it is not necessary to fully articulate every aspect of his model. Thus there will be a close focus on how this conceptualization links to knowledge, and how it can help understand the dynamics of knowledge processes.

Hales (1993, 20) defines power resources as, 'those things which bestow the means whereby the behaviour of others may be influenced and power relations arise out of the uneven distribution of these resources.'

This definition is therefore based on a similar conception of organizations as that outlined earlier in the chapter, where power in not regarded as being evenly distributed. Secondly, this definition, like the objectivist definition of knowledge, regards power to be a discrete resource/entity that people can possess, or have access to, and which they can use in attempting to modify the behaviour of others. Further, Hales argues that power resources have this ability through three specific properties they possess (see Table 7.2). Firstly, they are relatively scarce and only available to some. Secondly, they are desired because they can satisfy certain wants. Finally, there are no alternatives available.

 Power (Definition no. 1)

Power is a (scarce) resource whose use allows people to shape the behaviour of others.

Hales identifies four basic types of power resource: physical resources (the capacity to harm or physically restrict the actions of others); economic resources (money); knowledge resources (scarce or desirable knowledge); and normative resources (meanings, values, or ideologies which are scarce or desirable). For Hales, political acts are those actions whereby people attempt to influence others through the use of these power resources (see Figure 7.2). Further, these resources are available to people either through personally possessing them, or by virtue of organizational position giving access to them. For example, money can be a source of economic power to either those who possess adequate amounts of it, or to those who individually have access to financial resources (such as through control

Table 7.2. Properties of knowledge that can make it a power resource

Property	Knowledge-power
Scarcity	Specialist knowledge/expertise which only a limited number of people possess. Knowledge which may be highly tacit, and which requires to be developed though experience.
Satisfy wants	Knowledge which may satisfy individual wants through its possession or use (such as status, or rewards), or knowledge which satisfies organizational goals and objectives through its possession or use (such as providing organizations which status, profits, market share, or product/market innovations).
No alternatives	Where the wants which are satisfied (see above) are only achievable through the possession or use of specific types of knowledge.

Table 7.3. Power resources and modes of influence (adapted from Hales 1993)

Power resource	Personal	Positional
Physical	Individual strength, means of violence	Access to/control over means of violence
Economic	Individual wealth	Access to/control over economic resources
Knowledge (administrative)	Individual expertise	Access to/control over relevant knowledge
Knowledge (technical)	Individual expertise	Access to/control over relevant knowledge
Normative	Individual beliefs/values, personal qualities	Access to/control over ideas and values

over budgets). Thus, for each power resource, there are two separate modes of influence available: personal or positional (see Table 7.3).

Power and knowledge

This conceptualization of power therefore shows the close relationship with knowledge, as knowledge represents one of the four fundamental types of power resource. Secondly, power can be derived from knowledge either through someone possessing it (personal knowledge power), or through having access to knowledge by dint of organizational position. Thus, for example, a senior manager employing external consultants/advisers could be argued to be using their position to gain access to important knowledge-power resources. Thirdly, Hales makes a distinction between two types of knowledge, each of which can be an important power resource: administrative knowledge (knowledge of organizational processes, rules, regulations, etc.); and technical knowledge (specialist knowledge of particular work activities/tasks, or knowledge relevant to such activities). Finally, the connectedness of the relationship between knowledge and power means that *all* behaviours involving the use of knowledge to some extent involve the use of power, and can be understood as political acts driven by attempts to pursue particular objectives (see Figure 7.2).

Thus, for example, in the context of knowledge-sharing both willingly sharing knowledge, or hoarding and protecting knowledge from others could be interpreted as a political act shaped by particular interests/objectives, involving the use of the knowledge-power an individual possesses. A willingness to share knowledge with others may be driven by a desire to contribute to organizational performance or to receive status and rewards from being seen to use personal knowledge, whereas a reluctance to share knowledge may be due to concerns that one is giving away what makes one powerful, or from a desire to prevent certain individuals/groups gaining access to one's knowledge.

Social capital

One important modification that requires to be made to Hales' model is to take account of social capital. The role of social capital in shaping organizational performance and its role in affecting knowledge processes has increasingly been acknowledged since the mid-1990s (Adler and Kwon 2002; Nahapiet and Ghoshal 1998; YliRenko et al. 2001). Social capital relates to the networks of mutual acquaintances that people possess, and is defined formally, by Nahapiet and Ghoshal (1998, 243) as 'the sum of the actual and potential resources embedded within, available through, and derived from the network of relations possessed by an individual'. Arguably, however, social capital can be conceptualized as a potential power resource, and can be added to Hales' model as a fifth dimension of knowledge power. As with the other sources of power in Hales' model, social capital can be a source of power through the personal social capital that people possess, or as a positional power resource, available to people as a result of their formal organizational position.

Stop and think

Social upbringing (class, religion, gender, ethnicity), organizational position (seniority increases likely access to important social networks), and personal endeavour are all argued to be important in the development of social capital? Are any of these elements more important than the others?

The final part of Hales's model requiring elaboration is how the use of power is shaped by the response of those subject to it (see Figure 7.2). Such judgements can have important implications for behaviour, as if someone's power is deemed as legitimate, then people are more likely to comply than if it is regarded as being of dubious legitimacy. This is equally true for positionally based or personally possessed power resources. Thus while managerial power is, to some extent, a function of organizational position it is one of the problematic aspects of management that such power can't be assumed to be *automatically* deemed as legitimate by workers (Hislop et al. 2000). For example, behaviour such as verbally abusing workers, or not adequately consulting them, may undermine the extent to which power related to managerial position is deemed legitimate by workers.

For Hales, the legitimacy of each power resource is likely to vary (see Figure 7.4). Thus for example the use of physical power, such as threatening violence, is likely never to be

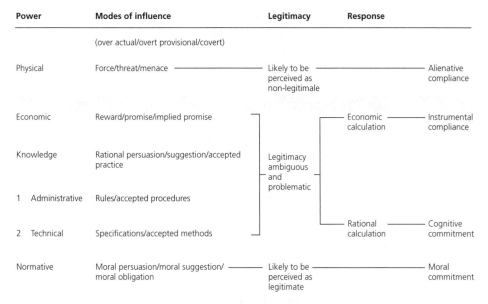

Power	Modes of influence	Legitimacy	Response
	(over actual/overt provisional/covert)		
Physical	Force/threat/menace ───────────	Likely to be ─────── perceived as non-legitimale	Alienative compliance
Economic	Reward/promise/implied promise		Economic ──── Instrumental calculation compliance
Knowledge	Rational persuasion/suggestion/accepted practice	Legitimacy ambiguous and problematic	
1 Administrative	Rules/accepted procedures		
2 Technical	Specifications/accepted methods		Rational ──── Cognitive calculation commitment
Normative	Moral persuasion/moral suggestion/ ──── moral obligation	Likely to be ──────── perceived as legitimate	Moral commitment

Fig. 7.4. The perceived legitimacy of, and response to attempts to use different power resources (from Hales 1993)

deemed as legitimate. In contrast, the legitimacy of knowledge-power resources are typically ambiguous, with their legitimacy being evaluated by workers dependent upon contextual factors. These issues can be illustrated by examining the politics of knowledge dissemination processes, which can involve negotiations and conflict regarding the legitimacy of different and competing knowledge claims (see Chapter 3, p. 34–5 for a previous example of such a dispute).

ILLUSTRATING THE ISSUES

The UK accounting profession: disputed knowledge

Mitchell et al. (2001) describe a number of cases where the validity of their knowledge and findings were disputed, and which involved them in highly political battles over the accuracy of their truth claims. While the specific details of the conflict are not relevant, the general dynamics of the dispute illustrate how processes of knowledge dissemination, equally as much as processes of knowledge sharing, creation, application, etc., involve the use of power resources, and can be highly political in nature.

Primarily, based on the accumulated evidence and knowledge they possessed, and the analysis of it that they made, they challenged the 'public face of respectability'. (529) which represents the dominant image of the UK accounting profession. However, attempts were made to silence this knowledge, and prevent it becoming public by those with a vested interest in maintaining the dominant image. This was attempted primarily through threats of (libel) lawsuits. Using Hales's framework, individuals/groups in possession of economic and knowledge power resources (social and cultural capital) attempted to use this power through the political tactic of threatening lawsuits. However, Mitchell et al. did not regard the knowledge claims of those challenging them as legitimate, and resisted the attempts to prevent their work being published. Ultimately they were successful in their endeavours and have published their findings in various books and journals.

Stop and think

Using Hales's framework (Table 7.3) what type/s of power resource does threatening libel action involve the use of? Does this example suggest that all these different power resources are interrelated?

Thus, while McKinlay (2002, 79) comments that knowledge management can be regarded as a 'brake on corporate forgetting' the case of Mitchell et al. suggests that knowledge management can involve deliberate attempts to engineer processes of forgetting. Knowledge management is therefore not only about remembering and managing knowledge, but actively marginalizing, discarding, and forgetting knowledge not deemed as legitimate. Thus, the dissemination of knowledge can be a highly political process involving conflicts to establish the legitimacy of competing knowledge claims.

Foucault and power/knowledge

It is impossible to examine the relationship between power and knowledge without taking account of the work of the French philosopher, Michel Foucault, as arguably he is the single most influential author in this area. As will be seen, Foucault's conceptualization of power, and characterization of the relationship between power and knowledge, is quite different from that elaborated by Hales. This section begins by giving a brief overview on the way Foucault theorizes power and its relationship with knowledge. Following this there will be two subsections where a Foucauldian framework is used to examine the dynamics of different organizational knowledge processes.

One of the main themes in Foucault's work is (self) discipline and the role of power/knowledge in attempting to produce (and reproduce) it. However, before considering how discipline is produced it is necessary to start by examining Foucault's definition of power, where it is worth quoting him in full.

[T]he power exercised on the body is conceived not as a property, but as a strategy . . . this power is exercised rather than possessed; it is not the 'privilege', acquired or preserved, of the dominant class, but the overall effect of its strategic positions—an effect that is manifested and sometimes extended by the position of those who are dominated. (Rabinow 1991, 174, quoting from Foucault's Discipline and Punishment)

Thus Foucault suggests that power, rather than being a discrete resource that social actors can utilize, is something which is produced and reproduced within and through the dynamics of evolving social relationships. Further, Foucault suggests that power and knowledge are so inextricably interrelated that they are fundamentally inseparable, and coined the phrase power/knowledge to symbolize this (Foucault 1980). To properly appreciate Foucault in this respect, it is again worth quoting him in full:

Power produces knowledge . . . power and knowledge directly imply one another; that there is no power relation without the correlative constitution of a field of knowledge, nor any knowledge that does not presuppose and constitute at the same time power relations. (Rabinow 1991, 17, quoting from Foucault's Discipline and Punishment)

The implication of this insight for understanding the dynamics of knowledge processes is therefore profound, as all uses of knowledge, or attempts to shape and manage knowledge within organizations, inevitably involve the use of power.

 Power (Definition no. 2)

Power is produced and reproduced through the evolution of social relations. What it is and what it does are thus the same thing.

IT based knowledge management: The power of the panopticon
As outlined above, central to Foucault's analysis in this area is the topic of discipline, and how it is achieved. The objective of disciplinary power it to define the parameters of what is acceptable and unacceptable, to punish those who transgress, and ultimately to produce docile, obedient, self-disciplining behaviour. For Foucault, the social transformation from feudalism to capitalism saw a change in the way discipline was achieved. Within capitalism, the use of expert knowledge/power and surveillance via panopticans represent two key disciplinary practices (Clegg 1998). Expert knowledge/power can play a disciplining role through providing an ideologically based justification for what behaviours are appropriate. A panoptican is a surveillance instrument, a tool which has the potential to monitor behaviour continuously, but where the observer is invisible to the person being observed. With such a mechanism, the threat of surveillance may be adequate to produce self-disciplining behaviour by the subject of the panoptican, as they can never be sure when or even if they are being observed.

That ICTs have the potential to be used as panopticans is vividly illustrated by Lyons in his books on surveillance in contemporary society (Lyons 1994, 2001). In relation to knowledge management, this represents one of the main ways in which Foucault's work has been applied.

The potential for ICTs to be tools of surveillance is well documented. For example, the extensive literature on call centres illustrates the bewildering diversity of ways in which the behaviour and work of call centre staff can be monitored via their use (Bain and Taylor 2000; Ball and Wilson 2000; Taylor 1998; Taylor and Bain 1999). ICTs represent an almost perfect example of a panoptican, as the act of observation is (virtually) invisible, and workers don't know when and if they are being observed. The idea of ICTs as a panoptican has also been applied to the understanding of ICT-mediated knowledge processes by both McKinlay (2000, 2002) and Hayes and Walsham (2000). However, they come to quite different conclusions.

The analysis developed by Hayes and Walsham, based on a case study company's use of groupware technology (Lotus Notes[1]), concluded that ICTs did represent effective pan-opticans and had a significant disciplining effect on worker behaviour. In their study workers were concerned that what was said on Lotus Notes would be visible to senior management, which made some workers reluctant to articulate views not felt to be compatible with senior management perspectives. The particular forums where management participation was deemed likely thus typically resembled a 'public façade' (84), where workers censored themselves to present management with a particular impression. This was argued would lead to a process of 'homogenization' where diversity would be damaged. Thus, based on this analysis, a potentially negative effect of the use of ICTs for knowledge management is that because of such factors they may not reflect, or perhaps even damage the diversity of knowledge and attitudes which typically exist in organizations.

McKinlay (2000, 2002) presents an alternative analysis, which suggests that the disciplinary power of ICT-based knowledge management systems has been somewhat exaggerated. McKinlay's analysis, based on a case study of the UK divisions of an American pharmaceutical corporation, suggests that ICT-based knowledge management systems have a limited ability to capture highly tacit knowledge. Further, workers have the ability to resist the disciplinary gaze of such systems through creating and communicating within 'unregulated social processes' (2002).

Stop and think

Based on your own experience, do ICTs represent technologies with significant disciplinary power? Can their gaze be avoided, resisted, or subverted?

Knowledge workers and (willing) self-discipline

The typical image of the relationship between knowledge-intensive workers and their employers is of a win: win scenario, where such workers are highly skilled, have a lot of autonomy in their work, whose knowledge is highly valued, and whose contribution to organizational performance is regarded as key (see Chapter 4). Such analyses typically do not describe any negative consequences that may be experienced by such workers. Deetz (1998) takes a critical perspective to such assumptions, and uses a Foucauldian framework to consider how such work involves a process of (self) subordination/discipline which can have damaging effects for such workers. This analysis also reveals much about the power dynamics involved in the relationship between knowledge workers and their employing organizations.

In many ways, the knowledge workers (consultants) examined by Deetz did comply with the dominant image. They were highly paid, highly educated, relatively happy, had good career prospects, and did a relatively high-status job. Further, they had a high degree of work autonomy, which reinforced the sense of status they had. There was also evidence of goal alignment between the company and the employees, where the consultants consistently under-reported the actual hours they worked for clients, accepted the long working

[1] Lotus Notes is a specific, widely used IBM software system which allows groups of people to electronically communicate, collaborate, and share/modify documentation collectively.

hours which were common, and were prepared to do what was deemed necessary by clients to get the job done.

However, these consultants were not totally free from organizational control systems. Normative control systems were used through an extensive system of culture management (Kunda 1992). This operated through the usual mechanisms of vision statements and socialization programmes and shaped what were regarded as desirable/acceptable behaviours, values, and attitudes.

Deetz argues that there was a dark side experienced by the consultants, but that they committed willingly to it. The Faustian pact they negotiated involved subordinating their selves/bodies to the organization in exchange for the attractive levels of pay, status, and job security that working as a consultant provided. Self-discipline/subordination involved them controlling themselves in order to further the organization's objectives. One of the aspects of the dark side for these workers was that the adoption of a self-identity as a consultant involved accepting the demands of clients, even when they were unreasonable. Such demands typically required these consultants to work long hours. To do this successfully involved the consultants subordinating their own bodies and non-work lives to their job. Thus when the body (through illness or tiredness), or non-work commitments (such as family), conflicted with work objectives they were regarded negatively, as they inhibited the achievement of work-related objectives.

Part of the reason for this willing self-subordination, where these workers placed stressful work demands on their bodies and their families was due to the perception that, while work conditions were good, a climate of fear wasn't far below the surface, where if they hadn't committed the hours necessary, or achieved the required results, then negative consequences may have ensued. Thus, even for high-status, knowledge-intensive workers, issues of conflict and power are not absent, and only a little amount of digging is required to expose them.

Conclusion

While two contrasting perspectives on power have been examined, they both point to the conclusion that to analyse and effectively understand the full dynamics of organizational knowledge processes requires power to be accounted for. The chapter has identified three key reasons why this is the case. First, power is embedded in the employment relationship between workers and the organizations they work for, and the potential conflict that exists between workers and their employers over how workers' knowledge is used cannot be fully understood without taking account of power. Secondly, understanding the dynamics of intra-organizational conflicts over how knowledge is used, for example where certain groups or individuals may be unwilling to share knowledge with each other, can also only be fully understood when power is accounted for. Finally, power and knowledge are closely interrelated, if not inseparable.

As a consequence, one of the most general conclusions of this chapter is that the centrality of power to knowledge processes means that any analyses of such processes that neglect to account for power are relatively impoverished. For example, taking account of power helps to explain and understand the human/social dimension of knowledge processes, such as whether people are willing or reluctant to participate in organizational knowledge processes. Thus, Walsham suggests (2001, 603) 'what we know affects how influential we are [thus] . . . there may be good reasons why individuals may not wish to participate in, or may modify some aspect of their sense-giving activities, for reasons related to organizational politics.'

Knowledge management was also shown to be concerned with more than simply managing all the knowledge that exists in organizations. Key to knowledge management processes are decisions about what knowledge is important/irrelevant, and what knowledge is reified/marginalized, and power plays a fundamental role in such processes. Finally, based on the work of Foucault the chapter showed how power is implicated in ICT-mediated knowledge management processes, through the potential for surveillance and monitoring which is possible with such technologies.

REVIEW QUESTIONS

1 In general, how compatible are the interests of workers and their employers over how workers knowledge is used? Does the requirement by organizations to derive economic value from it mean conflict is likely or inevitable?

2 The chapter assumed that power and knowledge are closely related, if not inseparable. Can you think of any ways in which knowledge can be used in organizations which do not involve the use of power in one way or another?

3 Compare the two conceptualizations of power examined. Can you relate either/both of them to your own experience?

4 What type of workers, if any, are likely to be empowered through the utilization of knowledge repositories to store and codify knowledge?

FURTHER READING

- S. Deetz (1998). 'Discursive Formations, Strategized Subordination and Self-Surveillance' in A. McKinlay and K. Starkey (eds), *Foucault, Management and Organization Theory*, London: Sage, 151–72.

  Provides an interesting counterbalance to the mainstream perspective on knowledge workers through using a Foucauldian-based analysis to illustrate how power and conflict is experienced by such workers.

- A. Mckinlay (2002). 'The Limits of Knowledge Management' *New Technology, Work and Employment*, 17/2: 76–88.

  Critiques the ICT as panoptican perspective by Illustrating the limitations of ICT-based knowledge management practices.

- N. Marshal and T. Brady (2001). 'Knowledge Management and the Politics of Knowledge: Illustrations from Complex Product Systems' *European Journal of Information Systems*, 10: 99–112.

Provides theoretical and empirical support for the argument that issues of power and conflict require to be accounted for in analysing organizational knowledge management initiatives.

- P. Gray (2001). 'The Impact of Knowledge Repositories on Power and Control in the Workplace' *Information Technology and People*, 14/4: 368–84.

  Speculated on how the use of IT-based knowledge repositories can affect the distribution of power in organizations.

8

Information and communication technologies and knowledge management

Introduction

As outlined in Chapter 4, one of the dominant themes in the early knowledge management literature was the importance of the role accorded to information and communication technologies (ICTs hereafter). This is visible in two ways. Firstly, ICTs had a central place in much of the early knowledge management literature (see p. 44), with the vast majority of this writing being optimistic regarding the role that they could play in knowledge management processes. Secondly, ICTs had a prominent role in many of the earliest knowledge management initiatives. Thus, Ruggles (1998), reporting on a 1997 survey, found that the four most popular types of knowledge management projects involved the implementation of intranets, data warehouses, decision support tools, and groupware (groupware relates to shared information spaces—such as Lotus Notes—which allow a range of people to work with the same documents simultaneously. More generally, they are technologies that support collaboration and communication). While these perspectives have been the subject of widespread criticism, this has *not* led to a position where ICTs are regarded as having no useful role. Instead, there has been an enormous evolution in how the relationship between ICTs and knowledge management processes is conceptualized. This chapter examines these changes.

 Information and communication technologies (ICTs)

ICTs are technologies which allow/facilitate the management and/or sharing of knowledge and information. Thus the term covers an enormous diversity of heterogeneous technologies including computers, telephones, e-mail, databases, data-mining systems, search engines, the internet, and video-conferencing equipment.

Hendriks (2001) described the bringing together of ICTs and knowledge management as involving the clash of two titans, as such an enormous amount of ink has been spilled on examining both topics, and the interrelationship between them. Attempting to do justice to the scale and scope of the debate on these linkages in the space of one chapter is therefore a difficult task.

The chapter begins by examining the role ascribed to ICTs in knowledge management processes when an objectivist perspective on knowledge is utilized. Following this, practice-based perspectives on the relationship between ICTs and knowledge processes will be examined, with the vast differences between these perspectives becoming visible as the chapter progresses. However, there isn't a consensus amongst those writing from a practice-based perspective, therefore this section of the chapter examines three areas of disagreement/debate. These debates centre on: (1) the extent to which ICTs can facilitate the sort of perspective-making processes described in Chapter 4; (2) the extent to which communication mediums have fixed or variable degrees of information richness and (3) the extent to which trust can be developed and sustained in social relations mediated by ICTs. Following this, the chapter closes by examining the dynamics of implementing ICT-based knowledge management systems.

Characterizing ICT-supported knowledge management processes

The following two sections examine the substantially different ways that the objectivist and practice-based perspectives on knowledge suggest that ICTs can be used in organizational knowledge management processes. While, as outlined in Chapters 3 and 4, the objectivist perspective has been the subject of widespread criticism, this perspective still underpins many contemporary knowledge management initiatives.

Objectivist perspectives

Chapter 2 outlined in detail both how the objectivist perspective on knowledge conceptualizes knowledge and how it characterizes knowledge-sharing processes. However, it is worth briefly restating some of the key assumptions of this perspective, as they help explain the roles that this perspective assumes ICTs can play in knowledge management processes. Firstly, this perspective conceptualizes knowledge in entitative terms, with knowledge being regarded as a discrete object that can exist separately from the people who possess and use it. Secondly, there is an optimism embedded in this perspective that much knowledge either exists in an explicit form, or that it can be made explicit through a process of codification (Steinmueller 2000). Thirdly, this perspective conceptualizes knowledge-sharing as being based on a transmitter–receiver model (see Figure 2.1), and assumes that it is relatively straightforward to share codified knowledge.

Building from these assumptions those utilizing an objectivist perspective believe that ICTs can play a direct role in knowledge management processes. Based on this viewpoint, which Swan and Scarbrough (2001) refer to as the 'knowledge management as technology' perspective, ICTs simply represents one channel/medium through which explicit

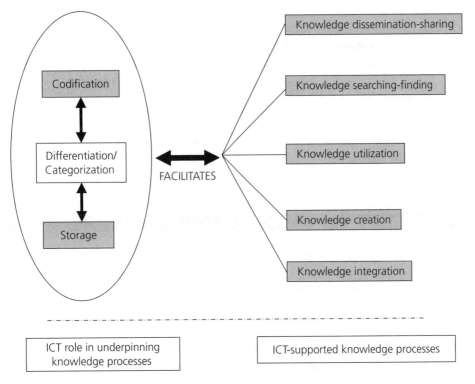

Fig. 8.1. Objectivist perspective on ICT roles in knowledge processes

knowledge can be shared. Figure 8.1 outlines the various roles that ICTs can play in knowledge management processes, and the interrelationship between them. These roles can be understood to exist at two levels.

The two primary, underpinning roles that ICTs can play in the management of knowledge, from which five further roles are linked, are firstly, in the codification of knowledge, and secondly in the storage of knowledge in some repository. Intermediate to them are the processes of categorization and differentiation, where distinctions are made between the discrete pieces of codified knowledge that exist, based on some system of categorization. Once the codified knowledge that exists has been through these processes, ICT systems can then play a key role in utilizing these frameworks for the storage of knowledge. Thus, for example, structured electronic databases represent one example of an ICT-based knowledge repository.

As illustrated in Figure 8.1, linked to from these roles, are five further ways in which ICTs can be used to manage an organization's knowledge (see Table 8.1). For example, one common use of search engines is for finding people within directories of expertise (thus the search role is underpinned by an electronic storage system, where the expertise of relevant people is categorized and structured into a searchable electronic database). Another example would be where Lotus Notes (a type of groupware technology) were used in a multidisciplinary project team for the sharing and simultaneous integration of the knowledge possessed by different project team members.

Table 8.1. ICT applications relevant to knowledge management roles

Knowledge management roles	ICT application
Searching for/Finding Knowledge	Search Engines, Web Portals
Creating Knowledge	CAD (computer-aided design) Systems
Utilizing Knowledge	Decision Support Systems
Sharing Knowledge	Intranets, e-mail
Integrating Knowledge	Groupware

Stop and think

Internet search engines such as Google are good examples of technologies that can be used for information/knowledge searching. Such technologies make the internet useful through providing a way of identifying relevant sources of knowledge on requested topics. What advantages and disadvantages have you personally found from using them? Are these advantages and disadvantages likely to also be applicable to organizationally based search engines?

As outlined in Chapter 4, there was a strong emphasis on ICTs in many of the earliest knowledge management initiatives. This was, to a large extent because, at that time, the objectivist perspective on knowledge was popular and widely accepted. However, the introduction to Part 2 of the book (p. 41–2) showed how a large proportion of these technology led initiatives failed because they focused almost exclusively on technological issues and typically, played down, if not completely ignored, social, cultural, and political factors which have since been shown to be key in influencing the willingness of people to participate in knowledge management initiatives. However, as can be seen by the example from Nortel Networks described below, such a neglect, while being common, is not intrinsic to ICT-based knowledge management initiatives. Therefore, technology-based knowledge management initiatives do *not* have to be technology led projects when they are being designed and implemented. This issue will also be returned to in the penultimate section of the chapter.

 ILLUSTRATING THE ISSUES

Nortel network: ICTs and knowledge management

Massey et al. (2002) examined how Nortel Networks used a 'process oriented' knowledge management strategy to successfully re-engineer its new product development (NPD) process. This was done through the development and implementation of a knowledge management tool called 'Virtual Mentor', which was described as an electronic performance support system (EPSS). This system linked together all relevant 'disparate knowledge resources' that were relevant to their product development process (including internal knowledge and expertise, which was highly dispersed, as well as customer knowledge, and relevant, archived historical knowledge). Virtual Mentor was designed to be of value to the three categories of worker they identified as being key to the NPD process: idea generators, decision-makers, and process owners. Process owners being the people responsible for the tracking the progress of the evolving NPD process. Massey et al. argue that the development and implementation of this system was a significant factor in the economic success that Nortel Networks experienced between 1994 and 2000. One of the central elements to the success of this project was that while it was a technology-based knowledge management project, technological issues did not dominate. Instead, Nortel Networks began by defining the stages in their NPD process, before considering the people-related issues flowing from this process. The technical specification and design of Virtual Mentor was thus the third and final stage in their NPD re-engineering project.

Stop and think

The success of Nortel's knowledge management system was that the technology was designed to be compatible with existing work practices, rather than vice versa. Based on your understanding of organizational knowledge management projects, which approach is most commonly used?

While the widespread criticism of this technology-based perspective on knowledge management has exposed a number of severe limitations in it (see the following section for a brief discussion of these issues), evidence suggests that the knowledge management initiatives of many organizations are still embedded in an objectivist-based perspectives on knowledge, and that some of these organizations have been successful in their knowledge management initiatives. Consider, for example, the case of Global Bank's IT support initiative described in Chapter 2 (see pp. 24–5), and Nortel Networks, just examined. Further examples include: the knowledge codification project undertaken by the UK consulting firm examined by Morris (2001); the media organization examined by Robertson (2002), whose knowledge management system was in essence a searchable repository of employee expertise and know-how; and, the World Bank, where the objectives of its knowledge management strategy in the late 1990s was to make itself a 'technology broker, transferring knowledge from one place where it is available to the place where it is needed' (van der Velden 2002, 30).

Practice-based perspectives

Even over the short space of time that knowledge management has been regarded as an important topic there has been a significant evolution in the role that ICTs are conceptualized as being able to play in such processes. The objectivist perspective just outlined, where ICTs were considered able to play a direct and significant role in knowledge codification and sharing processes, while still being utilized, is much less prevalent than it was in the mid to late 1990s. Consequently, the optimism possessed by those utilizing this perspective regarding the ability to codify tacit knowledge, and then store and share it electronically has also largely dissipated. Over time, therefore, there has been an evolution in thinking regarding the role of ICTs in organizational knowledge processes which

Table 8.2. Criticisms of the objectivist perspective on knowledge

Criticisms of objectivist perspective on knowledge
Overestimates extent to which tacit knowledge can be made codifiable
Underestimates extent to which tacit and explicit knowledge are inseparable
Underestimates extent to which organizational knowledge is fragmented
Underestimates extent to which knowledge is context-dependent
Overconfident on ability for knowledge to be collected in central repository

has seen practice-based perspectives on knowledge become more fully embraced. As will be seen, the practice-based perspective regards ICTs as having a less direct, but equally important role in supporting and facilitating the social processes that underpin interpersonal knowledge processes.

The critique of the objectivist perspective on technology, which to some extent underpins the shift in thinking regarding the role of ICTs in knowledge management processes, was outlined in detail in Chapter 3. However, it is worth briefly restating the main points of this critique (see Table 8.2), as it helps in understanding the role that ICTs are assigned by those utilizing a practice-based perspective on knowledge. Firstly, the objectivist perspective is criticized for overestimating the extent to which tacit knowledge can be codified, with the practice-based perspective arguing that much tacit knowledge can never be made explicit. Secondly, the objectivist perspective doesn't acknowledge the inseparable character of tacit and explicit knowledge, which means that there is no such thing as fully explicit knowledge, and the electronic communication of any (partially) explicit knowledge will typically mean that its tacit components are lost, or not fully communicated and shared. Thirdly, it underestimates the extent to which knowledge in organizations is fragmented, dispersed, and specialized. Fourthly, it is argued to underestimate the extent to which knowledge is context-specific, which means that such knowledge is difficult to remove from its context and be understood fully in a different context. Fifthly, and finally, to some extent as a consequence of all of the above criticisms, the objectivist perspective is argued to suffer from what Tsoukas (1996) called the 'synoptic delusion', the idea that it is possible to collect an organization's knowledge in a single repository.

One consequence, flowing from this general critique of the objectivist perspective on knowledge, is that the role that analysts using an objectivist perspective assumed ICTs could play in knowledge processes became questioned (Hislop 2002*b*; Walsham 2001). Thus, those writing from a practice-based perspective believe that the role of ICTs in the codification and storage of knowledge in electronic repositories is limited, as such knowledge is stripped of the tacit assumptions and values which underpin it.

Further, the transmitter—receiver metaphor of knowledge-sharing is regarded as inappropriate, as the sharing of knowledge does not involve the simple transferal of a fixed entity (explicit knowledge) between two people. Instead, the sharing of knowledge involves two people actively inferring and constructing meaning from a process of interaction (Hislop 2002b). This relates to the processes of perspective making and taking which were described in Chapter 4, where those interacting develop an understanding of the values, assumptions, and tacit knowledge which underpin each other's knowledge base (Walsham 2001). Communication processes in such interactions, to be successful, require to be relatively rich, open, and based on a certain level of trust.

The role which those writing from a practice-based perspective believe that ICTs can play in knowledge processes is thus somewhat indirect, being related to facilitating and supporting the social relationships and communication processes which underpin knowledge processes. Walsham (2001, 599), usefully summarized this by arguing that, 'computer-based systems can be of benefit in knowledge-based activities . . . to support the development and communication of human meaning.'

Debates within the practice-based perspective regarding ICTs and knowledge processes

Within the practice-based perspective, however, there isn't a consensus on the role that ICTs can play in knowledge management processes. This section examines three of the key debates, and will simultaneously provide a deeper understanding of how those utilizing a practice-based perspective conceptualize the role of ICTs in knowledge management processes.

ICTs and perspective making/taking

The first area of debate relates to the question of whether ICTs can facilitate the rich interaction that is usually necessary for perspective making and taking processes to be successful. Walsham (2001) answers this question in the positive, and believes that ICT-mediated communication does have the potential to facilitate processes of perspective making and taking. Boland et al. (1994) also believe that it could be possible to design IT systems to do this, suggesting, 'information technology can support distributed cognition by enabling individuals to make rich representations of their understanding, reflect upon those representations, engage in dialogue with others about them, and use them to inform action.' (457).

However, as will be seen later, Boland et al. argue that to do this requires a radical transformation in IS design philosophies. DeSanctis and Monge (1999, 696) also take a positive view regarding the ability of ICTs to allow a rich form of interaction by arguing that rather than the loss of social cues which occurs when communicating via most ICTs being negative, that such a loss may in fact facilitate understanding, 'by removing the distraction of irrelevant stimuli'.

Stop and think

Is a potential advantage of ICT-mediated communication that people are less likely to judge others on potentially superficial factors such as looks? How does the process of making initial judgements of strangers vary between face-to-face situations and ICT-mediated situations?

However, other writers are more critical, fundamentally arguing that the difficulties of facilitating rich interactions via ICTs should not be underestimated (Hislop 2002*b*). This is primarily because the loss of social cues (tone and pace of voice, gesture, facial expression) which occurs when using most ICTs significantly degrades the communication process, and limits the extent to which knowledge can be shared via such mediums (Goodall and Roberts 2003; Roberts 2000; Symon 2000). Further, there may be a limited role for ICTs particularly in the sort of intercommunity knowledge processes examined in Chapter 6. This chapter showed how knowledge-sharing in such circumstances is complicated by the lack of shared identity and limited overlap in the knowledge base of people. These difficulties are arguably exacerbated when such knowledge-sharing is electronically mediated, as the social cues that are important to the sharing of such factors are lost (Walsham 2001). McLoughlin and Jackson (1999) make similar conclusions, arguing that rich knowledge-sharing in virtual interactions is most likely to be successful where there is a positive, pre-existing social relationship between people.

Finally, a perspective, somewhat intermediate to the above two positions suggests that while ICTs alone may have a limited ability to facilitate a rich form of communication, they can have a role when combined with face-to-face interactions (Nandhakumar 1999). Maznevski and Chudoba (1999) reach such a conclusion in their study of global virtual teams, suggesting that 'effective global virtual teams . . . generate a deep rhythm of regular face-to-face incidents interspersed with less intensive, shorter incidents using various media' (473).

ICTs and media richness

One finding that emerges from the above debate is that face-to-face communication has different characteristics from electronically mediated communications. Looking in more detail, it can also be seen that different ICTs have different communication characteristics (see Table 8.3). However, the characteristics and degrees of information richness of different communication mediums, are the subject of disagreement, and are the second area of debate examined.

In the information systems literature Information Richness Theory (IRT) suggests that different mediums have fixed and static levels of information richness, where 'communication richness (or leanness) is an invariant, objective property of communication media' (Ngwenyama and Lee 1997, 147). Further, this theory adopts a rational choice approach to people's selection decisions with regard to the communication mediums they use, with people selecting the communication medium most appropriate to the task being undertaken. From this perspective, it is possible to rank different mediums in terms of their 'objective' levels of information richness, with face-to-face interaction being the richest, and e-mail being one of the leanest. Table 8.3 is thus laid out to reflect such a ranking.

However, this theory has been the subject of an increasing level of criticism, which questions the idea that each communication medium has fixed and objective information richness characteristics. This is therefore why there is a question mark in Table 8.3 beside the ranking arrow. Instead of communication mediums having fixed and objective information richness characteristics, as IRT suggests, others suggest the leanness or richness of any communication process is something which emerges from the, 'interactions between the

Table 8.3. Characteristics of various communication mediums

Medium	Communication characteristics
Face-to-Face Interaction	• Information rich (social cues such as facial expression, voice, gesture visible. Plus, synchronous communication, potential for rapid high-quality feedback/interaction) • Most relevant for sharing of tacit knowledge • Spontaneous/informal interactions possible when people geographically proximate • Conditions amenable to development of trust (other factors excluded) • Expensive when people geographically dispersed
Video conferencing	• Information rich (social cues, and virtually real time, synchronous medium) • Expensive to set up • Set up time inhibits spontaneity
Telephone	• Intermediate information richness (tone of voice conveys some social cues, but gesture, expression invisible. Also synchronous, facilitating detailed, immediate feedback) • Cost variable • Spontaneous/informal interactions possible irrespective of geographic proximity • Can facilitate development of trust where face-to-face interaction difficult interaction difficult
E-mail	• Suitable for sharing of highly codified knowledge • Relatively low information richness (all social cues lost) • Inexpensive (cost unrelated to geographic proximity) • Asynchronous, with variable feedback speed • Spontaneous/informal interactions possible irrespective of geographic proximity • Permanent record of interaction exists • Development of trust based on e-mail alone difficult

'Increasing Information Richness?'

people, and the organizational context' (Ngwenyama and Lee 1997, 148). Thus the richness of any communication process will not be determined by the technical characteristics of the communication medium, but will instead be shaped by a range of social and technical factors. Relevant social factors include the degree of mutual understanding which exists between people, the willingness of people to make the effort to communicate and understand, and the abilities of people to effectively use a communication medium. Thus, 'low richness' mediums like e-mail can be used for complex, information-rich interactions if organizations encourages it, or people become adept at using it (Markus 1994; Ngwenyama and Lee 1997; DeSanctis and Monge 1999). Thus, if people are more comfortable and competent using e-mail, compared to 'richer' communication mediums, such as groupware, this may help explain the preference for e-mail reported in a number of studies (Ngwenyama and Lee 1997; Markus 1994; Pauleen and Yoong 2001; Robertson et al. 2001).

Organizational level factors, such as the character of the organizational culture can also affect both the type of medium used, and the way in which it is used. Thus, if an organizational culture places an emphasis on accountability and documentation, this may encourage the use of e-mail, as, compared to other communication mediums this provides a good, documented record of conversations and interactions. Alternatively, an organizational culture that emphasizes teamworking, openness, and good interpersonal working relations, may encourage the use of face-to-face meetings, and telephone conversations.

 ILLUSTRATING THE ISSUES

Robertson et al. 2001: explaining the predominance of e-mail

Robertson et al. examined the communication and knowledge-sharing patterns in a knowledge-intensive organization: a scientific consultancy. Much of the work in this organization was knowledge-intensive, and required multidisciplinary project teams to share and integrate their knowledge together. The preferred mode of communication and sharing of knowledge was through either telephone conversations, or face-to-face meetings, which supported a rich inter-action. However, a surprising finding in the study was the significance of the extent to which e-mail was used, and the lack of use that was made of Lotus Notes, even though it had been implemented organization-wide. According to IRT theory, groupware technologies such as Lotus Notes, are a richer communication medium than e-mail, therefore this theory would suggest that Lotus Notes would be of use for the type of knowledge-intensive interactions typically required by the consultants. Robertson et al. suggest that there are a number of social and contextual factors which explain this communication pattern. Firstly, the consultants had become adept e-mail users, and were able to make innovative use of it. Secondly, few consultants had invested the time to learn how to use Lotus Notes, which created a vicious circle where people didn't feel encouraged to make the use of it, as they were unsure that others would be adept with it. Finally, the organizational culture, for a variety of historical reasons, also encouraged and reinforced the use of e-mail, as one of the main methods of communication.

Stop and think

In such an organizational context what would management require to do to persuade its workers to make greater use of Lotus Notes?

ICTs and developing/retaining trust
The final area of debate and disagreement examined, which links closely to the first topic of debate examined, is the extent to which trust can be developed and sustained in social relations which are mediated by ICT-based modes of communication. The literature on this topic shows that the extent of face-to-face interaction that occurs between people affects more than just their ability to develop an understanding of each other. It also affects the basic nature of the social relationship, and the extent to which trust can be developed and sustained. The debate in this area is over the question of whether trust can be developed and sustained by electronically mediated communication alone.

One school of thought suggests that it isn't possible to develop and maintain trust in social relations mediated purely by ICTs. Roberts (2000) thus argues that face-to-face contact is a vital element in the establishment of a relationship of trust. Research conducted by Maznevski and Chudoba (1999) reinforces this perspective, as one of the benefits for the successful teams who used occasional face-to-face meetings as well as electronically mediated interactions was that the face-to-face meetings improved the social relationship and the level of trust that existed amongst project team members.

Finally, the research conducted by Nandhakumar (1999) on global virtual teams also supports this perspective. This research examined patterns of information and knowledge-sharing within a global virtual team. The communication of the team was mediated by a PC-based ICT system which included desktop video conferencing, multimedia e-mail and groupware applications, which included an intranet and file transfer software. In this research the absence of co-location was found to significantly affect the development of trust. The project team examined consisted of people who had never previously met, or worked together, therefore there was no pre-existing personal relationship, and initially trust was relatively contractual and weak. However, project team members actively initiated face-to-face interactions with other team members to develop a more personal type of trust. Overall, Nandhakumar concluded that ICTs in and of themselves were not adequate for either the development or maintenance of trust in working relations. This conclusion can be illustrated with the following quotation from one of the project team members interviewed, 'to start establishing a relationship I think you need to have the physical contact more because you have this indefinable thing about relationships and body language and you don't get it in the same way [in electronic interactions] . . . so . . . as you do the teambuilding you need to have some physical contact' (52).

ILLUSTRATING THE ISSUES

Pharma-co: communication within a virtual project team

Pharma-co decided in the mid-1990s to implement a new information management system into their production sites, which would better link them to other organizational functions (for further details on Pharma-co's project see pp. 34–5). Pharma-co's production sites were spread throughout Europe, Asia, and North America, with the greatest concentration of sites in the UK and USA. The project team set up to facilitate the design and implementation of the information management system were from two UK and two American sites. Therefore there was some necessity to work virtually. A number of different communication mediums were used to facilitate the development of social relations and knowledge-sharing including e-mail, video conferencing, telephone calls, and conferences, as well as occasional face-to-face meetings. The project manager in particular had to do a lot of travelling to maintain frequent face-to-face interactions with project members from all sites. While the project was ultimately successful in its work, electronically mediated working was found to be difficult and challenging, for a number of reasons. Firstly, video conferencing facilities were only available on two sites, so it was difficult to include all project team members when using them. Secondly, the project developed a routine of having a weekly voice conference linking all team members on all four sites. The project manager, however, found that this method of communication had its difficulties, primarily because of the loss of some social cues. Thus, in discussing the telephone conferences she argued that, 'from a project management point of view you are completely blind as to the reactions received, you don't know whether they are comfortable telling you that's what they are doing, whether they are being optimistic or pessimistic. Whereas when you are looking at them you can see either that they are uncomfortable telling you this because they are not very confident about it, or that they are holding something back.'

Finally, language differences also complicated communication and knowledge-sharing. Thus, knowledge-sharing was initially inhibited by differing definitions of key terms between the UK and American team members.

However, some writers are more positive, and argue that it is possible to build and sustain trust in interpersonal relations that are totally mediated by ICTs. Pauleen and Yoong (2001) in a study on the role of ICTs for relationship building in virtual teams argue that social relations can be developed and built amongst strangers by the strategic use of a range of electronic communication mediums such as telephone, e-mail, and video conferencing. They also suggest that the specific balance of the most appropriate communication mediums is likely to vary between contexts, and will be shaped by factors like national and organizational cultural norms, individual personality, and the range of mediums available.

Stop and think

Do you agree with Pauleen and Yoong's conclusion that through the judicious use of a range of ICT-based communication mechanisms it is possible to develop effective working relations with strangers who have different cultural values without any face-to-face interaction?

Jarvenpaa and Leidner (1999) are also positive that trust can be developed in totally virtual social relations, though they found that the type of trust developed in temporary virtual teams was extremely fragile. The virtual teams examined by Jarvenpaa and Leidner were 'separated by time and culture', as they involved remote interaction between people of different nationalities who not only had no previous knowledge of each other, but who had no opportunities to meet face-to-face. In the teams examined time was not available for the development of personal-based trust, but with some groups what has been labelled as swift trust developed, which allowed them to work together effectively. Swift trust is utilized in situations where there isn't the luxury of time to develop social relations, and is typically inferred presumptively based on the limited information that team members have of each other. However, this type of trust was found to be fragile, precarious, and easy to destroy. Jarvenpaa and Leidner (1999, 807) found that certain actions and behaviours facilitated the development of this type of trust (see Table 8.4). For example, in the early stage of a group's life, trust is more likely to be developed if group members communicate an enthusiasm for the task to be undertaken, and show a willingness to engage in social communication to establish a more personal basis to social relations. Further, they found that at more mature stages of a group's working life, trust was sustained if group members provided timely responses to queries, and if groups were able to manage the transition from social-based interactions to task-based interactions. Thus, Jarvenpaa

Table 8.4. Trust facilitating behaviours and actions (adapted from table 4, Jarvenpaa and Leidner 1999, 807)

Communication behaviours and actions that facilitated trust in early group life	Communication behaviours and actions which helped maintain trust over time
• Social communication	• Predictable communication
• Demonstrate enthusiasm	• Substantial and timely responses
• Cope with technical uncertainty	• Successful transition from social to procedural to task focus
• Show individual initiative	• Positive leadership
	• Phlegmatic response to crises

and Leidner conclude that (a weak form of) trust can be developed in ICT-mediated social relations if people behave and act in certain ways.

Implementing ICT-based knowledge management systems

Up to now, the focus of this chapter has been on one central theme, the extent to which, and ways in which ICTs can be used to facilitate knowledge management processes. This section changes focus to consider the question of *how* ICT-based knowledge management systems should be designed and implemented. Chapter 4 illustrated the high failure rate of the earliest ICT-based knowledge management initiatives. In broad terms, these failures could be the result of two general causes. Firstly, it may be that these systems were designed for knowledge-related functions for which ICTs are unsuited. This represents one of the main critiques that writers from a practice-based perspective have utilized, for example, suggesting that the objectivist-based early initiatives underestimated the difficulties of codifying tacit knowledge. However, another, equally relevant explanation for the failure of these early knowledge management initiatives is that they were inappropriately designed and implemented. This section therefore considers this question.

A critique of the implementation methods of the early knowledge management initiatives

As described in Chapter 4, one of the main problems of the early ICT-focused knowledge management initiatives was that they neglected 'people'-related issues, by typically assuming unquestioningly that people would be willing to share their knowledge. In these early knowledge management initiatives the neglect of 'people' meant that inadequate account was taken of the social and cultural context into which the systems were to be implemented. Instead these projects were typically very much technically led, and technically focused, i.e. on how to physically store knowledge, rather than on whether people would be willing (or able) to store their knowledge in such systems.

These problems are not exclusive to the implementation of knowledge management systems. For example, Symon (2000), in discussing research on the use of electronic communication systems, concludes that it is typically problematic to assume unquestioningly that people will be willing to use these systems. Orlikowski et al. (1995) also in relation to electronic communication systems argued that when such systems are not adapted adequately to the social conditions of the local context that there is a significant chance that such systems will be underused. Finally, McDermott (1999) argued that a neglect of social and cultural issues in the design and implementation of information technology runs the risk that such systems will reinforce rather than transform existing cultures, values, and behaviour.

ILLUSTRATING THE ISSUES

Globalbank: the problems in a technology led KM project

In Chapter six (see p. 76–7) the problems Globalbank experienced with its intranet project were described. One of the main problems, which adversely affected this project, was that staff from different business units didn't adequately collaborate with each other, and share relevant knowledge. A significant part of the explanation for why this happened was that the project, whose overall coordination was the responsibility of corporate IT staff, was focused primarily on technological issues, such as whether the IT infrastructure in place was adequately for the functions required, agreeing protocols for site development, and deciding on the content and style of the intranet sites. The project team, while acknowledging the culture of autonomy and antagonistic competitiveness which existed between divisions, did little to improve or change these social relations. This meant that the level of trust between divisional staff was typically low as nothing had been done to break down and challenge the historical antagonisms which existed. Ironically, the result of this was that a project whose aim was to attempt to reduce cross-organizational boundaries, and improve levels of intra-organizational communication and knowledge-sharing, instead helped to reinforce the existing culture of divisional autonomy.

However, being sensitive to the socio-cultural context means taking account of the specific and distinctive characteristics of each organization. This therefore makes it difficult to provide a general checklist of prescriptions and answers about how to be successful in such ventures. What works in one organizational context may be completely inappropriate in another, different organizational context. A better way of dealing with this issue is not to try and give such standard, generalized answers. Walsham (2001) instead suggests that a better way to develop an understanding of relevant socio-cultural factors is to ask a set of sensitizing question, such as:

- What type of knowledge-sharing processes does the existing organizational culture encourage and discourage?

- How do existing power relations affect knowledge processes?

Once these questions have been answered it should then be possible to design and implement ICT-based knowledge management systems which take account of these factors.

An alternative design philosophy

Boland et al. (1994) are optimistic that ICTs can be designed to support processes of perspective making and taking. But they also acknowledge that achieving this will require a significant shift of emphasis in system design philosophies (Tenkasi and Boland 1996). This is primarily because, while the objectivist perspective on knowledge and knowledge-sharing has been widely criticized, it still represents the dominant paradigm in the main-stream information systems literature (Schulze and Leidner 2002). This is made visible by a number of the assumptions made by this literature:

- Objective knowledge exists and is transmittable through words and language which has a fixed meaning.
- The knowledge base of organizations is characterized by consensus, and a significant common knowledge base, making knowledge-sharing unproblematic.
- ICT systems for knowledge-sharing are based on the transmitter–receiver model (see Figure 2.1).

From this perspective, system design is concerned with designing communication channels that maximize signal/information richness and minimize 'noise' levels (Bolisani and Scarso 2000). Instead Tenkasi and Boland (1996) argue that, from a practice-based perspective, design objectives should shift to facilitate processes of perspective making/taking between people who can't be assumed to have a lot of knowledge in com-mon. This therefore requires the creation of open systems that allow the surfacing and sharing of different interpretations, taken for granted assumptions, and values.

Conclusion

A significant number of writers suggest that ICTs can play an important role in knowledge management processes. However, there is a significant debate in the contemporary knowledge management literature regarding the role that ICTs can play in knowledge management processes, which this chapter has examined. Thus, rather than attempt to present a coherent and unitary perspective, this chapter has attempted to do justice to the debate by presenting a range of perspectives.

In broad terms there has been a retreat from the optimist embodied in the early knowledge management literature that knowledge processes can easily be mediated and facilitated via the use of advanced ICTs. There is now, thus, a greater acknowledgement of the not insignificant difficulties of having knowledge processes mediated by ICTs.

One contrast in the literature can be made between analyses utilizing objectivist and practice-based perspectives. Writing which utilizes an objectivist conceptualization of knowledge typically argues that ICTs can have an important and direct role in knowledge processes, for example in the structuring, storage, and dissemination of codified knowledge. By contrast, writing which adopts a practice-based perspective on knowledge, questions this role for ICT systems in knowledge processes. This work emphasizes the difficulty of both codifying knowledge, and sharing codified knowledge electronically. Writing embedded in this perspective thus tends to suggest that ICTs can have a more indirect role in knowledge processes, facilitating interpersonal interaction and processes of perspective making/taking. However, as was shown, it is deceptive to present these two perspectives as being unified, as within the practice-based literature there are debates on a number of issues, including the extent to which trust can be built via social relations mediated by ICTs.

The managerial implications that flow from these insights are quite significant. For example, if different types of behaviour are appropriate for the development and maintenance of trust in face-to-face and ICT-mediated interactions, this affects the types of behaviours and attitudes that organizational management should encourage and reinforce.

However, one general conclusion that can be made on this topic is that, whatever the role that ICTs have in knowledge processes, for such systems to be effective, their design and implementation requires to be sensitive to the socio-cultural context into which they are being implemented. The danger of not doing this, as was well demonstrated by the high failure rate of the earliest technology led knowledge management projects, is that the chances of such projects succeeding are relatively low.

REVIEW QUESTIONS

1 Arguably, an either/or logic predominates in much of the literature which compares technology-mediated and face-to-face methods of communication and knowledge-sharing processes, where they are considered to exist at the opposite ends of a spectrum, and where the use of one mode of communication is regarded as being likely to limit the extent to which the other is used (Woolgar 2003). However, is this necessarily the case? To what extent may the use of either form of knowledge-sharing support and facilitate the use of the other? For example, is it possible that the use of technology-based knowledge systems, such as a searchable directory of expertise, may also lead to an increase in face-to-face based knowledge-sharing mechanisms, for example through meeting people found through using such directories?

2 When ICTs are used for knowledge management purposes there appears to be a preference for using off-the-shelf products and then attempting to customize/modify the organizational context, rather than customizing or designing technological systems to be compatible with existing organizational practices. Why is this the case?

3 The critique of Information Richness Theory (IRT) discussed challenged the idea that any communication medium has an objective and fixed level of communication richness, and that instead the richness of any communication process would be shaped by the relationship between people, and their skills at using different communication mediums. To what extent do you agree with this argument? Could this argument not be challenged by suggesting that certain communication mediums are inherently richer communication mediums compared to

others, for example phone conversations, where voice tone can be heard, and e-mail, which is a purely text-based medium?

FURTHER READING

- A. Massey, M. Montoya-Weiss, and T. O'Driscoll (2002). 'Knowledge Management in Pursuit of Performance: Insights from Nortel Networks', *MIS Quarterly*, 26/3: 269–89.

  Presents a detailed analysis of a successful ICT-based knowledge management initiative, which did take account of social/contextual factors.

- J. Roberts (2000). 'From Know-How to Show-How? Questioning the Role of Information and Communication Technologies in Knowledge Transfer', *Technology Analysis and Strategic Management*, 12/4: 429–43.

  Examines the difficulties of sharing knowledge, particularly tacit knowledge, via ICTs.

- G. Walsham (2001). 'Knowledge Management: The Benefits and Limitations of Computer systems', *European Management Journal*, 19/6: 599–608.

  Reviews the literature on IT-based knowledge management, and concludes that ICTs can facilitate knowledge management efforts, but from a practice-based perspective.

- R. Boland, R. Tenkasi, and D. Te'eni (1994). 'Designing Information Technology to Support Distributed Cognition', *Organization Science*, 5/3: 456–75.

  Argues that ICTs can be designed to support and facilitate perspective making/taking processes.

9

Organizational culture, HRM policies, and knowledge management

Introduction

As the introduction to Part 2, and Chapter 4 detail, social and cultural factors have been found to be key mediating factors, affecting the dynamics and likely success of knowledge management initiatives. This is primarily because such factors have increasingly been recognized as playing a fundamental role in determining whether workers will be willing to actively participate in knowledge management initiatives. Inevitably, this has led to organizations deliberately attempting to manage their cultures to produce appropriate knowledge behaviours.

Overall this chapter examines two broad topics. Firstly, how organizational cultures shape the attitudes and behaviours of their staff to knowledge processes, and, secondly, the ways in which management can use culture, and Human Resource Management (HRM hereafter) practices such as recruitment and reward, to produce appropriate attitudes and behaviours. The attitudes and behaviours that are relevant to knowledge management initiatives are outlined in Table 9.1. Thus, the use of culture management and HRM policies can be seen to be concerned not only with attempting to produce appropriate knowledge behaviours and attitudes, but also with making workers committed and loyal to their employer, so that valuable knowledge is not lost through staff turnover (Leidner 2000).

Table 9.1. Attitudes and behaviours relevant to knowledge management initiatives

Attitudes	Behaviours
• Positive attitude towards knowledge management initiatives	• Active participation in knowledge management initiatives
• Level of loyalty and commitment to the organization, and the goals it is pursuing	• Having continuous employment for significant periods

The chapter begins by examining the linkages between knowledge management, human resource management, and general business strategies. The second major section then shifts focus to examine the topic of organizational culture, and considers its importance in relation to knowledge management initiatives. The third and final section then considers how specific HRM practices can be used to affect not only attitudes and behaviours to knowledge processes, but also levels of organizational loyalty and commitment.

Linking HRM, business, and knowledge strategies

Before it is possible to articulate the type of HRM policies and practices that can support an organization's knowledge management efforts it is necessary understand the type of knowledge management strategy that organizations are pursuing. This is because not only is there an enormous diversity in the type of knowledge management strategies that organizations can pursue (see Hendriks 2001 for a useful taxonomy), but crucially the HRM implications of these different strategies are quite distinctive. This raises a number of related questions including: what is the link, if any, between an organization's knowledge management strategy and its business strategy; and how is an organization's business strategy related to its general HRM strategy. This section therefore examines how the strategic context (see Figure 9.1) shapes the type of HRM practices and policies organizations utilize.

Before considering this topic further it is necessary to say that the knowledge management–strategy relationship, as articulated in the knowledge management literature, has idealistic and rationalistic overtones. Thus, there are assumptions that business strategies are developed on the basis of thorough and objective analyses of the business/market environment, and that the implications of these business strategies are then used in a logical and structured fashion to determine organizational practices (such as HRM policies, IT strategy). In Mintzberg et al.'s terms (1998), strategy follows the Design School or Planning School models, which neglects the extent to which strategy is ad hoc, emergent, based on limited searches and hunches, or that business strategies are as much the result of political battles as careful market analyses. Arguably, this is because the issue of strategy has been given inadequate attention in the knowledge management literature (Zack 1999), and that as a consequence strategy models are thus relatively basic and unsophisticated.

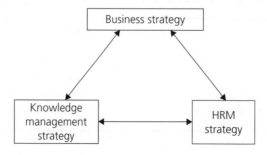

Fig. 9.1. Linking business, knowledge, and HRM strategies

A number of writers and analysts suggest that it is fundamentally important to link knowledge management initiatives to concrete business strategies (Hansen et al. 1999; Hunter et al. 2002; McDermott and O'Dell 2001; Pan and Scarbrough 1999; Skyrme and Amidon 1997). Zack (1999) suggests that this is the case because doing so represents the primary way that such initiatives can be made to effectively contribute to the creation of economic value and competitive advantage. Thus, in relation to Figure 9.1, the starting point in deciding on what type of knowledge management initiative to implement should be an analysis of an organization's business strategy to identify the role of knowledge in it. The development of knowledge and HRM strategies should therefore be informed by this analysis and link back to the business strategy by developing and reinforcing it.

Different writers have characterized the diversity of knowledge management strategies that organizations pursue in a variety of ways. Hansen et al. (1999), in what is one of the most well-known frameworks differentiate between two broad knowledge strategies: codification and personalization (see Table 9.2). The codification strategy is most relevant for companies whose competitive advantage is derived from the reuse of codified knowledge and is centrally concerned with creating searchable repositories for the storage and retrieval of codified knowledge. The personalization strategy, by contrast, is most relevant for companies whose competitive advantage is derived from processes of knowledge creation. The personalization knowledge strategy focuses on ways to improve the face-to-face sharing of tacit knowledge between the different workers who possess relevant knowledge.

Hunter et al. (2002) develop an alternative framework that has four specific knowledge strategies (see Table 9.3). The first two strategies, building and leveraging human capital, have in common the fact they are focused on the development and use of human capital. The second two strategies, deepening knowledge processes and diffusing knowledge, have in common the fact that they involve the development of human processes. Their

Table 9.2. Codification and personalization knowledge strategies (from Hansen et al. 1999)

Knowledge strategy	Codification	Personalization
Business-Knowledge Link	Competitive advantage through knowledge re-use	Competitive advantage through knowledge creation
Relevant Knowledge Process	Transferring knowledge from people to documents	Improving social processes to facilitate sharing of tacit knowledge between people
HRM Implications	• Motivate people to codify their knowledge • Training should emphasize the development of IT skills • Reward people for codifying their knowledge	• Motivate people to share their knowledge with others • Training should emphasize the development of inter-personal skills • Reward people for sharing knowledge with others

framework, based on an analysis of the knowledge strategies pursued by five large Scottish law firms, is similar to that of Hansen et al., in that the knowledge strategies relate to particular business strategies, and that, different HRM implications flow from each knowledge strategy.

ILLUSTRATING THE ISSUES

Castco and Swed-Truck: strategy and knowledge

Castco and Swed-Truck are two organizations which had historically been organized into separate and discrete divisions which had operated independently from each other, had interacted relatively infrequently, and which had little in the way of common standards and working practices. In the late 1990s senior management in both organizations, based on an analysis of their changing market conditions, decided that this had to change, and that there would be organizational benefits from increasing the amount of interdivisional knowledge-sharing and through increasing the degree to which working practices were standardized. To achieve this, both organizations embarked on change programmes that involved the development and implementation of common, organization-wide information management systems. These systems not only required the development of common standards and working practices, but also facilitated interdivisional communication and knowledge-sharing.

Stop and think

Using the strategy typologies outlined in Tables 9.2 and 9.3 classify the type of knowledge management strategy adopted by Castco and Swed-Truck.

Table 9.3. Hunter et al. (2002)'s four knowledge strategies

Focus	Knowledge strategy	Objective
Human capital	Building human capital	Increase the amount of knowledge capital possessed by the organization through the recruitment and retention of staff.
	Leveraging human capital	More effectively utilizing existing knowledge capital, for example through use of ICT-based knowledge-sharing systems.
Human process	Deepening knowledge utilization	Improving the quality of interaction between staff to improve level of (tacit) knowledge-sharing and perspective making/taking.
	Knowledge diffusion	Improve extent to which key knowledge is diffused and made accessible to all relevant workers.

Stop and think

How realistic is the strategy model portrayed in the knowledge management literature? Does it present too rational a model of the strategy-making and implementation process?

Hansen et al. (1999) make clear that the HRM implications of the codification and personalization knowledge strategies are different, and argue that it is thus important for organizations to ensure that their knowledge and HRM strategies are aligned (see Table 9.2). For example, with the codification strategy, the main motivation issue is persuading workers to codify their tacit knowledge, whereas with the personalization strategy it is related to persuading people to share their knowledge with others. HRM policies and practices thus need to be directed towards the achievement of these quite different objectives. Thus, for example, in terms of recruitment and selection, it will be important to identify and recruit people with suitable personalities to these different knowledge activities (knowledge reuse versus knowledge creation). Equally, training and development implications also require to be different, with companies pursuing codification strategies requiring to emphasize the development of IT skills, whereas those organizations pursuing a personalization strategy require to place a substantially greater emphasis on developing the social networking and interpersonal skills of their workers. Finally, payment and appraisal systems should reward behaviours appropriate to the organization's knowledge strategy.

Organizational culture and knowledge management

This section examines two interrelated topics: the extent to which and ways in which organizational culture can affect attitudes towards and participation in knowledge initiatives, and secondly, the extent to which appropriate, positive knowledge cultures can be created by deliberate management efforts. While there is general unanimity regarding the importance of culture in affecting knowledge initiatives, as will be seen, opinions vary greatly on the second topic, which to some extent reflects debates in the wider culture literature.

Before proceeding any further it is necessary to define what organizational culture is. While every piece of writing on culture typically gives its own specific definition, a useful one is that provided by Huczynski and Buchanan (2001, 624), who define organizational culture as 'the collection of relatively uniform and enduring values, beliefs, customs, traditions, and practices that are shared by an organization's members'. This definition is useful as it highlights the collective nature of culture and also suggests that culture exists both at the level of ideas and behaviours.

   Orgnizational culture

The beliefs and behaviours shared by an organization's members.

As outlined below, and in subsequent sections, culture is closely interrelated with HRM policies and practices. Thus, for example, a culture that emphasizes and encourages active participation in knowledge initiatives can be reinforced by HRM practices such as payment systems or training and development schemes. However, culture is not reducible purely to the HRM practices employed by an organization. Based on the definition of culture used here it includes elements such as the general management style, modes of communication, degree of formality in operating practices, all of which may affect attitudes and behaviours to knowledge management activities. For example, Kim and Mauborgne (1998) show how the extent to which organizational decision-making processes are deemed fair, and the extent to which workers are involved in them, which represents a fundamental aspect of organizational culture, can be crucial in shaping attitudes to knowledge sharing.

Creating appropriate knowledge cultures

McDermott and O'Dell (2001) suggest that the reason why cultural issues are such a prominent reason for the failure of many of the earliest knowledge management initiatives is that organizations have taken the completely wrong approach. Their case study evidence suggests that organizations which are successful with their knowledge management initiatives, 'build their knowledge management approach to fit their culture' (2001, 77). This is because organizational cultures are much more resilient than any knowledge management initiative, thus organizations which attempt to shape the culture to fit with their knowledge management initiative, rather than vice versa, are likely to find that their knowledge management initiatives fail. Further, the success of such initiatives is also predicated on organizations having suitable knowledge cultures already in place.

To align a knowledge management initiative with the organization's culture they argue that it is necessary to link it to both the visible and invisible elements of the culture (see Table 9.4). In terms of visible elements, the knowledge management initiative needs to be focused on addressing existing business problems, needs to match the existing 'style' of the organization (such as the degree of bureaucratic rigidity), and that reward and appraisal systems should make visible the importance of appropriate knowledge

Table 9.4. Linking knowledge management initiatives to organizational culture (from McDermott and O'Dell 2001)

Visible elements of culture	Invisible elements of culture
KM initiative should link to existing business problems	KM initiatives should link to core organizational values
KM initiatives should reflect existing organizational style	KM initiatives should link into existing networks of social relations.
HR practices should link to appropriate knowledge behaviours	

behaviours. In terms of the invisible aspects of an organization's culture, knowledge management initiatives should reflect existing core values, and should link into existing networks of social relations. In a similar vein Schulze and Boland (2000) argue that knowledge management initiatives are likely to fail if they involve the development and use of work practices which are incongruent with existing work practices.

Embedded in McDermott and O'Dell's analysis is a pessimism that large scale culture change can be achieved, and that if appropriate knowledge behaviours are not a part of the existing culture, then it is likely to be very difficult to change the culture to make them so. An alternative perspective, which is the mainstream perspective in the know-ledge management literature, is that organizational cultures can be changed to produce appropriate knowledge related behaviours and values. Analysts based in the perspect-ive therefore argue that one of the key tasks likely to underpin the success of knowledge management initiatives is the modification of an organization's culture in ways that encourage and support desired knowledge behaviours and attitudes (De Long and Fahey 2000; Ribiere and Sitar 2003).

Stop and think

Do management how the power to control and influence organizational culture, or is culture something beyond the control of management?

Contrary to McDermott and O'Dell, Pan and Scarbrough (1999) argue that appropriate knowledge cultures can be developed, but admit that doing so is a complex, daunting, and time-consuming process. Their argument is based on a detailed examination of one organization: Buckman Laboratories. This organization has arguably been a pioneer of knowledge management, and was one of the earliest organizations to actively manage and utilize its knowledge base to improve business performance. Buckman Laboratories has been relatively successful in these efforts, and has, in the words of one top manager interviewed by Pan and Scarbrough (1999, 369), 'created a culture of trust encouraging active knowledge-sharing across time and space among all of the company's employees across the world.'

This knowledge-sharing culture was something that had to be built and actively developed via a culture change programme. Pan and Scarbrough argue that key to the success of this programme was the role played by the organization's leader, Bob Buckman, who initiated and strongly championed the idea of developing a knowledge-sharing culture. The skills attributed to Bob Buckman by Pan and Scarbrough—of having a clear vision, a strong commitment to implementing it, and an ability to communicate it to others—fits closely with the typical characteristics of charismatic leaders (Bryman 1992; Nadler and Tushman 1990). Thus, for Pan and Scarbrough, knowledge-sharing cultures can be developed, given adequate levels of commitment and leadership from senior organizational management. Ribiere and Sitar's (2003) strong leadership is a key element to successful knowledge-related culture change.

The difference of perspective between McDermott and O'Dell and Pan and Scarbrough regarding the ability of management to deliberately manage culture change reflects similar debates in the wider culture literature (Ogbonna and Harris 1998). One factor that complicates the management of culture is the existence of subcultures, which may have their own interests and value systems, and whose strength of identity can affect attitudes to change (Harris and Ogbonna 1998; Hofstede 1998; Sackman 1992). A weakness of the knowledge management literature that examines culture is that the issue of subcultures, and how they may affect attempts to develop appropriate knowledge cultures, is relatively neglected (De Long and Fahey 2000 being one of the rare exceptions).

HRM policies and practices

As outlined in the introduction, the human and social aspects of knowledge processes are related to and affected by more than simply the attitudes and behaviours of staff towards these particular activities. Of equal importance is the more general attitude of employees towards their employing organization. This is for two primary reasons. Firstly, the level of commitment workers feel towards their employing organizations is likely to shape their attitudes and behaviours towards knowledge processes. Secondly, and equally import-antly, the level of commitment that workers have for their employers shapes the extent to which they are likely to continue working for them. The next section considers how HRM practices can affect levels of commitment and employee retention, while the sub-sequent section looks at how HRM policies can shape attitudes and behaviour towards knowledge processes specifically. This is an analytical separation only, because there is a close relationship between employees' attitude towards their employing organization, and their attitude towards the knowledge activities of their employer.

Employee retention, organizational commitment, and the psychological contract

Retaining workers who possess valuable knowledge should arguably be as important an element in organization's knowledge management strategy as motivating workers to participate in knowledge activities. This is because the tacit and embodied nature of much organizational knowledge means that when employees leave an organization, they take their knowledge with them. Thus staff turnover means an inevitable leakage and loss of knowledge (Leidner 2000). As Byrne (2001, 325) succinctly put it, 'without loyalty knowl-edge is lost'. However, paradoxically, while many writers comment on the importance of retention, very few knowledge management studies examine the topic of retention in any detail. An exception to this is the literature on knowledge workers, examined in Chapter 14.

To examine the topic of retention it is necessary to utilize the concepts of organizational commitment and the psychological contract. Commitment was defined and discussed in Chapter 4. The psychological contract represents the unwritten expectations or obligations that exist between an employee and the employing organization. For example, workers may have expectations of work which is intrinsically interesting, high levels of job security, or good promotion prospects. Most literature focuses on the employee's psychological contract, which is acknowledged to be highly subjective (McDonald and Makin 2000).

Fig. 9.2. Linking the psychological contract, organizational commitment, and organizational behaviours

The importance of the psychological contract is that the extent to which workers perceive it to be fulfilled (or not), or the type of psychological contract that workers develop, can importantly shape their attitudes and behaviour. The relationship between the psychological contract, organizational commitment, and attitudes/behaviours at work is summarized in Figure 9.2. Thus, the extent to which workers perceive their psychological contract to be fulfilled will affect their level of organizational commitment, which will in turn affect the attitudes and behaviours of employees at work.

 Psychological contract

The unwritten expectations and/or obligations that exist between a worker and their employing organization

A common distinction is made between transactional and relational contracts (Rousseau 1990; McDonald and Makin 2000; Morrison and Robinson 1997). Transactional contracts are where the level of organizational loyalty and commitment workers have is limited, where there may be a limited sense of goal alignment between employees and their employer, and where the employment relationship is regarded primarily in economic terms. Relational contracts, by contrast, exist where there is a sense of goal alignment between employee and organization, where loyalty and commitment levels are significant, and there is an emotional as well as economic component to the employment relationship. Flood et al. (2001) in a study of knowledge workers found that a positive psychological contract did result in higher levels of organizational commitment, while Robertson and O'Malley Hammersley (2000) found that levels of organizational commitment affected employee-retention levels and attitudes to knowledge processes.

The type of psychological contract and level of organizational commitment that workers have has also been found to affect a wide range of organizational attitudes and behaviours, including:

- Controllable absences—higher commitment levels are associated with lower levels of such absences (Iverson and Buttigieg 1999; Somers 1995)
- 'in-role' behaviours, i.e. tasks and duties which are part of a worker's formal responsibilities. Quality and timeliness of work likely to be positively related to commitment levels (Kim and Mauborgne 1993; Meyer et al. 1993)

- 'citizenship behaviour', i.e. behaviour beyond a worker's formal responsibilities. Such behaviour is positively related to levels of commitment (Coyle-Shapiro and Kessler 2000; Organ and Ryan 1995)

Empirical evidence also suggests that when workers perceive that there has been a violation in their psychological contract, for example when expectations are not met, this can have negative consequences for levels of organizational commitment and loyalty (Atkinson 2002; Coyle-Shapiro and Kessler 2000). However, in the HRM literature this is an area of intense debate relating to such topics as: the typical content of the psychological contract—does it include expectations of job security, career prospects, etc.; is the psychological contract undergoing change—are expectations of job security declining (Smithson and Lewis 2000; Beaumont and Harris 2002); and have contemporary changes in the employment relationship given rise to a 'contract culture' where transactional psychological contracts are typical?

Stop and think

Is job security likely to be a significant part of the psychological contract of many contemporary workers, or is job security something that no one realistically expects to have guarantees over any more?

The final issue dealt with in this section is the question of what organizational management can do to induce high levels of commitment and loyalty from their workers. Developing high levels of commitment is generally not simple and straightforward (Meyer and Allen 1997). However, empirical evidence suggests a number of factors within managerial control can affect commitment levels including: levels of worker involvement in organizational decision-making (Gallie et al. 1998); the use of recruitment practices which attempt to achieve a fit between employee and organization (Iverson and Buttigieg 1999); and a general sense of equality (Burchell et al. 2002). Robertson and O'Malley Hammersley (2000) explain the high retention rate in the company they examined, which can be interpreted as indicating high levels of commitment, as being related to the specific management practices it adopted. These included providing workers with high levels of autonomy over their work, as well as over their training needs, creating a culture of trust and involvement through having open and participative decision-making, encouraging extensive communication, and having a flat organizational structure.

ILLUSTRATING THE ISSUES

Staff retention, organizational commitment, and HRM practices

Buck and Watson (2002) report on research into how HRM practices in higher education institutes in the USA affected levels of organizational commitment and turnover amongst staff. This was done through postal and web-based surveys of a range of institutions. They found that there was a positive correlation between level of job enrichment and commitment, but a negative correlation between training and organizational commitment. Thus, commitment was most likely to be developed through job enrichment practices such as providing workers with high levels of autonomy and discretion. However, the provision of training may have a negative effect on commitment levels through providing workers with more marketable skills, and raising their awareness of the benefits from pursuing a multiple company career.

Stop and think

To what extent are these findings specific to the type of occupation examined? For what other type of job is there likely to be expectations of autonomy? Think about a range of occupations/jobs and what the psychological contract of the workers doing them may be. For example, what are the typical expectations of workers doing routine administrative jobs?

In conclusion, this section suggests that fulfilling the psychological contract and inducing high levels of commitment amongst an organization's workforce can contribute importantly to an organization's knowledge management strategy through helping to retain key knowledge within the organization. Secondly, there are a wide range of HRM and general management practices that can be utilized as a way of developing commitment levels in workers. However, as outlined in Chapter 4, a point worth reinforcing is that very few detailed empirical studies have been done on how workers' commitment levels affect their attitudes and behaviours to knowledge processes (see Hislop 2002*a*).

HRM policies and knowledge attitudes/behaviours

This final section of Chapter 9 examines the role that HRM practices can play in shaping attitudes to knowledge and learning processes. This is done through focusing centrally on the ideas and analysis contained in one challenging, interesting, and stimulating book: *Beyond Knowledge Management* by Garvey and Williamson (2002). This book considers in detail what an effective culture of knowledge-sharing and learning looks like, as well as considering the specific HRM and management practices that can be utilized to facilitate such behaviour, and thus is of central relevance to the issues addressed here. The analysis presented here is also supplemented by the use of a number of other relevant books and articles.

Characterizing an effective knowledge culture
Before considering what HRM practices can be useful in supporting organizational knowledge processes, it is necessary to consider in more detail what constitutes effective knowledge and learning processes, and the character of organizational cultures that support them. Two key concepts elaborated by Garvey and Williamson are the corporate curriculum and knowledge productivity (see Table 9.5). For Garvey and Williamson, a corporate curriculum which is necessary to support learning and knowledge development is one which is respectful of existing knowledge, but which is simultaneously accepting of new ideas, knowledge, and frameworks. Relatedly, high levels of knowledge productivity are likely when people are able to modify, update, and transform existing knowledge through a process of critical reflection, dialogue, and experimentation.

Table 9.5. Corporate curriculum and knowledge productivity (Garvey and Williamson 2002)

Corporate curriculum	Organizational-level climate and framework of values which shape both attitudes to learning and new ideas, as well as what's defined as valid knowledge.
Knowledge productivity	Individual-level ability to produce new insights/knowledge, through an openness to new ideas, and through integrating them with existing knowledge and experience.

This involves not a rejection of existing knowledge, but a reflection upon it without either reifying it (an overemphasis on tradition which creates a blindness to the new) or rejecting it (an inability to effectively learn from the past).

Garvey and Williamson's analysis is fundamentally embedded in the epistemology of practice framework outlined in Chapter 3. Thus, knowledge productivity and learning are achieved as much through action, experimentation, and risk taking as through a process of abstract reflection and formal education or training. Further, learning is most likely to occur when the corporate curriculum is egalitarian, and respectful of all knowledge and experience. This requires circumstances where people are able to openly express their opinions without fear of sanctions. Such circumstances create the potential for open, critical dialogues through which perspective making and taking is likely to occur, and which provides circumstances favourable to deep-rooted knowledge sharing and learning. However, as discussed in Chapter 7, the embeddedness of power in the employment relationship, combined with the inherent potential for conflict that exists within organizations, means that creating such circumstances is not likely to be a straightforward task.

HRM practices and the creation of a culture of learning and knowledge development

As with Pan and Scarbrough (1999), Garvey and Williamson believe that organizational management does have the ability to put in place practices and structures that can encourage, support, and develop a culture of learning. To be knowledge productive requires a certain mode of thinking and is thus to some extent the responsibility of the individual. Thus, Garvey and Williamson (2002, 125) make clear that the first step in being knowledge productive is for workers to develop a critical sense of self-awareness. However, there is also a fundamentally important role that organizations can play in creating a corporate curriculum that is supportive of such modes of thinking, learning, and working.

 ILLUSTRATING THE ISSUES

Rewarding (self) development

Garvey and Williamson (131) describe an oil company where its pay and appraisal system is used to support a learning culture. To reinforce the importance of (self) development activity by staff, workers are rewarded for both meeting commercial performance targets and for undertaking and utilizing self-development activities. To signal the importance of both these elements they are embedded in the annual appraisal/pay scheme and together constitute 30 per cent of a worker's pay. Development needs are an intrinsic part of the annual appraisal/review, and staff are expected to provide evidence of the self-development activities they have undertaken. This scheme was regarded as successful, as it had a positive effect on the amount of time and effort staff devoted to development activities.

Stop and think

While such a scheme is likely to be successful at encouraging self-development, to what extent is there a risk that it may distract workers from a central focus on the achievement of organizational goals?

This example shows how appraisal, pay, and training systems can be used to encourage appropriate knowledge and learning behaviours. Yahya and Goh (2002) and Hansen et al. (1999) also conclude that appraisal schemes can provide a useful way of reinforcing the importance of knowledge-related behaviours that organizations regard as appropriate.

Garvey and Williamson also argue that investing in training can help create an environment supportive of appropriate knowledge and learning behaviours, as such investments reflect a corporate curriculum which is supportive of learning. However, for Garvey and Williamson training should not centre 'narrowly' on skills-based training, but should instead be related to developing social skills of self-reflexivity, how to learn through experimentation and risk taking, and how to conduct critical dialogues with others. The importance of training was also emphasized by Hunter et al. (2002). In their analysis, training was most important for organizations pursuing a strategy of building social capital (see Table 9.3), where providing training represents one key way of doing this. Finally, Robertson and O'Malley Hammersley (2000) also regard the provision of training as one key way of creating a supportive knowledge culture. However, for the knowledge workers they examined this was achieved through providing the staff with the autonomy and resources to identify and undertake what they individually regarded as their own training needs.

Stop and think

Can people be trained to be knowledge productive, or are such skills/abilities/attitudes shaped by personality and intelligence?

Pay and reward systems provide another avenue through which HRM practices can be utilized to facilitate and develop appropriate knowledge cultures. As illustrated by the above example, this can be done through linking pay to development activities. It could also be achieved, as suggested by Hansen et al. (1999), through rewarding knowledge behaviours which are consistent with the knowledge strategy being pursued (see Table 9.2).

In conclusion, this final section has outlined the role that HRM practices such as training, appraisal, and reward systems can play in supporting and reinforcing appropriate knowledge behaviours. This therefore suggests that management has potentially significant scope to affect the human, social, and cultural factors that are so crucial to the success of knowledge initiatives.

Conclusion

The central focus of this chapter has been on the relationship between organizational culture and knowledge management initiatives, and has found the relationship to be both important and complex. The culture an organization has was shown to be an important factor shaping the attitudes of workers to knowledge initiatives, and the extent to which they are prepared to use and share their knowledge. One general conclusion emerging from the chapter is that organizational management, through shaping their culture, and utilizing relevant HRM policies, can influence the attitudes of their workers towards knowledge initiatives. However, it was also shown that there is an active debate on this topic, with some writers raising questions regarding the extent to which effective knowledge cultures can be achieved through culture management initiatives. Thus, McDermott and O'Dell (2001) suggest that attempting to modify an organization's culture to fit in with the objectives of a knowledge management initiative is likely to be a recipe for failure.

The chapter also showed how attempting to develop the commitment and loyalty of workers can be a key part of an organization's knowledge management strategy. This is because not only does the typically tacit and embodied nature of knowledge mean that when workers leave an organization they take much of their knowledge with them, but that the level of commitment a worker feels towards his employer is also likely to affect his willingness to participate in knowledge management initiatives (Hislop 2002a). However, developing such commitment and attitudes is by no means straightforward.

Finally, the chapter also illustrated the importance-specific HRM practices such reward systems can have in shaping the attitudes and behaviour of workers to knowledge initiatives. However, as was considered at the start of the chapter, to be most effective, such practices require to be effectively linked to the business and knowledge management strategy being pursued, as different business and knowledge strategies typically have quite different HRM implications.

REVIEW QUESTIONS

1 Do most organizations have a single, dominant culture, or is it more typical that they have distinctive subcultures with their own values and knowledge? What factors affect the extent to which organizational culture is coherent?

2 Some research suggests that money alone is unlikely to motivate people to share their knowledge. Can pay systems be used to motivate people to develop or display suitable attitudes and behaviours towards knowledge processes?

3 Given the embeddedness of power and conflict within organizations, are Garvey and Williamson unrealistic about the ability of organizations to create open, egalitarian cultures where knowledge and ideas can be shared freely?

FURTHER READING

- D. Hislop (2002*a*). 'Linking Human Resource Management and Knowledge Management: A Review and Research Agenda', *Employee Relations*, 25/2: 182–202.

  Considers how levels of organizational commitment may affect knowledge-related attitudes and behaviours.

- S. Pan, and H. Scarbrough (1999). 'Knowledge Management in Practice: An Exploratory Case Study', *Technology Analysis and Strategic Management*, 11/3: 359–74.

  Presents a positive case study of culture change at Buckman Laboratories, where an effective knowledge-sharing culture was developed.

- R. McDermott, and C. O'Dell (2001). 'Overcoming Cultural Barriers to Knowledge Sharing', *Journal of Knowledge Management*, 5/1: 76–85.

  Considers how organizational culture and knowledge management initiatives are interrelated.

- L. Hunter, P. Beaumont, and M. Lee (2002). 'Knowledge Management Practice in Scottish Law Firms', *Human Resource Management Journal*, 12/2: 4–21.

  Considers how knowledge management strategy can be linked to specific HRM practices through the analysis of some case studies in large Scottish law firms.

Learning, innovation, and knowledge management

These two chapters have in common a focus on deliberate processes of learning within organizations. However, each chapter considers quite different types of learning. Thus while Chapter 10 examines organizational learning in general, Chapter 11 has a more specific and narrow focus on processes of organizational innovation. However, this is not to suggest these topics are unrelated. There is obviously much overlap between the chapters, as processes of innovation management are very much about learning. However, as Meeus et al. (2001) argue, while innovation processes can be characterized as a type of learning, they represent a very specific and distinctive type of learning. It is beyond the scope of this introductory section to define what is meant by the terms 'learning' and 'innovation'. This is primarily because, as will be seen in each chapter, doing so is not straightforward and involves engaging with debates and competing definitions.

Chapter 10 examines the contemporary literature on learning in organizations. Interest in this subject predated the explosion of interest in knowledge management by a few years. However, there is an enormous overlap between the subjects. In fact it is impossible (and inaccurate) to define learning and knowledge processes as being separate and distinct phenomena. Trying to define where learning ends and knowledge processes begin is a futile process, as knowledge processes can be characterized as being about learning, or to put it the opposite way, learning processes can be characterized as knowledge processes. One of the central focuses in Chapter 10 is the debate over the concept and character of 'the learning organization' that, as will be seen, can be characterized as involving two diametrically opposed perspectives.

Chapter 11 by contrast focuses more narrowly on organizational innovation processes, which includes R&D activities, as well as what some people term new product development (NPD). This chapter starts from the basic premiss that innovation processes are fundamentally knowledge processes, which is the way Nonaka, arguably the most well-known writer in the contemporary knowledge literature, characterizes innovation processes.

10

Learning and knowledge management

Introduction

As Figure 1.1 indicates, a growth of interest in both learning in organizations and knowledge management occurred at very similar times. This is to a large extent no accident, and indicated the interrelatedness of these issues. Ultimately, learning, whether at the level of the individual, group, or organization, is about improving and developing knowledgeability: changing ideas, values, and/or behaviours through a change or transformation in understanding. This can involve the acquisition and application of new knowledge/practices, the reconfiguration of existing bodies of knowledge/practices, refining existing knowledge/practice, or the application of existing knowledge/practice to a novel context. Thus, while the precise relationship between learning and knowledge management is unclear, their relatedness is unquestionable (Thomas et al. 2001). The purpose of this chapter is to consider the ways the learning literature links with the topic of knowledge management, and how it can help to understand the dynamics of organizational knowledge processes.

Given the enormity of the body of work on organizational learning this represents a formidable task. In the space of one chapter it is impossible to outline, let alone examine in detail, all the issues raised by the organizational learning literature. Thus, deliberately, this chapter narrowly focuses on the learning literature from the late 1990s and is further only concerned with how this literature relates to the subject of knowledge management. Even with this narrow focus, the increasing overlap of interest that occurred between the learning and knowledge management literature between 1995 and 2002 (on the importance of social and cultural issues, on group-level processes, and on social constructivist/practice-based perspectives on knowledge—Easterby-Smith et al. 2000; Vince et al. 2002) means that there is still much to examine.

As with the general perspective of the book, a critical perspective, is taken to the descriptive, prescriptive, and optimistic literature on learning which conveys the idea that it is relatively straightforward to become a learning organization. This is because, despite the rhetoric which suggests that all organizations are becoming learning organizations, there are many who argue that learning is still something that few organizations do well or do at all (Farr 2000; Hedberg and Wolff 2001; Salaman 2001; Snell 2001; Weick and Westley 1996). This chapter examines the factors that help explain why this is the case, and why genuine learning can be difficult to achieve within the context of work organizations.

The chapter begins by very briefly examining the difficulties involved in defining what learning is. After this, the next major section examines the dynamics of learning in organizations, and the relationship between individual, group and organizational-level learning processes. The largest section in the chapter then examines the debate on the learning organization concept, which provides a useful way of discussing some of the key issues which link the learning and knowledge management literatures. As will be seen, issues raised by the critics of the learning organization rhetoric, such as the need to account for power, as well as the broad context of the employment relationship, link closely with some of the key issues developed in Part 2 of the book, and in Chapter 7 in particular.

Characterizing learning

It would seem sensible to begin the chapter by defining learning. However, such a task is by no means easy due to the diversity of definitions which exist. In fact, one of the characteristics of the literature on learning in organizations is a lack of theoretical consensus (Berthoin Antal et al. 2001; Crossan et al. 1999). Ironically, the only consensus in this

Table 10.1. Typologies of learning

Frameworks	Concepts/Levels	Description
Learning Modes	Cognitive	Learning as a change in intellectual concepts and frameworks (at individual or group level).
	Cultural	Change in intersubjective, group-based values, concepts or frameworks.
	Behavioural/Action based	Learning occurs primarily through action followed by a process of critical reflection.
Learning Types	Single-loop	Incremental changes within a coherent framework of theory.
	Double-loop	Learning where existing theories/assumptions are questioned and reflected on.
	Deutero	The highest level of learning which involves the process of learning and reflection itself being questioned.
Learning Levels	Individual	Changes in the behaviour or theories and concepts of an individual.
	Group	Changes in group level, shared understandings or practices.
	Organizational	Institutionalization at organizational level of changes in behaviour/theory.
	Interorganizational	Learning at supra-organizational level—for example within a network or sector.

subject area appears to be on the lack of consensus that exists within it! The heterogeneous and relatively fragmented nature of the literature on learning is partly because it is such a broad, multidisciplinary topic. Thus learning in organizations has been written about by economists, management scientists, psychologists, sociologists, historians, and anthropologists, all of whom conceptualize it in different ways.

Thus, instead of providing a single definition of learning, Table 10.1 gives an overview of some of the most important ways that learning in organizations has been characterized (for a more detailed examination of the different taxonomies of learning which exist see Pawlovsky 2001). These typologies are not examined in detail because not only do constraints of space make it impossible to do justice to the depth of debate, but the debate on these typologies became somewhat dormant during the mid-1990s (Easterby-Smith et al. 2000). Thus, most of the contemporary learning literature makes only passing reference to these frameworks. Presenting such a summarized overview illustrates the complexity of the topic and the diversity of ways in which learning has been conceptualized.

The dynamics of organizational learning

While the central concern of the chapter is on learning within organizations, this does not mean that there is an exclusive focus on organizational-level learning. As will be seen, learning in organizations can be characterized as involving a dynamic reciprocity between learning processes at the individual, group, and organizational level. Before presenting a conceptual model that outlines the interrelationship between these processes it is useful to define and discuss the term organizational learning. Organizations can be understood to learn, not because they 'think' and 'behave' independently of the people who work within them (they cannot), but through the embedding of individual and group learning in organizational processes, routines, structures, databases, systems of rules, etc. (Hedberg 1981; Shrivastava 1983). For example, organizational learning would be where insights developed by an individual or group result in a systematic transformation of the organization's work practices/values. However, it is wrong to equate organizational learning as being simply the sum of individual and group learning processes (Vince 2001). Organizational learning only occurs when learning at the individual or group level impacts on organizational-level processes and structures. But such a transition is by no means automatic. For this to be achievable organizations need to be able to sustain critical reflection on their established norms and practices. It is thus possible, as will be seen in the example of Hyder presented later in the chapter, that learning can occur at individual and group levels, but *not* produce learning at the organizational level.

Organizational learning

The embedding of individual- and group-level learning in organizational structures and processes, achieved through reflecting on and modifying the norms and values embodied in established organizational processes and structures.

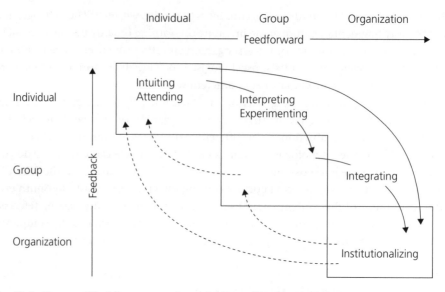

Fig. 10.1. The modified Crossan et al. model (from Zietsma et al. 2002)

This complex interrelationship between learning at different levels is taken account of in the Crossan–Zietsma framework of organizational learning. This framework was initially devised by Crossan et al. (1999), but was usefully modified by Zietsma et al. (2002) with the addition of two action-based learning processes to supplement the more cognitively focused processes of Crossan et al. The relationship between the six learning processes and three levels of learning in the Crossan–Zietsma framework is illustrated in Figure 10.1.

Descriptions of the learning processes, and the levels at which they exist are outlined in Table 10.2. In the framework, the six learning processes link the three levels of learning through two opposing dynamics: feed forward and feedback loops. The feed forward loop, alternatively referred to as an *exploration*-based learning process, involves the development and assimilation of new knowledge. Exploration thus starts with individual-level learning, through intuition or attending, and then builds to both group- and organization-level learning through interpretation, experimentation, integration, and institutionalization processes. The feedback loop, by contrast, referred to as an *exploitation*-based learning process, involves the utilization of existing knowledge, whereby institutionalized learning guides and affects how groups and individuals act and think. However, while feed forward and feedback learning loops involve moving between learning processes at different levels, such movement cannot be assumed to happen automatically or unproblematically. Thus, for example, it can be difficult for someone to take an individual-level insight, articulate it to a group, and for this to develop into a shared, agreed upon, collective insight.

One of the core themes in the Crossan–Zietsma framework is the tension that exists between exploration (the development and acquisition of new knowledge) and exploitation (the utilization of existing knowledge). This tension exists because processes of exploration may bring into question, challenge, undermine and even replace institutionalized norms

Table 10.2. Characteristics of learning process in Crossan–Zietsma model

Process name	Level	Process description
Intuition	Individual	Cognitive process involving the preconscious recognition of patterns. Intuition is highly subjective and rooted in individual experience.
Attending	Individual	Action-based individual process of actively searching for and absorbing new ideas.
Interpretation	Individual-Group	Explaining personal insights through words or actions. It can be an individual process, where an individual actively interprets their own insights, or a group process where individual insights are shared and discussed collectively.
Experimenting	Individual-Group	Attempting to implement and utilize new learning through actual practices of change.
Integration	Group-Organization	Developing shared understandings and practices, which can occur through both dialogue and coordinated action.
Institutionalization	Organization	The process of ensuring that routinized action occurs through embedding insights in organizational systems & processes.

(knowledge and practice) embedded in exploitation processes. This is a potentially serious tension because, as Crossan et al. argue (1999, 534) 'learning that has become institutionalized at the organizational level is often difficult to change.' Thus the institutionalization of learning has the potential risk that such a process can introduce rigidities and an inability to adapt and change through a blinkering process that leaves institutionalized norms unquestioned. Thus when institutionalized norms become powerful and dominant, for example through being successful, they can turn into what has been defined as 'competency traps' where organizations become locked in to previously successful routines through not noticing or effectively accounting for changed circumstances (Bettis and Prahalad 1995; Levinthal and March 1993). To help explain the Crossan/Zietsma framework, an example of its application is presented immediately below.

ILLUSTRATING THE ISSUES

Resisting and embracing learning: the case of MacMillan Bloedel

Zietsma et al. (2002) present an interesting case study of an organization which for long periods actively resisted change, but which eventually undertook a radical transformation. MacMillan Bloedel (MB) is a Canadian forestry company, which for a long time was in the vanguard of defending the use of 'clear cutting' forestry management in the face of extensive and widespread opposition from a range of protesters. In terms of the Crossan framework this was because MB was focused on exploration/feedback learning processes, which involved the utilization and refinement of existing practices and values. In MB, these institutionalized norms were extremely powerful and dominant, which actively inhibited, if not prevented, feed forward, or exploration-based learning which challenged the existing values in any way. In MB this meant the logic of clear-cutting forestry management was never seriously questioned. This occurred because MB developed a specific form of competency trap, which Zietsma et al. labelled a 'legitimacy trap', which significantly inhibited learning. A legitimacy trap occurs where the arguments of an individual/group are ignored or regarded as worthless as the legitimacy of the group/individual to make relevant arguments are questioned. In the case of MB, the arguments of the protesters were disregarded as senior management believed that they did not understand the detailed technical and economic factors affecting forestry business practices. Resistance to the arguments of the protesters was also related to individual-level emotional issues. Thus, many of MB's senior managers were reluctant to listen to the arguments of the protesters as they felt this challenged and undermined the morality of their traditional values and business practices. However over time, change and learning did begin to occur, with various isolated individuals in MB (including public relations staff and field managers) adapting their thinking. This occurred not simply through a process of intuition, but also through an active process Zietsma et al. label as 'attending' (see Table 10.2), where these individuals actively engaged in a dialogue with the protesters to develop a better understanding of their perspective and arguments. These isolated, individual learning processes then developed into isolated group-level learning through processes of group-level interpretation and experimenting. This involved groups of individuals coming together not only to share their views, but actively experiment with alternative forestry management practices. Finally, after a new CEO was appointed this learning became institutionalized, with the viewpoints of the protesters becoming accepted and discussed at board level. This institutionalization of learning became highly visible when MB eventually gave up clear-cutting practices altogether and shifted to a different style of forestry management.

Stop and think

How significant was the appointment of the new CEO to organizational-level learning occurring at MB? To what extent are competency traps that inhibit organizational learning related to the attitudes and behaviours of senior management in organizations?

The learning organization: emancipation of exploitation?

As outlined in the introduction, the literature on organizational learning is characterized by a diversity of theoretical perspectives. One specific topic that has produced an enormous amount of debate and heated argument is the learning organization. It is worthwhile examining the contours of this debate, as doing so sheds light on some key issues.

Crudely, those engaged in this debate can be classified into two broad camps: the visionaries or utopian propagandists and the sceptics or gloomy pessimists (Friedman et al. 2001). The visionary/propagandists camp, whose most well-known and prolific writers include Peter Senge (1990) and Mike Pedler (Pedler et al. 1997), is largely dominated by consultants and industrial practitioners (Driver 2002). This camp portrays the learning organization as an achievable ideal with significant benefits for both organizations and their workers. The sceptic/pessimistic camp, which is largely populated by academics, challenges this perspective and pours scorn on the claims of the learning organization propagandists (Levitt and March 1988; Weick and Westley 1996). Primarily these writers, with Coopey (1995, 1998) being one of the most incisive, argue that despite the emancipatory rhetoric of the learning organization discourse, in reality it is likely to provide a way to buttress the power of management and is thus likely to lead to increased exploitation of and control over workers, rather than in their emancipation and self-development.

This section examines the two dominant perspectives in this debate, simultaneously uncovering and focusing on key issues such as power, the nature of the employment relationship, and trust, which have been shown in Part 2 to be key to understanding the dynamics of knowledge processes, and which thus helps to link the learning and knowledge literatures.

The learning organization: the advocates vision

Constraints of space make it impossible to elaborate all the different learning organization frameworks developed by its different advocates (Pedler, Senge, Garvin, among others). This section focuses centrally on the way Pedler et al. conceptualize it. However, there is much commonality to these frameworks, therefore, there is a general resonance between the broad characteristics of these different models. Pedler et al. (1997, 3) define the learning organization as an, 'organization which facilitates the learning of all its members and consciously transforms itself and its context'. Their learning organization framework is also elaborated into eleven specific characteristics (see Table 10.3). A key element of this definition is that there is a mutual, positive synergy between the organizational context and the learning of its members. Thus in a learning organization, the organizational context should facilitate the learning of organizational staff, with this learning in turn sustaining and contributing to the ongoing transformation of the organizational context.

One of the articulated organizational advantages of the learning organization framework is that it is appropriate, in contingency theory terms, to the contemporary business environment, which is typically characterized as being highly competitive and turbulent (Harrison and Leitch 2000; Salaman 2001). Thus, in such circumstances organizations require to continually adapt and change, with the adoption of the learning organization framework being argued to make this possible. One of the defining characteristics of a learning organization is therefore that it is flexible, and that this provides organizations with the ability to achieve and retain a position of competitive advantage. Implicitly (and sometimes explicitly) the learning organization is regarded as the antithesis of traditional bureaucracies, which are regarded as having highly centralized and hierarchical systems of management and control. Instead, the learning organization is typically conceptualized as having a relatively flat structure, open communication systems, limited top down control, and autonomous working conditions (Driver 2002).

Table 10.3. The learning company framework of Pedler et al. (1997)

Focus	Core characteristics	Description
Strategy	(1) Learning Approach to Strategy	Strategy making-implementation-evaluation structured as learning processes—for example with experiments and feedback loops.
	(2) Participative Policy-Making	Allow all organizational members opportunity to contribute to making of major policy decisions.
Looking in	(3) Informating	Use of IT to empower staff through widespread information dissemination and having tolerance to how it is interpreted and used.
	(4) Formative Accounting and Control	Use of accounting practices which contribute to learning combined with a sense of self-responsibility, where individuals/groups encouraged to regard themselves as responsible for cost management.
	(5) Internal Exchange	Constant, open dialogue between individuals and group within an organization, and encouraging collaboration not competition.
	(6) Reward Flexibility	New ways of rewarding people for learning contribution which may not be solely financial, and where principles of reward system are explicit.
Structures	(7) Enabling Structures	Use of loose and adaptable structures which provide opportunities for organizational and individual development.
Looking out	(8) Boundary Workers as Environmental Scanners	The bringing in to an organization of ideas and working practices developed and used externally—an openness and receptivity to learning from others.
	(9) Intercompany Learning	Use of mutually advantageous learning activities with customers, suppliers etc.
Learning Opportunities	(10) Learning Climate	Facilitate the willingness of staff to take risks and experiment, which can be encouraged by senior management taking the lead. People not punished for criticizing orthodox views.
	(11) Self-Development Opportunities for All	Have opportunities for all staff to be able to develop themselves as they see appropriate.

Learning organization (propagandists)

An organization which supports the learning of its workers and allows them to express and utilize this learning to the advantage of the organization, through having an organizational environment which encourages experimentation, risk taking, and open dialogue.

However, the advocates such as Pedler are clear that the benefits of utilizing the learning organization framework are by no means confined to improving organizational performance. Instead, an inherent element of these frameworks is that management and workers alike will benefit from their adoption. In fact one of the articulated consequences of utilizing these frameworks is that the divisions between management and workers are likely to become blurred. As is clear from all eleven characteristics of the learning organization framework (see Table 10.3), workers benefit through the creation of a working environment where levels of participation in major decisions are high, where the opinions of all are valued, and where there are opportunities for workers to be creative and develop themselves.

Stop and think

To what extent are bureaucratic organizational structures antithetical to organizational learning? Are flexible or network structures (see Chapter 12) more conducive to, and supportive of organizational learning?

One element, which is argued to be necessary and central to the creation of such a working environment, is a particular type of leadership style (Sadler 2001; Snell 2001). For example leaders in learning organizations require to be learners as much as teachers, and that they should also have roles as coaches or mentors. Such a leadership style is necessary not only to actively stimulate the curiosity and learning of workers, but to also make leaders sensitive and responsive to the opinions of workers. However, the contradictions of the learning organization advocates regarding the role and style of that organizational management should have are discussed later when looking at the critique of this perspective. Before doing this it is useful to illustrate its application in practice, with the results of this process pointing towards the criticisms of this perspective.

ILLUSTRATING THE ISSUES

A learning organization?

Harrison and Leitch (2000) applied Pedler's learning organization framework to what they describe as a knowledge-intensive company, a small software development company, which employed a large proportion of graduates. The company had a flat organizational hierarchy, and structured work around flexible, temporary project teams. Harrison and Leitch used a survey to identify whether the company demonstrated the characteristics of a learning organization.

The survey was sent to three levels of workers: the Managing Director (MD), senior managers, and project team members. Each respondent was asked questions on both how they perceived the company to be, and how they would like it to be, with the difference between these scores representing what Pedler et al. called a dissatisfaction index. One of most interesting findings was that a consistent difference existed, across all three levels of the hierarchy, in terms of the dissatisfaction index. Thus the MD had negative average score of -1.2%, indicating that he thought the company exceeded his expectations in terms of supporting staff learning. By contrast, the average score for senior managers was 18.2%, while that for project staff was 38.1%. Thus senior managers, and more specifically project staff, had different perceptions regarding the extent to which the organization supported their learning. However, there was evidence that the company displayed the characteristics of a learning organization as the MD addressed some of these concerns, despite his own feelings. One area where this was done was 'reward flexibility' (see Table 10.3), where issues raised by staff were dealt with. However, there were other areas of disagreement, such as in relation to 'structures' where no conclusive resolution was achieved. Harrison and Leitch conclude by suggesting that the consistency of difference in satisfaction levels, 'raises the possibility of substantial differences in internal policy-making and prioritization, which will bring into play issues of conflict and power relations.' (113).

Stop and think

Are such differences typical? To what extent are the interests of workers and managers with regards to learning likely to be in conflict? Further, does this suggest that there are few, true learning organizations?

Arguably, though this is not how Harrison and Leitch see it, the differences in satisfaction levels found could be interpreted as indicating that there are irreconcilable differences between senior management and workers, which make it likely that conflict will be inherent and unavoidable. This represents one of the main critiques put forward by Coopey of the learning organization framework, and is an issue that will thus be elaborated in detail in the following section.

The learning organization: the sceptics' perspective

The arguments of the learning organization advocates have produced an enormous amount of debate (Easterby-Smith 1997; Tsang 1997). This section examines the critique put forward by those who have been labelled the pessimists or sceptics. The critique is structured into three broad, but interrelated areas: the nature of the employment relationship, the need to account for power, and how individual factors, such as emotion, shape people's willingness to learn.

Commitment, trust, and employment relationship
Central to Coopey's (1995, 1998) critique of the learning organization rhetoric is that there is a fundamental contradiction that is not addressed, regarding the power and authority of management. On the one hand, as outlined previously, Pedler's vision of the

learning organization—characterized by the support and encouragement given to open discussion and risk-free critical debate, as well as the importance of democratic decision-making processes—requires organizational managers to share power much more than in traditional organizations. However, on the other hand, Pedler takes for granted the legitimacy of both shareholder rights, enshrined in company law, as well as management's authority and right to manage in their shareholders interests (Coopey 1995, 195). Thus, while the learning organization rhetoric suggests that more democratic decision making is necessary, it doesn't explain how this can be effectively achieved. Given that empirical evidence suggests that organizational management is often unwilling to share power, it is arguably unlikely that such a process will occur voluntarily (Boeker 1992; Dovey 1997; Kets de Vries 1991).

Stop and think

If management's authority to manage is enshrined in company law, does this limit the extent to which organizational decision-making can be made democratic?

Coopey's argument, which is compatible with the way the employment relationship is conceptualized in Chapter 7, is that within the socio-economic context of capitalism, power is structurally embedded in the employment relationship, and that this typically places workers in a subordinate position to management. Such institutional arrangements are argued to produce a 'democratic deficit' where the values, ideas, and interest of workers are largely downplayed and where the authority and knowledge of management is privileged and taken for granted (Coopey 1998). In such situations it is arguable that the vision of the learning organization articulated by its propagandists is unlikely to be achieved. Firstly, this is because necessary levels of empowerment are unlikely to be granted to workers. Secondly, without such levels of empowerment the level of trust in and commitment to their organizations that workers have is likely to be relatively low (Coopey 1998).

Power, politics, and learning

Neglecting to adequately account of power, politics, and conflict is another critique made against the learning organization propagandists. However, such neglect was typical of the majority of the learning literature until the mid-1990s (Berthoin Antal et al. 2001). Further, the propagandists not only downplay such issues, but are typically unwilling to even acknowledge that they are relevant to the analysis of learning processes (Driver 2002). However, since the mid-1990s, issues of power and politics have been given a greater level of attention (LaPolombara 2001; Easterby-Smith et al. 2000; Vince et al. 2002). The need to account for power and politics in learning processes flows from three closely interrelated factors (see Figure 10.2).

Firstly, as discussed in Chapter 7, power and knowledge are intimately interrelated. Thus if learning is about the development and use of knowledge, then account needs to be taken of issues of power (Vince 2002). Coopey (1998) for example, drawing on Foucault suggests that managerial authority relates to the inseparability of power and knowledge,

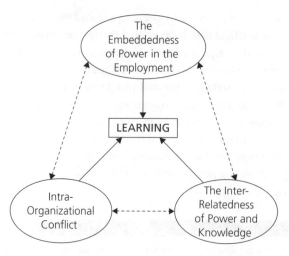

Fig. 10.2. Linking power and politics to learning

where management's power is reflected in the privileging of their knowledge, and vice versa. Secondly, as discussed in the previous section, the need to account for power in learning processes relates to the embeddedness of power in the employment relationship. Thirdly, and finally, some argue that power and politics need to be accounted for due to the typical lack of value consensus which exists in most organizations, and the potential for conflict and disagreement this creates (Huzzard and Ostergren 2002; Salaman 2001). This is another issue that was discussed previously in Chapter 7.

ILLUSTRATING THE ISSUES

Learning without a consensus

Huzzard and Ostergren (2002) examined the dynamics of learning in a Swedish trade union (SIF), where, during the 1990s, a lack of consensus existed over the fundamental objectives of the organization, as well as how it should respond to significant economic and social changes which undermined traditional notions of collectivity. In response to these environmental changes senior management in SIF attempted to implement a top down, centralized process of learning, where they described and explained how and why the union was changing. The intention was that through this process union members and officials would come to agree with the centrally planned changes. These changes were characterized as generally moving from a collectivist to a more individualistic orientation, from an adversarial to a partnership-based relationship with organiza- tional management, and moving from a focus on issues of collective bargaining over pay and con- ditions to supporting the career and work experience of members. However, little evidence existed that these ideas were accepted by local union members and officials. Thus, despite this initiative, members had a diversity of conceptions of the union's basic values and identity. Huzzard and Ostergren argue that attempting to develop a consensus in such a context was not feasible, and that learning would be more likely to occur if the value dissensus was embraced, and where people developed a better understanding of the perspective of others through an open process of communication.

Stop and think

How typical is the case of SIF? Is value consensus unlikely in most organizations? Do conflicting perspectives inhibit learning? To what extent can conflicts operate as catalysts to learning?

The critics of the learning organization rhetoric argue that taking adequate account of these factors means the vision of the advocates is unrealistic, and that there are likely to be some stark contradictions between their rhetoric and the way the adoption of learning organization practices impact on organizational relations. Thus, rather than workers having a greater potential for creativity and self-development, the use of learning organization practices may mean they are subject to greater levels of control. Further, rather than empowering workers, learning organization practices have the potential to bolster and reinforce the power of management (Armstrong 2000; Coopey 1995, 1998; Driver 2002; Easterby-Smith 1997). The adoption of the rhetoric and practice of the learning organization can be perceived as increasing the potential to control workers, because, as with the use of culture-based management practices generally (Kunda 1992), it involves a form of socially based control, where goal alignment between worker and organization is achieved through persuading workers to internalize the organizational value system (Driver 2002). Such control systems are more subtle, less visible, and have the potential to be more effective than traditional bureaucratic methods (Alvesson and Wllmott 2001; Gabriel 1999).

 Learning organization (sceptics)

An organization where socially based control systems are used to create value alignment around the benefits to all of learning, which has the potential to reinforce management power, and contradict the logic of emancipation embodied in the learning organization rhetoric.

Some writers however, conclude that conflict is not necessarily detrimental to learning processes, and that if conflict and differences of opinion are managed and negotiated through a certain type of dialogue, they can actually facilitate learning (Coopey and Burgoyne 2000; Huzzard and Ostergren 2002). For example, conflict can facilitate learning if it is dealt with in a communication process which does not privilege any particular point of view, where people are able to communicate without fear, where the communication is a two-way process, and where ultimately the objective of the process is not to achieve a consensus, but for people to develop a greater understanding of the viewpoint of others. Such processes therefore have much in common with the processes of perspective making and taking outlined in Chapter 3, which are an important element of the practice-based perspective on knowledge.

Emotion and attitudes to learning

The final factor that the learning organization advocates inadequately account for is the role of emotion in shaping attitudes and behaviours towards learning processes. However, a growing number of writers now acknowledge how emotion importantly affects the dynamics of learning processes (Scherer and Tran 2001; Vince 2001). At the individual level, learning can be regarded as potentially positive and exciting—discovering new knowledge, improving levels of understanding, developing more effective ways of working, etc. But, there is also a potential negative side—giving up the familiar, embracing some level of uncertainty—which may be anxiety-inducing for people (Kofman and Senge 1993). Learning is therefore likely to induce conflicting emotions for people. Learning and changing can also be understood to affect an individual's sense of self-identity (Child 2001), which may be regarded positively or negatively. Arguably, the attractiveness of defensive routines (Argyris 1990) is that they provide people with a sense of security and self-identity (Giddens 1991). Thus, a potentially frightening side of learning is that it can be felt to involve giving up that which makes people feel competent and secure. For example, in the case of MacMillan Bloedel examined earlier, part of the reason why senior management resisted change was because they felt that acknowledging the legitimacy of the protester's arguments raised questions about the morality of their actions and the company's strategy (Zietsma et al. 2002).

Learning can also be understood to have an emotional component due to the dynamic between individual and group or organizational level learning. Primarily, learning and change will inevitably involve, to some extent, challenging the existing balance of power, interests, practices, and values. Thus, learning may induce hostility and defensiveness because of its (potential) implications: people may be scared of challenging the existing norms (Salaman 2001). As Cooper and Burgoyne (2000) argue, the character of the organizational context will crucially affect the extent to which people will feel anxious and reluctant to raise or introduce learning that is likely to challenge existing values and practices. Pessimistically, they argue that few organizations create the 'psychic space' for people to raise such issues in a risk-free and supportive environment, with, for example, levels of consultation in key decision-making processes typically being 'pitifully low' (2000, 876). In such circumstances normalizing pressures are likely to inhibit the questioning of established norms, which may adversely affect the willingness or capacity of people to learn. Thus, Vince (2001) suggests, as a consequence of these ideas, that issues of power, politics, and emotion are intimately related.

ILLUSTRATING THE ISSUES

Conflict, emotion, and learning: the case of Hyder

Vince (2001) analysed the dynamics of learning at Hyder, a multi-utility and infrastructure company, which had evolved considerably from its origin as Welsh Water. Hyder actively supported individual learning, and believed that this would create organizational learning. However NO organizational learning occurred, which was explained by the intra-organizational dynamics which were shaped by issues of power and emotion. Hyder's evolution from Welsh Water into Hyder had resulted in two broad perspectives emerging over what the values underpinning the company should be. One camp saw the company as being primarily a Welsh utility, and that it should be driven by values of public service. The other camp saw the company as a global corporation that should be driven by commercial values. People in both camps used a range of methods in attempting to make their view of the company accepted. One of the main political tactics used was to develop change initiatives, which resulted in two competing initiatives being developed simultaneously. One was a corporate re-branding exercise to create the idea of one company driven by commercial values. The other change initiative, which used the rhetoric of employee empowerment, attempted to develop support around the public service perspective. Very little communication occurred between the camps and what was described as an 'iron curtain' developed between them. This reinforced the sense of competition, increased the level of anger and suspicion in both camps at the motivations of the other, and created a sense of entrenchment and defensiveness which ultimately reinforced their isolation. Individual learning was not able to contribute to organizational learning as it couldn't/didn't challenge the existing dynamics. This was partly shaped by emotions of defensiveness, as part of the dynamic was the fear of the consequences of challenging the status quo. As a consequence of this, open and acrimonious disputes were avoided (people publicly pretended they didn't exist, but simultaneously were attempting to defend their interests). Thus these organizational dynamics actively inhibited organizational learning.

Stop and think

This represents an example where conflicting viewpoints actively inhibited organizational-level learning. What could management at Hyder have done to make use of these different perspectives to actively facilitate organizational-level learning?

Conclusion

The chapter has shown that the enormous literature on organizational learning which has been produced since the mid-1990s is of great relevance to those wishing to understand the dynamics of organizational knowledge processes. This should be relatively unsurprising given the relatedness of learning to knowledge management. Through utilizing the Crossan–Zietsma framework the complexity of the relationship between learning at individual, group, and organizational levels was explored, showing how organizational learning cannot simply be regarded as the sum of the learning of an organization's workers.

The chapter also showed how the concept of the learning organization has been the subject of significant debate, with its advocates arguing that it provides both organizations and workers with many benefits, while the critics argue that the emancipatory rhetoric of the learning organization disguises and denies the way in which the practices of the learning organization may impact negatively on workers, for example leading to increased levels of exploitation and control. This debate was not resolved, but it did provide a useful way of revealing the diversity of factors which making learning within the context of work organizations difficult and complex (see Table 10.4).

Table 10.4. Factors affecting learning in organizations

Factor	Level
The emotional character of learning	Individual
Competency traps and the difficulty of giving up established values and practices	Individual-Group-Organization
The politics and power involved in implementing learning and challenging established norms	Individual-Group-Organization
The interrelatedness of learning, knowledge, and power	Supra-organizational
The embeddedness of power in the employment relationship	Supra-organizational

REVIEW QUESTIONS

1 The advocates of the learning organization suggest that critical self-reflection and open debate on norms and values are fundamental to learning organizations. However, Coopey and Burgoyne (2000) suggest few organizations provide the 'psychic space' where such reflection can occur. Do you agree with this analysis? If so, what factors are key in stifling such processes?

2 Compare the two definitions of the learning organization outlined in the chapter. Which do you most agree with, and why?

3 One of the main critiques of the learning organization literature is that managements are typically unlikely to 'give up' and share power in the way necessary to facilitate proper learning and self-reflection. Do you agree with this? If so, what, if anything can be done to persuade such managers that sharing power with workers has potential advantages for all?

FURTHER READING

- C. Zietsma, M. Winn, O. Branzei, and I. Vertinsky (2002). 'The War of the Woods: Facilitators and Impediments of Organizational Learning Processes', *British Journal of Management*, 13: S61–74.
  A fascinating case study that examines the dynamics of organizational learning processes and provides a useful modification of the Crossan framework.

- R. Vince (2001). 'Power and Emotion in Organizational Learning', *Human Relations*, 54/10: 1325–51.
  A useful examination of the relationship between individual- and organizational-level learning, which considers issues of emotion and power.

- J. Coopey (1995). 'The Learning Organization, Power, Politics and Ideology', *Management Learning*, 26/2: 193–213.
  One of the earliest and best critiques of the propagandists' perspective on the learning organization.

- J. Thomas, S. Sussman, and J. Henderson (2003). 'Understanding "Strategic Learning": Linking Organizational Learning, Knowledge Management and Sensemaking', *Organization Science*, 1/3: 331–45.
  Links together the topics of organizational learning and knowledge management via an empirical case study.

11

Innovation dynamics and knowledge processes

Introduction

Organizational innovation is concerned with deliberately designing and implementing changes to an organization's products, services, structures, or processes. The importance to organizations of such changes, and learning in general, is that the business context faced by most organizations requires it. This business context, shaped by a variety of factors such as rapid and profound change in computer and communication technologies, as well as processes of globalization and internationalization, can be characterized as being highly turbulent. Thus, for the vast majority of business organizations the continuous development and implementation of innovations is necessary to remain competitive.

At a common-sense level, innovation if often characterized as being primarily a knowledge-creation process. Thus, from this perspective, whether developing a new product, or transforming an organization' working practices, innovation is concerned with going beyond the realms of existing knowledge, and developing new knowledge and insights. This idea is challenged here. As will be seen, much organizational innovation is relatively incremental in nature, involving the modification rather than transformation and replacement of existing knowledge. Further, while knowledge creation is an important aspect of innovation processes, so is the ability to search for and identify relevant external knowledge, apply existing knowledge to new contexts, understand and absorb unfamiliar external knowledge, and to blend and integrate different bodies of knowledge together. Thus innovation processes are much more than knowledge-creation processes.

The general character of innovation processes (if its possible to talk about the general characteristics of such a diverse phenomenon) has evolved since the early 1980s. In general, innovation processes appear to be becoming more complex in nature and increasingly innovating organizations no longer possess all relevant knowledge internally. Thus, the importance of developing external networks has increased significantly, as has the need to integrate together diverse bodies of knowledge. Thus, Lam (1997, 973) suggested that, 'firms increasingly build cooperative ventures in order to sustain and enhance their competitiveness.' Because of these changes, this chapter has many issues in common with Chapter 6, on intercommunity knowledge processes, and with Chapter 12 on virtual and network organizations.

The next section of the chapter provides an overview on how the literature on organizational innovation has evolved since the 1980s and points to three key elements to innovation processes. These are their increasing interactivity, the role of knowledge, and the growing importance of developing and managing diverse networks. While these issues are closely interrelated, the chapter proceeds by examining each one separately.

Characterizing innovation processes

Before the knowledge dynamics of innovation processes can be examined in detail, it is worthwhile making a few introductory comments on the topics of terminology, the diversity in type of innovation that exists, and finally the evolution in the way that innovation processes have been conceptualized.

As outlined, the central focus of this chapter is on the way organizations systematically develop and change themselves with the objective of improving organizational performance. However, this encompasses a wide diversity of organizational activities from investing in large-scale, basic scientific research (such as pharmaceutical or chemical companies undertaking research on genetics), through the development and utilization of technology for the creation of new products (such as mobile phone companies incorporating photo and video functions into new generation mobile phones), to modifications in organizational processes (such as changing intra-organizational communication systems or developing knowledge management systems). A diversity of labels can be utilized to refer to these processes including new product development (NPD), research and development (R&D), and innovation. In this chapter the term 'innovation' is used, as it is generic enough to refer to all of the above types of change.

 Innovation

The deliberate modification, or transformation, by an organization of its products/services, processes, or structures.

As should already be apparent, organizational innovations are extremely diverse in character. For example, they can be incremental, where the scale of change is small, or radical, where the innovation involves large-scale and fundamental change. Secondly, innovations can be product/service focused (where a new product/service is designed or an existing product/service is modified), or process focused (where organizational processes and/or structures are modified). Finally, innovations can also vary in their content/focus. For example, Lynn (1998) differentiated between technological innovations (where innovations are made through the utilization of new technological developments) and market innovations (where existing products/services are sold to new markets). These represent significant differences, as they importantly shape the character of innovation processes, with, for example incremental and radical innovation processes being significantly different. However, equally, there are a number of general characteristics common to all innovation processes, and it is these common features that are examined here.

While the literature on organizational innovation has typically been characterized by a heterogeneity of diverse theoretical perspectives (Slappendel 1996; Wolfe 1994), one of the dominant streams in it is the stage model theory, where innovation processes are characterized as being divisible into a number of discrete stages (see Figure 11.1).

However, during the 1990s this neat and linear model was increasingly brought into question. As will be seen later, a number of writers, including Leonard-Barton (1995), argued that the problem with the stage model was that it disguised the extent to which these stages were interrelated (for example, with design modifications occurring during implementation). More broadly, others argued that innovation processes were becoming more interactive in nature, increasingly requiring extensive and repeated interactions throughout the whole innovation process between a diverse range of actors from both within the innovating organization (such as from different sites, business units, and functions), and from external actors such as customers, suppliers, consultants, universities, and public and private sector research institutions (Alter and Hage 1993; Jones et al. 2001; Powell 1998). The need for the development and utilization of such networks flows partly from the increasing complexity of innovations, which means that organizations

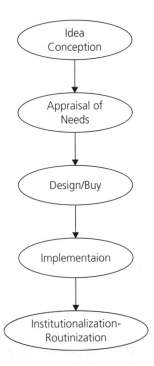

Fig. 11.1. Typical components in stage model of innovation

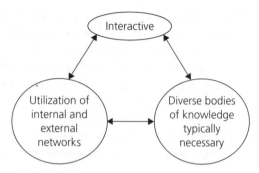

Fig. 11.2. Key characteristics in contemporary conceptualization of innovation processes

increasingly no longer possess all relevant knowledge internally, and who therefore require to develop networks with individuals and organizations in possession of relevant knowledge (Cohen and Levinthal 1990; Lam 1997; Sakakibara and Dodgson 2003; Tidd et al. 2001). Thus, contemporary writers typically conceptualize innovation processes as having three closely interrelated characteristics: they are highly interactive, they require the development and utilization of networks, and they involve the utilization of diverse bodies of knowledge (see Figure 11.2).

Innovation as an interactive process

The insight that innovating organizations need to interact with external actors is not totally new (Lundvall 1988; Pavitt 1984; von Hippel 1976, 1988). But, a number of factors that emerged during the 1980s mean that the extent and intensity of such interactions has increased significantly. Swan et al. (1999), for example, argue that advances in ICTs and the move to virtual and network forms of organization mean that innovations are increasingly becoming organization-wide in scope, requiring intra-organizational interactions between different functions and business units. Meeus et al. (2001) suggest that the growing complexity of innovations contributes to the increasing interactiveness of innovation processes, as the more complex an innovation, the more likely it is that all relevant knowledge will not be internally possessed. Finally, Jacquier-Roux and Bourgeois (2002), drawing on the influential work of Gibbons et al. (1994), suggest that the changing nature of knowledge production in society, from narrow, disciplinary based innovations, to trans-disciplinary innovations helps explain the increasing interactiveness of innovation processes.

Nonaka and Takeuchi (1995) usefully capture the characteristics of the stage and interactive innovations model, and the contrasts between them, through the use of sports metaphors. For them, the 'stage model' of innovation processes is comparable to a relay race where the baton (innovation) is dealt with in separate discrete stages by isolated individuals/groups, before being passed on to those responsible for successive stages. By contrast, interactive innovation processes are compared to the use of a ball in a rugby match, with the ball (innovation) being moved towards the try line through collaborative team-working, and continued interaction (such as passing or moving) between all the team's players. More formally, Meeus et al. (2001) define interactive learning as the continuous exchange and sharing of knowledge resources conducive to innovation processes, between an innovating firm and its customers and suppliers. This is a useful definition except for the unnecessarily narrow focus on customers and suppliers. As will be seen, innovation processes involve organizations interacting with a much wider range of organizations.

Stop and think

Of all the diverse factors identified, which are most important in making innovation processes more interactive?

The need for extensive and repeated interactions between organizations during innovation processes questions the linearity of the stage model, and suggests that the notion of innovation processes involving discrete, sequential stages is oversimplistic. As innovation processes become more interactive the more likely it is that there will be overlaps between different stages. One of the most visible ways in which this occurs is in the blurring of the boundary between design and implementation activities. Thus a number of writers suggest that the implementation of innovations can produce important changes to the characteristics of the innovation being implemented (Badham et al. 1997; Leonard Barton 1995; Swan et al. 1999). An important consequence of such dynamics is that innovations require to be understood as malleable and adaptable rather than having fixed and objective properties. Thus, different organizations may adapt similar innovations in quite different ways. For example, two organizations may utilize the same ICT-based knowledge systems (such as intranets, data-warehouses, etc.) in quite different ways, with one using it 'as designed' without modification, while the other customizes it significantly through collaborating with the systems designer.

ILLUSTRATING THE ISSUES

Interactive innovation in the energy industry

Jacquier-Roux and Bourgeois (2002) investigated innovation activity in the energy production industries and found that in the period between 1985 and 1998, paradoxically, as the R&D spending of the main oil and electricity production companies went down, there was a simultaneous overall increase in the production of knowledge in these sectors (measured in terms of number of patents granted). This was explained by the change in these sectors towards more interactive-based innovation processes, where the level of collaboration in innovation activity between the main oil and electricity production companies and equipment suppliers increase markedly. During the period examined significant changes had occurred in these sectors which encouraged the main producers to reduce their R&D spending. Primarily, deregulation and privatization, combined with a process of globalization in these industrial sectors, significantly increased the pressure on the main oil and electricity production companies to focus on short-term economic performance, which encouraged them to reduce their levels of R&D spending. Simultaneously, these companies started developing innovation partnerships with equipment suppliers as a way to sustain their R&D efforts and outputs. Prior to this, the main oil and electricity production companies had undertaken virtually all their R&D activity totally in-house.

Thus the strategy change undertaken by the main oil and electricity production companies resulted in the level of interaction between users and suppliers during innovation activities increasing significantly, and with equipment suppliers playing a greater role in such activities than had historically been traditional. These changes were visible in the evolving number of patents granted to these companies, with the patent activity of the main oil and electricity production companies declining, while the number of patents granted to equipment suppliers increased significantly. While these changes gave equipment suppliers a more important role in innovation activities a power asymmetry still existed which favoured the main oil and electricity producers. This was related to both their size (they were typically large multinational companies), and also their ability to be able to switch their business to different equipment suppliers if so desired.

However, some anecdotal evidence suggests that the use of interactive innovation processes has not been adopted uniformly in all countries. One of the basic assumptions of Nonaka and Takeuchi's (1995) analysis is that there are significant differences between Japanese and Western cultures with regard to knowledge, which results in the knowledge bases and knowledge processes of Western and Japanese companies being significantly different. Other writers argue that what have been labelled as 'national systems of innovation' exist, whereby the characteristics of innovation processes vary significantly between countries being shaped by the specific political, cultural, social, and economic context which exists in different countries (Maurice et al. 1980; Sakakibara and Dodgson 2003; Sorge 1991).

Lam (1997) presents some case-study evidence that reinforces this conclusion. The case study examined by Lam was outlined in Chapter 6 where the difficulties of knowledge-sharing during a collaborative innovation process between UK and Japanese companies were outlined. Lam suggests that part of the explanation for these difficulties was that the innovation processes utilized by these companies were significantly different. As touched on briefly in the illustrated example, the Japanese company utilized an interactive innovation process that involved significant amounts of communication and knowledge-sharing occurring between staff involved in all stages of the innovation process. Consequently, the boundary between the design and implementation phases was blurred, as most staff were involved in both activities, with much 'design' work happening during the 'implementation' phase. The innovation process utilized by the UK company was, by contrast, much closer to the stage model approach. Here, innovation was a very hierarchical and sequential process, with staff typically working on one specific phase only, and with limited knowledge-sharing occurring between staff working on the different stages. Unsurprisingly, these differences contributed to the problems experienced by these companies when they attempted to develop collaborative innovations.

Stop and think

To what extent do national systems of innovation exist, whereby different innovation philosophies predominate in particular countries?

In conclusion, this section has shown that one of the key characteristics of contemporary innovation processes is their typically interactive nature, requiring innovating companies to intensively work with a wide and diverse range of organizations, groups, and individuals. This characteristic of innovation processes thus links closely with the other key elements of innovation processes examined: the importance of networks and knowledge processes. However, as will be seen, and as was discussed in Chapter 6, this type of working relationship is by no means straightforward to manage. Firstly, there is a need for some common knowledge to exist (or be developed) between collaborating partners. Second, such work can involve collaboration between communities that may have distinctive and divergent cultures or values. Thirdly, the type of trust-based social relations that are conducive to knowledge-sharing may not initially exist. Finally, the tacit, context-specific, structurally and contextually embedded character of much organizational knowledge makes it difficult to share. These issues will be examined in detail in the following two sections.

Innovation and knowledge processes

This section examines the way the contemporary literature on innovation processes increasingly acknowledges the importance of knowledge. Their interrelatedness means that it is quite uncontroversial to suggest that innovation processes are fundamentally knowledge processes, involving the creation, utilization, management, and manipulation of knowledge. This is done in two contrasting ways, by examining firstly the influential work of Nonaka and his collaborators on knowledge creation, and secondly how the general characteristics of knowledge affect the dynamics of innovation processes. However, the interrelatedness of knowledge and networking issues means that totally separating them into discrete sections is impossible. Thus, some networking issues are dealt with here and, equally, some knowledge processes are considered in the following section on networks.

Knowledge creation

Nonaka and Takeuchi (1995) somewhat ambitiously develop a theory of organizational knowledge creation that both explains why certain Japanese companies have been successful innovators, and which attempts to blend together the best aspects of Japanese and Western business practices. This work has been developed and clarified primarily by Nonaka, along with a number of collaborators (Nonaka 1994, 1998; Nonaka et al. 2000, 2001). While their theory is centrally concerned with the dynamics of knowledge creation, they also consider important contextual factors such as the most appropriate organizational forms and management strategies. However, here the focus is primarily on their conceptualization of knowledge processes.

Nonaka and Takeuchi's theory of knowledge creation can't easily be characterized as embedded in either the objectivist or practice-based perspectives on knowledge, as it embodies elements of both. Thus, while one of its fundamental premises is the tacit–explicit dichotomy of knowledge (see Chapter 2), simultaneously it emphasizes the importance of human activity and social interaction to the creation and development of knowledge.

In Nonaka et al.'s theory of knowledge creation, as illustrated in Figure 11.3, interaction is required both between and within three separate, but interrelated layers. The first layer, SECI, represents the four modes of knowledge creation/conversion, with knowledge being created through the interaction between tacit and explicit knowledge (see Table 11.1). The second layer, labelled 'ba', refers to the shared context in which knowledge creation occurs, with there being four types of ba, each one related to a specific mode of knowledge creation. Ba can be a physical location (such as an office), a virtual space (such as an e-mail conference), or a mental space (collectively shared ideas, values, and experiences). The third and final layer of Nonaka et al.'s model refers to knowledge assets, with there again being four categories of knowledge asset including:

(1) *experiential* knowledge assets (tacit knowledge shared through experience);

(2) *conceptual* knowledge assets (explicit knowledge in the form of symbols and language);

(3) *routine* knowledge assets (tacit knowledge embedded in organizatiional routines and practices)

(4) *systemic* knowledge assets (systematized explicit knowledge).

Thus, as per Figure 11.3, knowledge is created through individuals collectively bringing together their specific knowledge assets, within particular contexts (ba), with this contributing to the creation of knowledge through the interaction and combination of these different knowledge assets through the four articulated modes of knowledge creation.

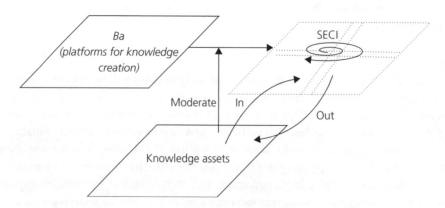

Fig. 11.3. The three layers of knowledge creation (from Nonaka et al. 2001)

Table 11.1. Nonaka et al.'s modes of knowledge creation and type of ba (from Nonaka et al. 2001)

Knowledge creation mode	Socialization	Externalization	Combination	Internalization
Type of knowledge linked	Tacit to Tacit	Tacit to Explicit	Explicit to Explicit	Explicit to Tacit
Example	Where a new member of a work group acquires the tacit knowledge possessed by other group members, for example through dialogue, observation, or co-operative working.	Where an individual is able to make their tacit knowledge explicit, for example through a process of communication and dialogue with others.	The linking together and integration of discrete bodies of knowledge, to create a more complex body of knowledge.	Where an individual converts explicit knowledge, codified in documentation, into tacit and embodied knowledge, through applying it to their work tasks.
Ba	Originating ba A physical location where face-to-face interaction occurs.	Dialoguing ba Inter personal interaction, though not necessarily face-to-face, where mental models, and tacit values can be shared.	Systematizing ba is a virtual rather than a physical place. For example, new (ICTs) facilitate the transferral, and absorption of explicit knowledge.	Exercising ba is the location where people actually carry out their work tasks and activities.

Characteristics of knowledge

Another way to consider the impact of knowledge on innovation processes is to examine the characteristics of knowledge. Three broad characteristics of knowledge can be identified as influencing innovation dynamics:

(1) the degree of tacitness;

(2) the level of complexity;

(3) the degree of relatedness between bodies of knowledge being linked together.

The importance of tacit knowledge to innovation processes is well recognized (Hislop et al. 2000; Powell 1998; Senker and Faulkner 1996; von Krogh et al. 2000), with some writers suggesting that the ability to effectively utilize tacit knowledge represents a measure of an organization's innovativeness (Leonard and Sensiper 1998; Subramaniam and Venkatraman 2001). For Leonard and Sensiper (1998) innovation occurs through interactions between people. This is because when an appropriate form of communication exists, people are able to gain an insight into the knowledge of others. When such insights are linked to a person's existing knowledge base, new knowledge and insights can be created. Thus, innovation involves a process of creative knowledge integration, which occurs when a 'creative abrasion' between contrasting viewpoints and knowledge bases occurs (Leonard and Sensiper 1998, 118).

The typically tacit nature of much organizational knowledge means that the sharing and communication of such sticky knowledge requires detailed and extensive social interactions to occur in a context of typically trust-based social relations (Leonard and Sensiper 1998; Subramaniam et al. 1998; Subramaniam and Venkatraman 2001). The impact of social relations on knowledge processes was examined in detail in Chapter 3, and in the context of innovation networks is returned to again in the following section.

ILLUSTRATING THE ISSUES

The role of tacit knowledge in new product development processes

Subramaniam and Venkatraman (2001) examined new product development processes in a number of large multinational companies and found that their ability to share and utilize important tacit knowledge was key. Specifically, they looked at the development of transnational products. These are products that are developed simultaneously for multiple markets, which contain both standardized features, and features that are responsive to individual local markets. Knowledge of consumer preferences in different local/national markets was thus important to such innovations. This knowledge was found to be largely tacit, being developed by people over time, through experience of working within a particular country/market. The transferral and sharing of such knowledge was an important aspect of these innovation processes. Subramaniam and Venkatraman found that the effective sharing of such knowledge required the use of rich communication mediums. Three particular ways which were examined, and all of which were found to be effective included: the use of face-to-face communication among teams with members drawn from different countries; the use of face-to-face communication among teams with members who had some overseas work experience; and the use of extensive communication amongst project teams which were not co-located. Thus, of the three methods examined two involved face-to-face interaction, while the third involved extensive communication via ICTs.

Stop and think

Is knowledge of local market conditions and preferences the sort of knowledge that is always likely to be tacit and which can only be developed over time, through experience? Can such knowledge be codified and communicated more easily?

Hansen, in two separate articles examining the characteristics of knowledge-sharing during innovation processes, suggests that the complexity of knowledge (Hansen 1999) and the degree of relatedness amongst bodies of knowledge being shared (Hansen 2002) can crucially affect the dynamics of innovation processes. Hansen defined complexity in terms of both the degree of tacitness and interdependence of knowledge. If knowledge is

highly interdependent, a full understanding of it is not possible without some understanding of related knowledge. Thus complex knowledge is knowledge that is both highly
tacit and simultaneously interdependent. The sharing of complex knowledge was found
to be most effective when strong trust-based relations existed between people involved in
the innovation process, as the sharing of such knowledge required extensive interactions.
In later work, Hansen (2002) also found that the interrelatedness of the different bodies
of knowledge being utilized in innovation processes also affected the dynamics of innovation processes. However, Hansen found that the interrelatedness of knowledge and the
nature of network relations amongst people participating in innovation processes were
inseparable. This issue is thus examined in the following section.

Stop and think

What, if anything, can organizations do to reduce the complexity of the knowledge used in innovation
processes? Is complex knowledge something that, by its nature, is irreducible to a simpler form?

In conclusion, this section has shown two different ways to examine the importance of
knowledge to the dynamics of innovation processes: through examining the knowledge
processes involved, and through examining the characteristics of knowledge. What the
chapter has also show is the interrelatedness of knowledge and networking issues. For
example, the typically tacit nature of much organizational knowledge means that gaining
access to such knowledge requires the development of networks with people who possess
relevant knowledge (Hislop et al. 2000; Powell 1998). Equally, this section has touched
upon how the character of knowledge affects the type of social relationship necessary for
effectively sharing it. These issues of networks, and the character of social relations within
them, are the central focus of the next section.

Innovation processes and network dynamics

As outlined previously, the importance of effectively developing and utilizing networks
in innovation processes has grown considerably, due to a number of factors. Firstly, innovations are increasingly organization-wide in scale, thus requiring intra-organizational
collaboration amongst staff from different functions and business units. Secondly, the
growing complexity of innovations means that all relevant knowledge is unlikely to be
possessed internally by the innovating company, requiring the development of external
networks to access such knowledge. This section examines the dynamics of such
processes, and considers the importance of the role of knowledge in shaping them.

Diversity: network partners and relations

When examining innovation networks, one of the most striking initial observations is
the diversity in both the type of network relations that organizations can develop
(see Table 11.2), as well as the range of different organizations involved in such networks.
Further, when these two dimensions are combined this helps to reveal the enormous
diversity in type of innovation networks that can exist. Thus, as illustrated in Table 11.2,

Table 11.2. Forms of collaboration

Type of collaboration	Duration	Character
Subcontract Relations	Short–Medium Term	Can vary from short-term, market-based contractual relations, to longer-term relations such as collaborative innovation development.
Licensing	Fixed Term	Fixed-term, contractual agreement between companies, where one company provides specific technologies, skills, and knowledge to another.
Strategic Alliances	Medium Term	A medium-term relationship, which can involve two or more companies, with a specifically defined remit, such as the development of a specific product.
Joint Ventures	Long Term	Long-term collaborative relationship between two or more companies, which can be wide in scope, and for relatively open-ended time periods.

network relations can vary from relatively short-term, low-commitment collaborations, to longer-term, more involved collaborations, such as joint ventures or mergers and alliances (Tidd et al. 2001).

In terms of potential network partners there is also a bewildering diversity. Thus organizations may develop research-based collaborations with universities, or private research organizations, as has been occurring in the biotechnology and pharmaceutical industries in the USA since the early 1980s (Powell et al. 1996; Powell 1998). Secondly, companies can develop network relations with suppliers (see Jacquier-Roux and Bourgeois example outlined earlier from the energy industries), customers, or both (as was found by Meeus et al. 2001 in their survey on innovation behaviour in a Dutch region). Thirdly, companies can develop collaborative relations with consulting companies. Finally, companies can develop innovation networks with other organizations, some of which may even be competitors. For example, the restructuring of American and European military industries following the end of the Cold War involved mergers, acquisitions, as well as a significant increase in the number of strategic alliances developed (Hislop 2000). Finally, collaboration amongst small firms within industrial districts represents another type of intercompany collaboration involving competing companies (Antonelli 2000; Sternberg 1999; Tell 2000).

*Absorptive capacity: the ability to identify and absorb external
sources of knowledge*

Before organizations can utilize external sources of knowledge and develop network relations they need to be able not only to identify sources of relevant knowledge, but also have the ability to absorb it. An organization's ability to do this is defined as its absorptive capacity (Cohen and Levinthal 1990). The results of an empirical survey conducted by Tsai (2001) suggests that absorptive capacity is of fundamental importance to innovation processes, with organizational innovativeness being directly correlated with levels of absorptive capacity.

 Absorptive capacity

The ability to recognize (search) and absorb (integrate) external knowledge that is important to innovation processes.

Cohen and Levinthal identified a number of factors that influenced an organization's absorptive capacity. A key element was the possession of prior knowledge. Thus a lack of prior knowledge will inhibit an organization's ability to identify and absorb external knowledge, although Meeus et al. (2001) suggest that this relationship works only up to a point, and that an organization's absorptive capacity can be inhibited by the possession of too much prior knowledge, as well as by too little. An organization's absorptive capacity is also affected by the role of key people such as boundary spanners, who work at the boundary between an organization and its environment, and are thus well placed to identify external sources of knowledge. Relatedly an organization's absorptive capacity is also shaped by the effectiveness with which boundary spanners can interact with and communicate their knowledge to other organizational members. Finally, Leonard Barton (1995) produced a list of ways in which organizations could enhance their absorptive capacity (see Table 11.3)

Cohen and Levinthal also suggest that a problem called 'lockout' (1990, 136–7) can develop when organizations have weak absorptive capacities. This is closely related to the concept of competency traps discussed in Chapter 10. Lockout happens when an organization's absorptive capacity is very low and it can become so unreceptive to

Table 11.3. Mechanisms for enhancing organizational absorptive capacity (adapted from Leonard Barton 1995)

1. Scan the environment as widely as possible to create an openness to a broad diversity of knowledge sources.

2. Scan the environment continuously rather than occasionally as this allows organizations to effectively keep up to date with contemporary developments.

3. Nurture and support technological gate-keepers as these are the people who can effectively keep colleagues up to date with the latest technological developments.

4. Nurture and support boundary spanners due to the importance of their role. Support multiple, rather than one boundary spanner, as having only one boundary spanner can be risky (if they leave or if they are ineffective).

5. Fight against a culture of NIH (not invented here) through encouraging and rewarding people for utilizing external sources of knowledge.

external environmental changes that it finds it impossible to implement innovations and change its products/services or working practices. Tsai (2001) also found that a lack of absorptive capacity can inhibit an organization's innovativeness, even if strategically placed at the centre of important networks.

Social relations within innovation networks

As outlined earlier in the chapter the characteristics of knowledge affect the characteristics and dynamics of the social relations within innovation networks. Thus, the typically tacit and complex nature of much of the knowledge utilized in innovation processes means that effectively sharing it requires not only that strong, trust-based social relations exist between individuals, but that an extensive amount of communication and interaction occurs. Hansen (2002) also reached a similar conclusion when considering how the relatedness of knowledge affected knowledge-sharing during innovation processes involving collaboration between different organizational business units. Hansen concluded that the quality of knowledge-sharing processes was affected by both the closeness of the relationship between network partners and the relatedness of their knowledge. Thus effective knowledge-sharing was found to be most likely when there was *both* a close relationship between collaborators *and* when a significant amount of common knowledge existed.

However, the difficulty faced by collaborators in innovation networks is that appropriate trust-based social relations may not exist, making the sharing of such knowledge extremely difficult. Thus in innovation networks involving diverse collaborators, whether from different parts of the same organization, or from completely different organizations, it is not uncommon that the collaborators will have only limited acquaintance with each other, may have only limited common knowledge, and may have divergent values and identities. Thus in this context, which, as described in Chapter 6, is likely to be typical for most intercommunity knowledge processes, before innovation-specific knowledge can be shared it will be necessary for the collaborators to develop their social relationship so that a certain level of trust exists, so that participants can develop some level of common knowledge, and which allows them to develop at least a basic understanding of the knowledge and values of others.

ILLUSTRATING THE ISSUES

Network-based innovation processes and contrasting work practices

Diamond Pension is one of the UK's largest pension and assurance companies. In the late 1990s, for a variety of strategic reasons, it decided to change the way that field sales staff were managed and supported. The core of these changes involved replacing a manual, paper-based sales support system with an automated one. This would allow sales management staff to more effectively set targets for staff, monitor their progress towards achieving them, and make comparing the performance of staff substantially easier. However, the three-person team responsible for this project quickly realized that no existing software systems were totally suitable for their requirements.

However, one very senior sales manager found a system that he liked, and was extremely keen to have it customized for Diamond Pension's purposes. After various negotiations involving the project team and the systems designers a collaborative development was undertaken. Diamond Pension agreed to give the software company the knowledge necessary to design the system, while the software company would then undertake the development work. They also agreed that once this had been done the software company would be able to sell this new product to other pension companies, with Diamond Pension benefiting financially from every additional sale made. The system modification work required the Diamond Pension project team to communicate a substantial amount of knowledge regarding the company's working practices so that the new system could be designed to be compatible with it.

Problems emerged during this work largely due to differences in the culture and working practices of the companies. Diamond Pension utilized relatively formal project management methods, where substantial amounts of documentation were required to keep track of all agreements made, progress on project development, and ongoing changes to the systems specification, etc. The software company, by contrast, which was relatively small, had a much more informal, ad hoc culture where documenting all work was deemed not very important.

Over time, however, largely through extensive communication between the project team and the software developers, which occurred through both face-to-face meetings, and many lengthy telephone conversations, an agreed way of working was negotiated. Ultimately Diamond Pension got the product they wanted, although it was delivered later than they had originally planned.

Stop and think

Is this situation likely to be typical in most collaborations between large and small organizations? Are large companies always likely to have more formalized roles, responsibilities, and procedures than small companies? What, if anything, can large organizations do to minimize the risks and problems in such collaborations?

Orlikowski (2002), using an analysis embedded in a practice-based perspective on knowledge, suggests that a sense of common identity as well as appropriate social relations and amounts of common knowledge can be achieved through organizations utilizing particular 'repertoires' of organizational practices (see Table 11.4). For Orlikowski, knowing and practice are mutually constituted, as knowing is something that is created and sustained through ongoing practice, and vice versa.

Orlikowski's analysis is based on a detailed study of a software development company titled Kappa (a pseudonym) that undertakes geographically dispersed software development work. Kappa is organized into fifteen separate development units, spread across four continents, each of which has design responsibilities on different projects. Design and product knowledge in Kappa is highly distributed, and Kappa deliberately splinters development responsibilities between sites, and creates project teams involving members from different development units. This is done with the objective of tapping into and linking together all their knowledge resources.

Orlikowski suggests that the repertoire of practices utilized by Kappa facilitate effective collaborative product development activities, as collectively they allow workers to span the

Table 11.4. Orlikowski's boundary-spanning practices

Practice & knowledge objective achieved	Description	How Achieved	Advantage	Disadvantage
Sharing identity: knowing the organization	Develop an understanding of 'kappa way of working' and develop common vocabulary	Training and socialization programmes	Facilitates communication and co-ordination. Builds sense of organizational loyalty	Development of groupthink
Interacting face-to-face: knowing the players	Establishes social relations between people	Extensive use of face-to-face meetings	Builds the inter-personal trust necessary to facilitate product development work	Financial and personal cost from extensive social interaction—burnout
Aligning effort: knowing how to co-ordinate across time	Allowing staff from different development units to interact and communicate easily	Use of standard project management methods and standard metrics for measuring time/effort on projects	Allows co-ordination of large groups of geographically dispersed people working on interrelated complex work	Creates a set of norms and practices which can become institutionalized and difficult to challenge. Can Inhibit improvization
Learning by doing: knowing how to continually develop capabilities	Encourage ongoing personal development	Rewarding and supporting learning and providing mentoring	Allows people to undertake development work which keeps their skills and knowledge up date	Knowledge lost through staff turnover. An investment which is difficult to retain
Supporting participation: knowing how to continually develop product innovations	Sustaining ability to continually introduce product innovations	Involving people in decisions. Tolerating criticism and risk-taking and mistakes. Also through frequent rotation of staff	Sharing of ideas and insights among geographically dispersed people. Provides voice to different groups	Can be costly, can also generate and exaggerate inter-unit conflict

diversity of boundaries which separate and divide them. Within Kappa Orlikowski identified seven separate boundaries which project teams had to work to overcome. These were:

(1) temporal boundaries (time zones);

(2) geographic boundaries (different locations);

(3) social boundaries (with people being involved in a diversity of projects simultaneously);

(4) cultural (thirty different nationalities worked within Kappa);

(5) historical (three different versions of the same product were being worked on simultaneously);

(6) technical (different IT infrastructures were used in different locations) and

(7) political (each development unit had its own responsibilities, targets, and interests).

Innovation processes: power, knowledge, and networks

A general, though typically implicit assumption, in the majority of the innovation literature on knowledge and networks, is that the primary purpose for the development of organizational networks, is to gain access to the knowledge that such networks can provide. However, this is not necessarily the only reason for the development of such networks. For example, the analysis undertaken by Hislop et al. (2000) showed that in the two case studies examined, one of which is briefly touched on in Chapter 3, the development of networks served a political as well as a functional objective. In the two cases examined in the study networks were developed and utilized by different staff for the dual purpose of giving access to relevant knowledge, as well as attempting to resolve conflicts raised by the innovation projects in particular ways.

As has been discussed extensively in Chapters 4, 7, and 10, issues of power and knowledge are inseparable. Therefore, when considering knowledge processes, issues of power, politics, and conflict require to be accounted for. This is as true for knowledge utilized for innovation processes are for other organizational activities. While the literature on innovation networks has generally been weak at addressing such issues (Jones and Beckinsale 2001), there are exceptions, and a number of studies have discussed such issues. Thus, for example, Leonard and Sensiper (1998) discuss the conflicts of interest which innovation projects can generate, while Ciborra and Patriotta (1998), as discussed in Chapter 4, showed how R&D staff were reluctant to voice certain opinions in electronic discussion forums for fear of the sanctions doing so might incur. Finally, in the case discussed earlier in the chapter, Jacquier-Roux and Bourgeois (2002) outlined how significant power asymmetries existed in the interorganizational innovation networks they examined. These few cases therefore illustrate the importance of accounting for power and politics in innovation processes.

Conclusion

Contemporary conceptualizations of innovation processes typically emphasize three interrelated characteristics (see Figure 11.2). First, they are highly interactive, involving dynamic, intensive communication between the innovating organization and a potentially diverse range of people, groups, and organizations. Such interactions can occur throughout the innovation process and bring into question the 'stage model' logic that suggests that innovations are developed in separate stages, by distinctive and separate groups of people who have little interaction with each other (Figure 11.1). Secondly, the development and utilization of networks is also regarded as a fundamental aspect of contemporary innovation processes. The reasons for this, to some extent, are related by a growing need for innovating organizations to access and utilize knowledge not possessed internally. Such networks can be with organizations as diverse as customers, suppliers, competitors, research organizations, universities, and government bodies. Thus, innovating organizations typically find themselves at the center of a complex web of diverse network relations. Thirdly, and finally, innovation processes are conceptualized as involving the complex interaction of a diversity of knowledge processes (not just knowledge-creation processes, but also search and identification, absorption, integration, etc.).

The chapter also showed how the sharing and communication of knowledge relevant for innovations, much of which is highly tacit, requires extensive communication between people who have a significant degree of common knowledge, and some shared sense of identity. However, the lack of one or all of these elements in many innovation networks makes the sharing of innovation-related knowledge, difficult, complex, and time-consuming. Thus, in this respect, the dynamics of knowledge processes within innovation networks has much in common with all intercommunity knowledge contexts examined in Chapter 6, where the degree of common knowledge and/or extent of shared identity may be limited.

REVIEW QUESTIONS

1 Rhetoric suggests that innovation processes are important for most companies as their environments are highly turbulent, requiring constant change and adaptation. Is there a certain element of hyperbole to such claims, or is constant change and innovation a reality for a large number of companies? Which sectors are the most dynamic and why?

2 The stage mode of innovation processes can be criticized as being too simplistic because it ignores the extent to which stages overlap, etc. However, to what extent do the innovation processes undertaken by most companies have some element of a linear trajectory between specific stages?

FURTHER READING

- W. Orlikowski (2002). 'Knowing in Practice: Enacting a Collective Capability in Distributed Organizing', *Organization Science*, 13/3: 249–73.

  Illustrates how organizational practices can be used to facilitate intra-organizational knowledge-sharing in a dispersed software company.

- M. Subramaniam and N. Venkatraman (2001). 'Determinants of Transnational New Product Development Capability: Testing the Influence of Transferring and Deploying Tacit Overseas Knowledge', *Strategic Management Journal*, 22: 359–78.

  Examines the difficulties involved in, and the mechanisms used for sharing tacit knowledge needed in new product development work.

- W. Powell (1998). 'Learning From Collaboration: Knowledge and Networks in Biotechnology and Pharmaceuticals Industries', *California Management Review*, 40/3: 228–40.

  Illustrates the importance and dynamics of interorganizational network relations in the US. pharmaceutical and biotechnology industries.

- M. Meeus, L. Oerlemans, and J. Hage (2001). 'Patterns of Interactive Learning in a High-Tech Region', *Organization Studies*, 22/1: 145–72.

  Illustrates the interactiveness of contemporary innovation processes, focusing centrally on customer and supplier relations.

Organizational contexts

The three chapters in this section examine the nature of knowledge processes in three different, but generic types of organization. The primary objective of these chapters is to examine the character and dynamics of the knowledge processes in a number of specific organizational contexts and apply the general ideas discussed in Parts 2 and 3 to particular organizational contexts. Thus the chapters in this section have a substantially different focus from all previous chapters. While previous chapters have been thematically focused on specific knowledge processes (such as R&D activity), or particular factors which influence knowledge processes (such as issues of power and conflict, organizational culture, or the use of ICTs), the chapters in this section each examining the nature of knowledge processes in particular organizational contexts.

One interesting conclusion, which will emerge more fully as these chapters are read, is that the character of the knowledge processes in each organizational context varies considerably (see Table 12). Each chapter focuses on examining both the nature of the knowledge processes in each context, as well as the key factors which shape these processes. This will involve some overlap with themes discussed in preceding chapters. Thus for example, the chapter on Network-Virtual organizations reconnects with the theme of cross-boundary knowledge processes discussed in Chapter 6, as Network-Virtual organizations represent one specific context where boundary-spanning knowledge processes are common. Equally, however, these chapters introduce and examine themes which have received little attention thus far in the book, such as in Chapter 13 where the relationship between organizational size and national cultural/business systems are linked to knowledge processes.

The final topic worth elaborating here is to explain the rationale for selecting the three specific organizational types examined. The main reason for focusing on knowledge-intensive firms, global multinationals, and Network-Virtual organizations is that they represent three of the most important and dominant organizational types in the contemporary business world. As touched on in Chapter 1, the last quarter of the twentieth century witnessed an enormous amount of change in the structuring of business organizations. This period has seen the importance of each of the organizational forms examined grow significantly. Thus, Chapter 12 shows how hierarchical organizational structures have evolved towards network and virtual organizational forms. Chapter 13 shows how the same period, due to a number of diverse influences, saw a growth in both the number of large multinational organizations which exist, as well as a quantitative growth in the

Table 12. The core knowledge issues related to organizational types

Organizational type	Knowledge issues
Network-Virtual Organization	• Cross-boundary knowledge processes (organization, function, business unit). • The difficulties of sharing contextually embedded knowledge. • ICT-mediated knowledge processes.
Global Multinational	• Cross-boundary knowledge processes (national culture, business system). • Organizational size and knowledge processes. • Organizational structure and knowledge processes.
Knowledge-intensive Firm	• How to make knowledge workers loyal to company (retention). • Conflict in the employment relationship? • Who are knowledge workers and how can they be motivated to share their knowledge?

size (number of employees) and degree of internationalization of these organizations. Finally, Chapter 14 shows how this time period also witnessed a significant growth in the number and importance of knowledge-intensive firms.

12

Knowledge processes in network/virtual organizations

Introduction

Arguably, moves towards network and virtual organizational structures represent one of the most important aspects in the contemporary restructuring of work. As has been outlined in Chapters 6 and 11, collaborative modes of working, which bring together diverse individuals and groups to collectively utilize their individual knowledge and expertise, have become increasingly popular. Further, as witnessed by the literature on multinationals, examined in Chapter 13, the network metaphor has also become a powerful analytical tool for understanding the nature and dynamics of contemporary modes of organizing (Fulk 2001).

Defining and characterizing network and virtual forms of organizatin will be done in the following section, but some examples can illustrate the mode of organizing referred to. 3 (formerly Hutchison 3G),[6] a UK multimedia communications company that is developing a mobile telephone with video capabilities, can be characterized as being a network organization. Thus, the development of its current video-telephone has involved close collaboration with a number of organizations including Nokia and NEC, to provide an infrastructure, Motorola and NEC, to produce handsets, a variety of content providers including the FA Premier League and nine game developers, and BBC Technology, who are responsible for producing and editing audio-visual content. Another example of a network and/or virtual-based organization was the multinational examined by Nandhakumar (1999), which developed an IT-based virtual teamwork project which had the objective of fostering collaboration not only between the company's business units, but also with external collaborating partners. However, as Castells (1998) makes clear, the existence of Japanese *keiretsu* (vertical networks built around a large, specialized industrial corporation), as well as Korean *chaebol* (hierarchically structured networks of companies dominated by a single large corporation), network forms of organizing are by no means totally new.

However, what factors explain the massive contemporary growth in the use of network-based modes of organizing? Primarily, it is argued that the highly competitive and turbulent nature of the market environment that most companies operate in, combined with the fast pace of technological change, requires organizations to be both continually

---

[6] Information on 3 was taken from their company website www.three.co.uk, on 11 July 2003).

innovative and highly adaptable. As will be illustrated in the following section, network and virtual structures are argued to provide organizations with these capabilities (Black and Edwards 2000; Jackson 1999).

The issues discussed in this chapter link closely with topics considered in other chapters. The first section, which examines the character of network and virtual forms of organization, links to Chapters 11 and 13. Secondly, the character of cross-boundary knowledge processes that were examined in Chapter 6 are returned to in the second section, which considers how the nature of knowledge affects the dynamics of knowledge processes in network modes of organizing. The third major section of the chapter then considers the sociocultural factors that affect people's willingness to share knowledge in virtual and network-based contexts, which links to issues of motivation discussed in Chapter 4, as well as the boundary-spanning organizational practices discussed in Chapter 11. Finally, the last major section in the chapter, which considers the role of ICTs in facilitating and enabling network and virtual forms of work, connects closely with a number of themes discussed in Chapter 8.

Defining and characterizing network/virtual forms of organizing

The focus of this chapter is on work that involves the spanning of traditional organizational boundaries (function, business unit, organization), is typically geographically dispersed, and where extensive use of ICTs is made to facilitate interactions. However, an excess of different labels is utilized to describe such work, including network-based organizing, virtual working, and dispersed working. For example, Ahuja and Carley (1999, 742) define a virtual organization as a, 'geographically distributed organization whose members are bound by a long-term common interest or goal, and who communicate and coordinate their work through information technology'.

To distinguish between network and virtual organizations it could be argued that virtual organizations involve dispersed, ICT-mediated working, while network organizations involve cross-boundary collaboration (functional, organizational, etc). However, maintaining a clear distinction between them is difficult, as much virtual working involves cross-boundary working, and equally much cross-boundary working is done by geographically dispersed teams. Thus Ahuja and Carley's definition could equally be a definition of a network organization. In this chapter, no distinction is made between network and virtual organizations. Instead, the all-encompassing but shorthand term N-V will be used to refer to both simultaneously.

 Network-Virtual Working

This is work that spans traditional boundaries, through either involving interorganizational working, or by intra-organizational collaboration that transcends functional or business unit boundaries. Further, collaborators are typically not co-located requiring the extensive use of ICT-mediated communication.

Table 12.1. Character and articulated advantages of N-V organizational structures

Characteristics	Advantages (compared to hierarchical structures)
• Multidirectional knowledge sharing—horizontally between functions, organizations and business units as well as vertically in hierarchy.	• More effective for horizontal, cross functional, inter-organizational knowledge sharing.
• Flexible and adaptable—structures easy to modify.	• More innovative—through better linking and integrating dispersed organizational knowledge.
• Dispersed working—work colleagues not collocated.	• Better knowledge searching—through knowledge developed from cross-functional and inter- business interactions.
• Dispersed knowledge—knowledge required to carry out work tasks geographically dispersed.	• More flexible and thus better suited to contemporary dynamics and competitive business environment.
• Technology-mediated working—ICTs are an important means of communication and coordination.	
• Flat' hierarchies—few layers of management.	
• Decentralized—'heterarchy', non-hierarchical.	
• Blurred boundaries—the boundaries between functions, business units, and organizations involved in networks become blurred.	

The characteristics of N-V forms of organizing, and their articulated advantages are closely interrelated (see Table 12.1). This is primarily because the advantages of these forms of organization fundamentally lie in their structural characteristics, which are argued to be well suited to the highly turbulent and competitive character of contemporary business environments, which require companies to be highly innovative, flexible, and continually adapting (Castells 1998; Cravens et al. 1996). Further, N-V work structures are usually defined in opposition to hierarchical forms of organization, which are characterized as being highly inflexible, and thus not suited to contemporary business environments. As well as being highly flexible, N-V organizations are also argued to be more effective than hierarchically based organizations at searching for, sharing, and creating knowledge, because they facilitate communication and interaction between business units and functions more effectively. Figures 13.1 and 13.2 illustrate these differences diagrammatically in relation to multinational corporations.

As Table 12.1 makes clear, one characteristic of N-V forms of organizing is that traditional boundaries, such as those between functions, business units, and/or organizations become blurred. Thus, appropriately, research on this topic includes work which examines both intraorganizational networks (such as Ardichvili et al. 2003), and interorganizational networks (such as Dyer and Nobeoka 2000). For the purposes of this chapter N-V forms of organizing are defined broadly to include both intraorganizational as well as interorganizational contexts.

An enormous number of writers and analysts argue that N-V modes of organizing are so important that they have become the new orthodoxy in the structuring of organizations. Fenton and Pettigrew (2000*a*) report the results of a large-scale survey of companies in Western Europe that substantiates such claims. Their results showed that during the course of the early 1990s, of the companies that participated in the survey:

- 30% reduced the number of layers in their hierarchy
- 50% used project-based working practices more
- 74% reported an increase in horizontal interaction
- 82% increased investment in IT
- 65% reported using outsourcing more
- 65% reported using strategic alliances more

Before concluding this section, it is, however, worth making a couple of important observations. First, while it is possible at an abstract level to talk in general terms about N-V forms of organizing, this disguises the enormous diversity of specific N-V organizational forms that exist. Thus, just as Chapter 11 showed that there is enormous variability in the types of innovation networks that firms undertake (see Table 11.2), there is equally as much diversity in the types of N-V structures. Cravens et al. (1996) developed a typology with four generic categories of N-V governance structure (see Figure 12.1), with the character of such structures varying dependent upon both the nature of the network relationship developed, as well as the level of environmental volatility. Thus they use the term 'hollow network' to describe collaborative networks in volatile environments that are characterized by relatively transactional relations, such as exist in the network that Nike, the sports shoe designer, develops with shoe manufacturers. Alternatively, they use the term 'flexible network' to describe the type of networks developed by the pharmaceutical and biotechnology firms examined by Powell et al. (1996, 1998), where the environment is equally volatile, but where network relations are more collaborative and long term in nature.

Another important observation to make regarding to the literature on N-V structures is that while many organizations have moved towards this type of organizational structure, there are few 'pure' N-V organizations (Stanworth 1997). Thus while many organizations

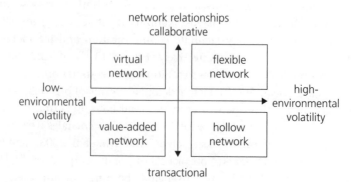

Fig. 12.1. Classification of network forms of organizing (from Cravens et al. 1996)

have restructured to produce flatter structures, and introduce cross-functional team-working, there are still elements of continuity with more traditional, hierarchical structures (Ahuja and Carley 1999; Goodall and Roberts 2003; Hales 2002).

N-V organizations and the 'problem' of dispersed knowledge

The focus of this section is on how the characteristics of knowledge affect the dynamics of knowledge processes in N-V forms of organizing. Most work in this area utilizes a practice-based perspective on knowledge, including the two papers examined here, by Cramton (2001) and Sole and Edmondson (2002). Therefore this section links closely to Chapter 3. As was discussed in that Chapter, and illustrated in Tables 3.1 and 3.3 the practice-based perspective on knowledge characterizes knowledge as being highly tacit, embedded in the work activities that people undertake, and context-specific.

These characteristics have quite profound implications for work in N-V organizations, because if knowledge is largely context-specific, the fact that people in N-V organizations are dispersed and work in different physical contexts means that the knowledge they possess is likely to be quite specific and specialized. Therefore, the knowledge dynamics in N-V organizations are equivalent to the type of cross-boundary knowledge processes examined in Chapter 6, where collaborating workers have limited common knowledge, a weak sense of shared identity, and possibly divergent values. However, the sociocultural issues of identity and values are considered in the following section.

Both the papers examined here, while focusing on slightly different themes, deal with the fundamental issue in N-V work contexts of how people who possess specialized knowledge, and have little common knowledge, effectively collaborate together and collectively utilize their knowledge. As suggested in Chapter 6 (see Table 6.3), not only do such workers have limited common knowledge, but this knowledge is likely to be 'sticky' and difficult to transfer, and epistemic differences may also exist in the assumptions underpinning their knowledge.

Cramton (2001) examines the difficulties involved in developing and sustaining 'mutual knowledge' (another term for common or shared knowledge—knowledge possessed by all those collaborating) in dispersed forms of collaboration. The specific context studied by Cramton was internationally dispersed student project groups (each of which had 6 members) that communicated exclusively via ICTs. Cramton found that significant difficulties existed in both developing and sustaining 'mutual knowledge', with this being visible in the frequent problems, conflicts, and misinterpretations which emerged within the groups studied, due to the limited ability of the students to either communicate relevant knowledge of their own specific context, or understand key knowledge related to the context of other project team members. While these difficulties were attributed to five specific factors (see Table 12.2), these factors all flowed from the fact that the knowledge possessed by the project team members was typically contextually embedded and difficult to communicate, particularly via ICTs.

One limitation of this study is that it is based on research on student projects, therefore the transferability of the empirical findings to work organizations is questionable.

Table 12.2. Factors inhibiting the development of 'mutual knowledge' in ICT-mediated dispersed work contexts (adapted from Cramton 2001)

Factor	Character	Problem
Communicating and Understanding Contextual Knowledge	Project team members found it difficult to communicate what was pertinent, contextual knowledge to others.	Team members could find it difficult to understand the behaviour and attitudes of others.
Unevenly Distributed Information/Knowledge	Not all information or knowledge was communicated to all team members (often accidentally).	• Limited the ability of team members not receiving full knowledge to participate in group activities. • Created conflict and antagonism related to interpretations regarding reasons for people's exclusion.
Divergent Interpretations of Saliency of Information/ Knowledge	When large messages with information/knowledge on multiple topics were sent, people found it difficult to communicate or interpret what was most salient.	Potential for conflict, as divergent interpretations on saliency affected how people behaved and expected others to behave.
Different Communication Speeds	Team members had differential access to e-mail, which affected the speed of their responses.	Potential for conflict, as the slowness of people to respond could be attributed to laziness rather than technical problems or structural factors.
Divergent Interpretation of Silence	The diversity of reasons for, and interpretations of, a lack of response to queries (silence as agreement, silence as busy, silence due to technical problems).	Potential for conflict if there were misunderstandings regarding the reasons for a group member's silence.

Symon (2000) suggests this is the case for much of the research on ICT-based communication in N-V organizations. For example, the study by Jarvenpaa and Leidner (1999) discussed in Chapter 8 was also on student-based virtual project teams.

Stop and think

How relevant and transferable are the findings of student-based studies to the context of work organizations? Does the lack of an employment contract in student-based contexts limit the generalizibility of such studies?

Sole and Edmondson (2002), in analysing the results of some longitudinal case studies into the knowledge dynamics within geographically dispersed product development teams, focus on the same key issue as Cramton: the difficulty of sharing knowledge between contexts. However, while Cramton examined the difficulties of developing 'mutual knowledge', Sole and Edmondson consider the difficulties involved in sharing what they refer to as 'situated knowledge' between the different locations that members of the product teams work at. Situated knowledge is a specific type of contextually embedded knowledge, being knowledge of the context itself, such as knowledge of the physical characteristics of the site, the people who work at it, and the capabilities of the facilities at the site. Drawing on the practice-based perspective on knowledge, Sole and Edmondson make clear that situated knowledge is highly context-specific, being acquired by people over time-through working at a particular site and formally and informally communicating with others who also work there. They conclude that sharing such knowledge across sites is likely to be a complex and time-consuming process, due largely to the lack of common situated knowledge that will typically exist in dispersed teams.

ILLUSTRATING THE ISSUES

Sole and Edmondson (2002): transferring situated knowledge between contexts

....

In one of the projects examined by Sole and Edmondson, difficulties were encountered when production of a new chemical required to be extended from pilot to production scale trials. The initial pilot trials had been done at one site, where the experimental scientist responsible gained a lot of knowledge and understanding of the production process. However, due to equipment constraints, the production scale trials had to be conducted at a site different to where the pilot trials had been done. This created a problem because staff at the new, production scale trial site didn't have the detailed knowledge of the pilot trial process. This knowledge was situated, and largely tacit, being possessed by scientists responsible for the pilot trial. The sharing of this knowledge between sites was not a quick or simple process, and was done by transferring the scientists responsible for the pilot to the new larger trial site. There the scientists were able to share their knowledge with local site engineers, who had a detailed understanding of the capabilities of the equipment and facilities on their site. While this introduced a delay to the product development process, this was found to be the only way that relevant staff could share their context-dependent, and largely tacit, situated knowledge.

Stop and think

Is situated knowledge always likely to be difficult to share and communicate? Are there work contexts where its transferral may be straightforward, such as in hotel, restaurant, supermarket, and shop chains, where work contexts are designed to be generic?

Overall therefore, a number of writers, drawing on a practice-based perspective on knowledge, suggest that the context specificity of the knowledge possessed by workers in N-V work contexts makes sharing knowledge and collaborative working in such contexts difficult.

The social dynamics of cross-boundary knowledge processes in N-V organizations

This section focuses on sociocultural issues that affect people's willingness to share and collectively utilize their knowledge within N-V organizations. As was made clear in Chapter 4, due to both the potential tensions that exist, because of the nature of the employment relationship between worker and employer over how a worker's knowledge is used, as well as the potential for interpersonal and intergroup conflict which exists in all organizations, people cannot be assumed to be willing to share their knowledge with others. Further, Symon (2000), in a review of the literature on the role of ICTs in N-V organizations concludes that people's willingness to use such ICTs should also not be taken for granted. Thus, the effectiveness of knowledge processes is fundamentally dependent upon people being willing to share and use their knowledge with others.

The dilemma of knowledge-sharing/hoarding

One way of characterizing the process by which people decide whether and how to participate in knowledge-related activities is to consider them as social dilemmas (Cabrera and Cabrera 2002; Dyer and Nobeoka 2000; Hollingshead et al. 2002). Cabrera and Cabrera argue that the dilemma people face over whether to share or hoard their knowledge is equivalent to the classical public-good dilemma. A public good is a shared resource which members of a community or network can benefit from, regardless of whether they contributed to it or not, and whose value does not diminish through such usage. A public park is an example of a public good. Knowledge can be considered a public good because people can benefit from using the knowledge of others without the value of the knowledge being reduced (Hollingshead et al. 2002). The choice for people in such a situation is thus to 'free ride' by using the knowledge available in a network without contributing to it, or to contribute knowledge to the network, and thus make it available to others. The dilemma in this situation for people is that while free-riding offers the greatest level of individual utility, if everyone acted as a free-rider, the value of the shared resource would diminish.

Stop and think

If a public good is a shared resource whose value does not diminish through use, to what extent can knowledge be considered a public good? Does the use of shared knowledge diminish or affect its value? Is there a risk that sharing it with large numbers of people may reduce its value?

Understanding the share/hoard knowledge decision individuals evaluate as a dilemma usefully emphasizes the complexity of this process, and also helps to explain why different people can make different decisions in quite similar circumstances. The rest of this section examines the range of factors that typically influence people's decisions on whether to share their knowledge or not, and what organizations can attempt to do to create a willingness among workers to share and use their knowledge.

Factors shaping attitudes to knowledge-sharing in N-V work contexts

Research shows that a wide range of different factors affect the willingness of workers to actively participate in the type of ICT-mediated knowledge processes that are typical in N-V modes of organizing. Thus, as discussed in Chapters 4 and 8, Hayes and Walsham (2000), utilizing a Foucauldian-based analysis suggest that the potential for surveillance in ICT-mediated knowledge processes will affect, and may inhibit, the participation of workers. Jarvenpaa and Staples (2000) conclude that factors such an individual's personal propensity to share knowledge as well as their perception of the quality of the knowledge in ICT-mediated media will affect participation levels.

McClure Wasko and Faraj (2000) also found that people actively contributed to ICT-mediated knowledge processes to show a commitment to and promote communities that they felt a part of. Finally, Ardichvili et al. (2003), based on a study of ICT-mediated knowledge-sharing in an N-V context in Caterpillar, a US-based multinational which designs and manufactures heavy construction and mining equipment, found a wide range of factors which affected the willingness of workers to both share their own knowledge and search for the knowledge of others (see Table 12.3)

These studies therefore show how the willingness of workers to actively participate in knowledge processes in N-V contexts is shaped by a complex range of factors. Conceptualizing knowledge use in N-V contexts as a dilemma involving workers conducting a risk/reward calculation, suggests that organizations can affect such attitudes

Table 12.3. Factors affecting knowledge-sharing/searching attitudes in virtual work groups (adapted from Ardichvili et al. 2003)

	Knowledge-sharing	**Knowledge-searching**
Factors creating a willingness to participate in knowledge processes.	• knowledge regarded as a 'public good' belonging to network, not individual. • commitment to organization and/or network. • personal benefits in terms of status/reward.	• helps integrate people into a new organization. • provides a medium through which people can interact with others who it would otherwise be difficult to communicate with. • have received useful advice from specific individuals previously. • network regarded as useful for keeping 'up to date'.
Factors inhibiting people's motivation to participate in knowledge processes.	• fear that contribution may be wrong. • feeling amongst newer staff of not having adequate experience to be able to contribute. • contributing is a time consuming process.	• people with established face-to-face communities may prefer to use them rather than virtual networks. • questions felt to require specific knowledge, and not relevant beyond narrow context.

through reducing the risks/costs and/or increase the rewards to workers for their knowledge-related behaviours (Cabrera and Cabrera 2002; Hollingshead et al. 2002). For example, reducing the costs/risks could involve minimizing the complexity and time involved in knowledge-sharing, or rewarding people (financially or otherwise) for appropriate behaviours.

Stop and think

Apart from providing financial rewards, and making the process simple, what else can be done by organizations to encourage workers to share their knowledge with others in N-V work contexts?

The following two subsections examine in detail two important factors that can have a particularly significant influence on the social dynamics of knowledge processes: firstly, the nature of the N-V collaboration being undertaken and secondly, the extent to which people identify with and trust others in such contexts, and who regard their knowledge as belonging to the network as a whole, has been found to be key to knowledge-sharing attitudes by a range of studies.

The nature of collaborative relations and knowledge dynamics

As discussed earlier, and illustrated in Figure 12.1, there is an enormous diversity in the type of collaborative networks that exist. One of the dimensions utilized by Cravens et al. (1996) in their taxonomy of network types was the nature of the relationship between network partners. In the Craven's taxonomy, network relations were characterized as existing on a spectrum between transactional-based relations, to more long-term, deeply involved, collaborative relations. Hardy et al. (2003) build from such insights and examine an important, but relatively neglected topic: how the nature of the collaborative relationship within a network affects the knowledge processes that occur within such networks. Further, Hardy et al. specifically focus on processes of knowledge creation.

Hardy et al. (2003) develop an analysis based on a detailed longitudinal case study of a range of collaborative relations developed by a single voluntary organization (see example immediately below). Thus while they develop an interesting analysis, the generalizibility of their conclusions have yet to be tested. They found the ability to create knowledge within collaborative networks was related to the level and character of the involvement between network partners, with involvement being measured in terms of three dimensions (see Table 12.4). The type of involvement that was most favourable to the creation of knowledge was collaborations that:

(1) had a deep level of interaction,

(2) were characterized by partnership based, rather than a transactional type of network structures, and,

(3) where knowledge flows were two-directional rather than unidirectional.

Hardy et al. (2003), drawing on a practice-based perspective on knowledge, suggest that the reason for this was because knowledge is highly tacit and contextually embedded, the interactions necessary between people to create new knowledge require to be extensive. Thus, high involvement relations are most likely to foster the type of interaction necessary for the creation of knowledge in network organizations.

ILLUSTRATING THE ISSUES

Network Relations and Knowledge Creation

Hardy et al. conducted a longitudinal, qualitative study of a range of collaborative networks developed by a single Palestinian non-governmental organization, Mere et Enfant, which was concerned with improving child nutrition within the occupied territories of the West Bank and Gaza Strip. Mere et Enfant had about sixty full-time staff, and developed an explicit strategy of utilizing inter-organizational networks to improve its effectiveness. Over the period studied (1994–7), Mere et Enfant developed eight separate collaborative networks with a range of organizations including Medicins Sans Frontiers, the Oslo School of Nutrition, Peace on Earth (a Japanese charity), the World Food Program, and Oxfam. However, not only did the purpose of each collaborative network vary, the nature of the collaborative relationship developed also varied significantly. Based on the analytical framework they developed, the type of relations that existed within each network were characterized as having variable levels of involvement (see Table 12.4). For example, the relationship developed with Peace on Earth had a high level of involvement, as the depth of interaction between staff was high, a partnership structure was developed, and information flows were both bidirectional and multidirectional. In contrast, the relationship developed with Oxfam had a low level of involvement. This was because there was a shallow depth of interaction between staff, a transactional structure was utilized, and information flowed unidirectionally (from Mere et Enfant to Oxfam). Hardy et al. found the type of high-involvement relationship developed with Peace on Earth was more conducive to the creation of knowledge than that developed with Oxfam.

Table 12.4. Factors affecting the character of involvement between partners in a collaborative network (adapted from Hardy et al. 2003)

Interactions among network partners	Type of collaborative structure	Direction of knowledge flows
Measured in terms of depth within hierarchy that staff are directly involved in networking activities.	1. *transaction*: no new structure created. Resource simply pooled or exchanged.	1. *Unidirectional*: from one partner to another only.
Shallow interaction as those which only involve senior management.	2. *partnership*: a specific structure created within which collaborating partners work.	2. *Bidirectional*: significant amounts of knowledge flow both from and to network partners.
Deep interactions are those which involve staff from a number of layers in the organizational hierarchy.	3. *representation*: where partners in a collaboration represent each other to external, third parties.	3. *multidirectional*: knowledge flows not only between network partners, but to third parties outside the network.

Trust, identity, shared values, and knowledge as a network good

In understanding what affects workers' motivation to share their knowledge with their co-workers, the concept of trust is of fundamental importance. As discussed in Chapters 3 and 4, if workers do not have a high level of trust in their co-workers, managers or, more abstractly, their organization, they are much less likely to willingly utilize their knowledge than if they had a high level of trust in these people, groups, and/or institutions. For example, Cascio (1999) and Mirchandani (1999) highlight the importance of a trusting relationship existing between N-V workers and their managers. Ardichvili et al. (2003) discuss the importance of the extent to which workers trust their employer in general. Finally, trust between co-workers is also vitally important (Ardichvili et al. 2003; Darthe and Snyder 2001; Nandhakumar 1999).

The importance of trust between co-workers is reinforced by the fact that N-V work contexts are equivalent to the sort of intercommunity, boundary-spanning, knowledge processes examined in Chapter 6, where workers who collaborate typically have a weak sense of common identity, limited shared of common knowledge, and possibly divergent values. In such contexts, the issue of trust is particularly significant, as the development of some level of trust is a likely to be necessary to create a willingness among workers to share their knowledge with others.

As illustrated in Chapter 6, trust is a complex concept, largely because it has been shown to be multidimensional. Thus, there are distinctive types of trust, which produce and affect social relations differently, and which are developed in dissimilar ways (see Table 6.4). In general, a willingness to share knowledge is most likely when the strongest forms of trust exist (Zucker's process-based and Newell & Swan's companion-based trust), and least likely when only weak forms of trust exist (institutional- or commitment- based trust).

What is indisputable is that when some level of shared knowledge, values, and identity exists in N-V work contexts, positive benefits flow, in terms of work attitudes and behaviours in general and more specifically in terms of people's willingness to collectively utilize their knowledge (Dyer and Nobeoka 2000; Jarvenpaa and Ives 1994; Orlikowsiki 2002). For example, Ahuja and Carley (1999) describe a successful virtual research network in which a strong sense of common interest and trust existed between participants. Further, Moon and Sproul (2002) argue that the successful development of Linux, open source software, which was developed by a self-organizing, voluntary group with a strong leader, was based on the sense of common identity and shared values that existed and was sustained by the project's collaborators.

A variety of methods can be utilized by organizations to create such conditions and attitudes. Two specific ways of doing this include facilitating and encourage communication between co-workers (such as through the creation of a diverse range of communication channels, or enhancing the richness of communication media) and through publicizing information about workers' knowledge-sharing contributions (Cabrera and Cabrera 2002). From a practice-based perspective on knowledge, the most effective way to develop trust, shared values, and common knowledge is through utilizing tasks that bring workers together. For example, in Kappa, the geographically dispersed software development company examined by Orlikowski (2002) that was discussed in Chapter 11 (see Table 11.4), it was a range of work practices which was fundamental in creating a sense of collective organizational identity. The example presented below of Toyota's supply chain network shows how such a sense of shared identity and common purpose can also be developed within interorganizational networks.

ILLUSTRATING THE ISSUES

Toyota: knowledge-sharing in a supply chain network

Dyer and Nobeoka (2000) suggest that Toyota has been successful in creating a supply chain network among its component suppliers, where extensive, interorganizational knowledge-sharing occurs. Further, they conclude that this knowledge-sharing pattern is a fundamental component in Toyota's ability to be sustainably innovative. It does this through dealing with the factors which typically inhibit knowledge-sharing, such as the free-rider problem, narrow self-interest, and concerns that there is a significant possibility of negative consequences flowing from knowledge-sharing. Firstly, Toyota utilizes a number of working practices that simultaneously allow the development of a sense of network identity, and facilitate the sharing of knowledge. This includes the creation and management of a Toyota specific supplier association that organizes formal conferences, training courses, and social events. This association provides a useful way of both creating a sense of identity and allowing the sharing of relatively explicit knowledge. There is also an internal Toyota consulting team that provides both intensive and extensive support to suppliers to address specific problems they may have. Finally, the sharing of knowledge between suppliers is facilitated through the use of 'voluntary' learning groups (Totoya is responsible for creating these groups, and the topics they focus on), and interfirm personnel transfers. These collective practices all facilitate the sharing of tacit knowledge through face-to-face interactions, and joint problem-solving activities that bring relevant staff together. Secondly, to further underpin appropriate knowledge-sharing behaviours among suppliers, Toyota has created a number of rules. The first rule is that free-riding is banned, and companies are only allowed to become Toyota suppliers if they agree to share knowledge with Toyota and its other suppliers. Secondly, there are also informal rules regarding the distribution of benefits that companies derive from knowledge they acquire within the network, where it is expected that, in the long term, economic benefits will be passed to the rest of the network through cost reductions passed on to Toyota. Through these various mechanisms, Toyota is able to create a common sense of purpose, and a shared sense of identity amongst its suppliers. Further, to some extent as a consequence of this, staff in these organizations regard their knowledge as being a public good which should be used for the benefit of all in the Toyota network. Thus people are less concerned to hoard their knowledge, or protect it for the narrow benefits of themselves or their own organization, and are willing to share it with others in Toyota's supply chain network, in the knowledge it should provide benefits for all in the network.

Stop and think

Dyer and Nobeoka take little account of issues such as power and conflict. However, Toyota is much more powerful than the suppliers it develops relations with. To what extent is the supply chain network that Dyer and Nobeoka describe the result of Toyota making use of its power to create the type of supply chain network that it wants? What scope are the suppliers likely to have to negotiate the conditions of their working relationship with Toyota and its other suppliers?

In conclusion, to understand what makes people willing to share and utilize their knowledge in N-V work contexts, it is necessary to understand the sociocultural factors that are so important in shaping such attitudes and behaviours. While this section has shown that it is possible for organizational management to use a range of interventions to create the sense of network-based identity and the type of trust which is typically necessary for people to be willing to share their knowledge with others, the difficulties of doing so should not be underestimated.

ICT-mediated knowledge processes in N-V forms of organizing

This section considers the relationship between ICTs and N-V forms of organizing, as well as the social dynamics of ICT-mediated knowledge processes in such work contexts, which involves returning to issues discussed in Chapter 8. The relationship between ICTs and N-V forms of working is of such fundamental importance that it is impossible to fully understand the character of, or catalysts underpinning N-V forms of working without accounting for the role of ICTs. The rapid pace in the evolution of ICTs represents one of the catalysts to the emergence of N-V form of organizing, as the contemporary function-ality of ICTs represent one of the enabling factors that make such forms of organizing possible. Thus it is almost impossible to find an analysis of N-V forms of organizing which don't make reference to the enabling role of ICTs (see, for example, Cravens et al. 1996; Jarvenpaa and Ives 1994; Staples et al. 1999; Jackson 1999).

ILLUSTRATING THE ISSUES

Shell: A web-based global knowledge management system
....

Carrington (2002) describes a web-based knowledge management system utilized by Shell International Exploration and Production (SIEP). SIEP is a worldwide operation, with staff being globally dispersed. A knowledge management system was implemented with the objective of helping people to share knowledge across sites. In all, eleven knowledge communities were set up, with three focused on specific business functions, and eight for support functions such as IT and HR, with the size of the communities varying from 700 to 4000. There are two aspects to the system. Firstly, people can ask for responses to specific questions, placed on a globally accessi-ble forum. Second, there is an indexed, searchable archive of previous questions and answers that people can use. The type of knowledge shared is typically 'hard factual stuff' (32), knowledge that is relatively objective and highly codified. For example, a Brazilian team had problems recov-ering a broken tool from a borehole and so decided to ask for answers on the forum. Within twenty-four hours they had received a variety of responses, and on the basis of them were able to solve their problem. People were initially reluctant to use the system, due to concerns about how much time would be involved, and whether they were 'giving away' precious knowledge. Knowledge-sharing was also inhibited by a system of divisional benchmarking which ranked divisions against each other. However, once these concerns were dealt with Shell believed the system had become successful, and estimate that it has helped them save over £100m.

Stop and think

One of the initial problems inhibiting knowledge-sharing on the global KM system was that while divisions were benchmarked against each other, the system involved sharing knowledge between divisions. To what extent is this issue likely to be typical in network forms of organizing? Further, does this mean that organizations moving towards network-based structures need to re-evaluate the way the performance of business units and functions is monitored and rewarded?

The problem with too much of this rhetoric, however, is that in its optimism it is somewhat blind to the limitations that persist, even now, in the information-processing and communication capabilities of ICTs, which inhibit N-V forms of organizing. The debates in the literature on the role of ICTs in N-V forms of organizing mirror the debates in the general ICT-based knowledge management literature described in Chapter 8.

For example, it is apparent that in the literature on the role of ICTs in N-V forms of working, both objectivist and practice-based perspectives on knowledge are utilized. Those writing from an objectivist perspective assume that knowledge can be codified and made explicit, and thus managed/shared directly via ICTs (see Shell example). Such writing emphasizes how databases, searchable archives, and structured discussion boards can be used to communicate and share knowledge within dispersed networks. Others utilize a practice-based perspective, where it is assumed that ICTs can play a more indirect role in facilitating the maintenance and development of the type of social relations which underpin knowledge processes. For example, Ardichvili et al. (2003) argue that ICTs can support and enhance processes of communication and interaction amongst pre-existing communities of practice.

Two issues related to ICT-mediated knowledge processes that are relevant to N-V forms of organizing are:

- While ICT- mediated communication may be able to help sustain social relations between people who already know each other, this form of communication is more problematic for the development of social relations between people with little knowledge of each other (McLoughlin and Jackson 1999).

- Social relations are unlikely to be strong if mediated *purely* by ICTs, and the development of a strong social relationship typically requires an element of face-to-face interaction.

The literature on knowledge processes in N-V organizations is typically sensitive to these issues and generally concludes that to develop and sustain the type of social relations conducive to effective knowledge-sharing requires a certain level of face-to-face interaction between workers. Thus, one of the most significant managerial implications flowing from this is that in organizations moving towards N-V structures it is important to ensure that there are adequate opportunities for workers to be able to interact and communicate face-to-face.

Conclusion

Evidence suggests that one of the main aspects in the contemporary restructuring of organizational forms has been to move away from hierarchical-based structures towards virtual- and network-based structures. The rationale underpinning this transition is that N-V forms of organizing, due to the way they transcend traditional organizational boundaries, and support horizontal as well as vertical communication in organizations, are more effective for sharing and integrating knowledge than hierarchical structures. The importance of such processes is in turn related to the dynamic character of contemporary business environments, which require organizations to be flexible and continuously adaptable.

ICTs and N-V forms of organizing were also shown to have a complex, symbiotic relationship, with the processing power, and pace of change of ICTs representing both a catalyst to and enabler of N-V forms of organizing. However, despite the (often blind) optimism regarding the ability of ICTs to facilitate N-V forms of organizing, the difficulties of managing and sustaining knowledge processes in an ICT-mediated context that were discussed in Chapter 8 were acknowledged. Thus, even with the powerful capabilities of contemporary ICTs, ICT-mediated communication still constrains the type of social interactions that can be undertaken, and affects the extent to which highly tacit knowledge can be effectively shared.

As N-V forms of organizing typically bridge and transcend traditional intra- and inter-organizational boundaries, through requiring the collaboration of people from different functions, business units, and/or organizations, knowledge processes in such contexts represent a specific example of the cross-boundary knowledge processes examined in Chapter 6. Thus the people collaborating in N-V forms of organizing will typically possess specific and specialized knowledge, and collectively may have a limited amount of common/shared/mutual knowledge, and possibly only have a weak sense of shared identity.

In N-V work contexts, creating a willingness among people to share their knowledge, and participate in collaborative knowledge processes was found to be predicated on the existence and development of trust and a shared sense of identity. When such trust exists people are likely to regard their knowledge more as a public good than an individual possession and are thus more likely to make it available to the network of collaborators, rather than to hoard it or and use it in a narrow, self-interested way.

REVIEW QUESTIONS

1 Based on your own experiences of, and knowledge of work, how common is the 'free-rider' problem in organizational life? Further, what affects whether people are likely to 'free-ride' on collective goods/knowledge? Is a sense of identity with and commitment to a community/network typically enough to make free-riding unlikely?

2 Network forms or organizing can be intra- or inter-organizational. How different will be the process of developing of a common/shared sense of identity in these two types of networks? What factors will affect the dynamics of such processes?

3   In analyses of the advantages of network and virtual organizational structures, stark contrasts are usually made with hierarchical structures, which implicitly assumes they are oppositional in nature. However, to what extent is this a false dichotomy? How compatible are hierarchical principles with N-V structures?

FURTHER READING

- J. Dyer, and K. Nobeoka (2000). 'Creating and Managing a High-Performance Knowledge-Sharing Network: The Toyota Case'. *Strategic Management Journal*, 21: 345–67.

  A detailed case study of how knowledge-sharing is encouraged and facilitated within Toyota's supply chain network.

- D. Sole, and A. Edmondson (2002). 'Situated Knowledge and Learning in Dispersed Teams', *British Journal of Management*, 13: S17–34.

  A theoretical and empirical examination of the problems of sharing context-specific knowledge in dispersed work environments.

- A. Ardichvili, V. Page, and T. Wentling (2003). 'Motivation and Barriers to Participation in Virtual Knowledge-Sharing Communities of Practice', *Journal of Knowledge Management*, 7/1: 64–77.

  Examines the sociocultural factors related to knowledge-sharing/searching in communities of practice where interaction is largely mediated by ICTs.

- C. Hardy, N. Phillips, and T. Lawrence (2003). 'Resources, Knowledge and Influence: The Organizational Effects on Interorganizational collaboration', *Journal of Management Studies*, 40/2: 321–47.

  Examines how the nature of collaborative relations affects knowledge creation processes.

13

Knowledge processes in global multinationals

Introduction

This chapter examines the dynamics of knowledge processes within large, global multinational corporations. The focus here is not on how companies grow to become global, but on the knowledge dynamics within already large, internationalized organizations. This represents an interesting and important context for the examination of such issues for a number of reasons.

Firstly, the economic importance of such organizations grew significantly in the last quarter of the twentieth century. Driven by a combination of interrelated processes such as market deregulation, rapid advances in information and communication technologies, and growth through mergers and acquisitions, not only has there been a process of globalization, whereby more and more companies are becoming globally active, but there has also been a growth in the number of large organizations, and in the size of already large organizations (Carchedi 1991, ch. 7; Korten 1995; WIR 1999). Von Krogh et al. (1996) characterize this trajectory as involving a two-stage evolution from international to multinational firms, and from multinational firms into global firms. Korten (1995, 121), using an element of hyperbole, suggests that this change has been so significant that it represented, 'the most rapid and sweeping institutional transformation in human history'.

Exemplars of the type of company considered here include: Ernst & Young, the professional service company which employs over 105,000 people, who work from over 670 locations in over 130 countries; Boeing the aerospace corporation which employs over 160,000 workers in thirty-eight states of the USA as well a seventy countries globally; and IBM the computer company which employs over 300,000 staff in more than 100 different countries globally.[7]

 Global multinational corporation

A large multidivisional organization which has sites throughout the world and whose business is global in character.

---

[7] This information was taken from the following websites on 16 June 2003 (www.EY.com, www.Boeing.com, www.IBM.com).

Secondly, global companies have typically been in the vanguard of attempts to develop knowledge management solutions/systems, have been some of the most enthusiastic advocates of the benefits of knowledge management, and have generally been the earliest at realizing the potential of knowledge management (KPMG 2000; McAdam and Reid 2001). Thus, for example on Boeing's corporate website (www.Boeing.com)[8] the third of its three corporate objectives is to, 'share best practice and technology across businesses'. Further, as illustrated by the example considered in Chapter 12, Shell International Exploration and Production (SIEP) have also become aware of the benefits of internal knowledge-sharing.

Finally, as will be become apparent as the chapter progresses, because global multi-national organizations have highly dispersed and fragmented knowledge bases, employ large numbers of employees, and involve the communication and interaction of people with diverse sociocultural beliefs, the dynamics of knowledge processes in such organiza-tions are quite particular.

In examining knowledge processes in this context the chapter links together issues already examined, with some new themes. Specifically, issues returned to include the distributed nature of organizational knowledge, the dynamics of knowledge-sharing across boundaries, and how social factors affect knowledge processes. These topics are then linked with two themes not examined thus far: organizational size and cross-cultural knowledge processes.

The chapter is structured into three sections, with the issues examined in each being illustrated and supported by different examples. The first section examines the relation-ship between the structuring of multinational corporations and the knowledge dynamics within them. Following this, the second section considers how organizational size affects the dynamics of organizational knowledge processes, and generally concludes that the greater the size of the organizations, the more complicated its knowledge dynamics are likely to be. The third section then concludes the chapter by examining cross-cultural knowledge processes, and considers how the sociocultural values that people possess affect organizational knowledge processes.

The structuring of multinationals and knowledge processes

As outlined in Chapter 3, the practice-based perspective on knowledge assumes that because the knowledge people possess is closely linked to the physical and cognitive activities they undertake, and is embedded in the social context in which such activity occurs, the knowledge base of all organizations will be fragmented into specialist sub-communities. From this perspectives, one of the key and most difficult tasks of manage-ment is to link together and coordinate the organizational knowledge base (Brown and Duguid 1998; Grant 1996; Kogut and Zander 1992; Tsoukas 1996). While the objectivist perspective has a different conceptualization of knowledge, and typically assumes that it can be more easily codified, those analyses of knowledge utilizing such a perspective

---

[8] Site accessed 16 June 2003.

also acknowledge the complexities of sharing and integrating knowledge within multinational corporations (Gupta and Govindarajan 2001; Szulanski 1996; Tsai 2001).

In global multinational corporations such as those outlined in the introduction to this chapter, which may employ tens of thousands of workers, operating from possibly hundreds of different sites, dispersed across the globe, the task of coordinating and integrating organizational knowledge is non-trivial. However, the flip-side of having such a diversified knowledge base is that it creates enormous potential for synergy to be developed through intra-organizational learning and interaction (Macharzina et al. 2001; Morosini 1998; Soderberg and Holden 2001; Van Maanen and Laurent 1993). Thus possessing a large, fragmented knowledge base has both potential benefits and problems.

One way of supporting and facilitating intra-organizational knowledge processes is through the structuring of organizations. However, the diversity of ways in which MNCs are structured in practice suggests that there is no consensus on the best way to facilitate intra-organizational knowledge-sharing. The rest of this section considers the knowledge-sharing implications of utilizing two particular structural forms: a centralized, hierarchical-based structure and a decentralized network structure.

The centralized hierarchical structure

This means of structuring a multinational corporation assumes that the home base of the corporation, the country out of which a multinational originates, provides a platform and a foundation from which global advantage can be achieved (Macharzina et al. 2001). In such organizations global expansion occurs largely through taking advantage of the home bases' capabilities, which are developed from, based in, and exploit national and regional systems of innovation. Porter (1990), for example, suggests that such a logic is highly prevalent. Laurent (1983, 1986) also supports such a perspective, and argues that all multinationals to some extent bear the stamp of the country from which they originate.

Based on this model the corporate centre, which will be based in the home country is typically large and where not only the vast majority of strategic decisions are made, but where research and development type knowledge-creating activities are also located (see Figure 13.1). Within such organizations knowledge flows unidirectionally, from the corporate centre out to the organizations business units, which are largely responsible for applying this knowledge to their local market context. Finally, another characteristic of this model is that there are few independent interconnections between different business units. The importance of such a structural logic is also reinforced by those writers who suggest that the extent to which multinationals are truly international has been exaggerated, and that the majority of multinationals are still home or region centred (Hirst and Thompson 1999; Rugman 2000).

Stop and think

To what extent are contemporary multinational corporations independent of the countries in which they originated? If you compare multinational corporations that originated in the USA, UK, France, Germany, Russia, China, Japan, etc, can you discern differences in the way they operate that are related to their country of origin?

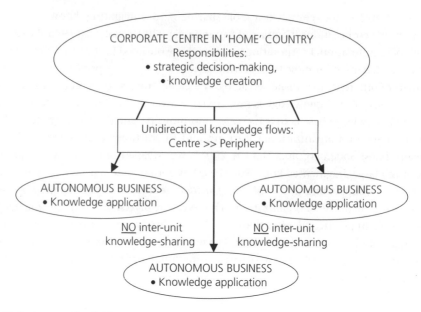

Fig. 13.1. A centralized, hierarchical structure for multinationals

ILLUSTRATING THE ISSUES

Dell: codification strategy and centralized structure

Hansen et al. (1999), as discussed in Chapter 9, suggested there were two broad knowledge management strategies that companies could pursue: a codification or a personalization strategy. Dell, the computer manufacturing and retailing company, was one company they described which followed a codification-based strategy. Such a strategy is IT-based, and involves the codification of knowledge into searchable repositories (see Table 9.1). With such an approach, the knowledge in the repository can easily be reused by anyone. Dell combines this type of knowledge management strategy, with a centralized, hierarchical structure. Dell utilizes a knowledge repository to sell computers direct to their customers, who define the specification of their machines (either on the web or via a telephone call with a customer sales assistant) through selecting components from the knowledge repository. Dell, which has over 34,000 employees worldwide, spread across thirty four different countries, utilizes a centralized corporate structure. Thus national/regional offices, whose main responsibilities are for selling computers, or providing after-sales support and servicing to customers, do not have much of a role in strategic decision-making, and are more concerned with administration and knowledge application than with knowledge creation (such as designing or managing the IT-based knowledge repository).

Stop and think

Is there a risk with such a strategy that Dell will be less sensitive to the particular demands of local markets than if it used a more decentralized strategy?

The decentralized network structure

As Chapter 12 shows, the network logic for the structuring of multinationals is currently extremely influential, with the path-breaking work of Ghoshal and Bartlett doing much to initiate this way of conceptualizing the internal structure of multinationals (Ghoshal and Bartlett 1990; Bartlett and Ghoshal 1993).

With a network-based structure, in contrast to centralized hierarchical structures, knowledge creation is not the sole responsibility of the corporate centre, with there being multiple centres of knowledge creation (see Figure 13.2). Secondly, knowledge can flow equally in both directions between the corporate centre and business units. Thirdly, there are many interconnections between interdependent business units, with a diversity of mechanisms being used (such as staff transferrals between units, matrix structures, etc.) to facilitate such interactions. Finally, these are typically complex organizational structures that don't have a clear hierarchy. Hedlund (1986, 1994) used the term 'heterarchy' to describe this structural form. Primarily, within a network structure, business units are not controlled in a top-down way by the corporate centre.

This structural form, as illustrated in Chapter 12, has a number of advantages over hierarchical structures in terms of knowledge processes. Primarily, the network structure more effectively facilitates the sharing of knowledge between business units (Tregaskis 2003; van Wijk and van den Bosch 2000). Grant (1996), in his development of the knowledge-based theory of the firm, also suggests that hierarchical coordination is bad for sharing

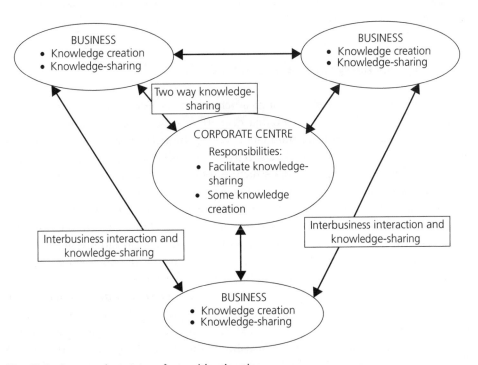

Fig. 13.2. A network structure for multinationals

and integrating knowledge. Grant, in what amounts to a knowledge-based justification for organizational delayering argues that the disadvantage of hierarchical structures is that they are ineffective at sharing tacit knowledge, as they primarily utilize systems of rules and regulations to coordinate activity and integrate knowledge, which are poor for sharing tacit knowledge. The most effective means of sharing such knowledge is through processes of direct interaction between people, where there are minimal levels of hierarchy, such as in the network form.

ILLUSTRATING THE ISSUES

N. V. Philips: the network structuring of a multinational

Ghoshal and Bartlett (1990) use the Dutch electrical goods company as an exemplar of how a multinational can be conceptualized as a network. Philips can be considered to be a multinational company as it has operating units in over sixty countries worldwide. While the company's corporate base in Holland is undoubtedly the single most important hub in the organizational network, Philips's structure is closer to a network than a hierarchy. Thus, many of its business units are extremely large, constituting some of the largest organizations in the counties they are located in. There are also different centres for research and development. Thus, many of Philips's business units are not simply responsible for the application of knowledge created at the corporate centre, but have knowledge creation responsibilities as well. Finally, there is also a diversity of interconnections between business units, facilitating the sharing of knowledge between them. Thus for example the business units in regions such as Africa, Europe, the Americas, and Asia-Australasia are linked together in regional networks.

A contingency perspective on structure

Birkinshaw et al. (2002), in an interesting article that deserves to be widely read, provide an analysis that challenges the logic that network forms of organization represent the most effective way of organizing multinational companies in *every* situation. Overall their analysis takes a contingency-based perspective to organizational design, and concludes that the design of an organization's structure should account for the character of its knowledge base. Their analysis considered how the level of observability and the degree of system embeddedness of an organization's knowledge were linked to the degree of autonomy and integration between business units. Observability refers to the ease with which an activity can be understood by simply looking at an organizational process, or its products, whereas system embeddedness refers to the extent to which knowledge is a function of the system or context in which it is developed and used.

While their analysis was based on research into the R&D activities in a handful of Swedish multinationals, making it difficult to generalize widely, they found a strong relationship to exist between organizational structure and the degree of system embeddedness of organizational knowledge. Specifically they found that the degree of system embeddedness of organizational knowledge was inversely proportional to the level of

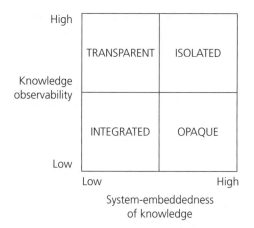

Fig. 13.3. A typology of organizational knowledge bases (from Birkinshaw et al. 2002)

inter-unit integration. Therefore, when the knowledge in an organization is highly system embedded, the level of inter-unit integration is likely to be low, due to the difficulties and problems involved in sharing such knowledge.

Based on the two dimensions of knowledge they utilized they developed a typology, characterizing the knowledge in R&D units into four generic types (see Figure 13.3). Birkinshaw et al. (2002) suggest that different structures are thus likely to be appropriate for each type of knowledge base. Extrapolating from this framework it could be argued that hierarchical structures are most appropriate when organizational knowledge is 'transparent' (i.e. when it has a high-level observability and a low level of embeddedness) as in such circumstances knowledge can be relatively easily codified and shared. Further, network forms of organization may be most appropriate when organizational knowledge is 'integrated' (i.e. when knowledge has a low level of observability, and a low level of embeddedness), as the effective sharing of such knowledge requires extensive and direct social interaction between people.

Overall therefore this section has outlined two different ways in which multinational companies can be structured, and shown how the knowledge dynamics within them vary substantially. In general, network structures are more conducive to processes of knowledge-sharing/searching than hierarchical structures. Further, drawing on Birkinshaw et al.'s (2002) analysis it was concluded that the most appropriate structure for a multinational corporation to adopt may depend on the dominant characteristics of their knowledge base. This analysis has significant managerial implications, as it suggests that in the development of business and knowledge strategies, as well as the design of organizational structures, attention requires to be paid to the character of the organizational knowledge base.

Organizational size and knowledge processes

As far back as 1987, Whitley suggested that organizational size required to be taken more seriously as a variable of analysis in the study of organizational behaviour. However, in general terms, his call has gone unheeded. The literature on knowledge management is no exception in this respect, as the relationship between organizational size and the dynamics of knowledge processes has in general terms been neglected (exceptions include Fenton and Pettigrew 2000b; van Wijk and van den Bosch 2000; Becker 2001; and Forsgren 1997).

As has been discussed extensively elsewhere in the book, the typically fragmented, specialized, and dispersed nature of the knowledge base in most organizations means that one of the key tasks for management is to coordinate and integrate organizational knowledge. In general, as organizational size increases, the more complicated the process of knowledge coordination becomes, as the organizational knowledge base becomes more and more fragmented and dispersed. Drawing on Brown and Duguid's (1991) metaphor of an organization as a 'community of communities', the more organizational (sub) communities that exist, the more likely it is that process of coordinating and facilitating their interactions will increase in complexity.

ILLUSTRATING THE ISSUES

Rabobank: the knowledge dynamics in an expanding network

Van Wijk and van den Bosch (2000) studied the evolution in the structuring of Rabobank, the Dutch-based banking and financial service company between 1988 and 1997. By the late 1990s it employed 44,000 workers with operations in over 100 countries. During the time studied, due to a variety of external and internal drivers, it evolved its internal organizational structure away from a hierarchical one towards a network-based structure. Part of the catalyst underlying this evolution was that the mergers and acquisitions undertaken by Rabobank increased the size of the organization such that business units were increasingly at arm's length from the corporate centre, and also increasingly didn't know where relevant knowledge was located.

The utilization of a network structure, it was felt, would help address these problems. However, the large size of the organization was found to make difficult the development of a single organizational network. The relationship between organization/network size and the dynamics of knowledge processes was also visible on a smaller scale, in one business unit SPECTRUM, which had been in the vanguard of developing and implementing the network-based structure. During the time that this division was studied (approximately six years), it grew from having only thirty employees to having 350. The expanding size of the SPECTRUM division significantly affected patterns of horizontal communication between staff working in its different product areas, which is one of the characteristic elements of a network structure. In general, the increasing size of the organization inhibited horizontal communication. Thus, when the division had been relatively small, such communication was widespread, but as the division grew it became increasingly uncommon, with each product group becoming more and more compartmentalized.

Stop and think

What implications do these findings have for the relevance of network structures to large organizations? Do they mean that the knowledge-related benefits of using network-based structures diminish with increasing organizational size?

However, increasing organizational size does not simply make the process of coordination more complex, it can fundamentally alter the type and character of interactions that are possible. As has been discussed in Chapters 3–6, the tacit and context-dependent character of most organizational knowledge means that effectively sharing knowledge requires extensive social interactions to occur in a context where enough trust exists for people to be willing to participate in such a process. As was extensively discussed in Chapter 6, this is particularly the case when knowledge has to be shared between people who are not members of the same community, as they may have different value systems and limited common knowledge.

Developing and sustaining the type of social relations necessary for such knowledge processes to be effective is time-consuming. Thus Hansen (1999), as well as Gargiulo and Benassi (2000), argue that sustaining strong social relationships requires continuous interactions between people and a sustained reciprocal exchange of knowledge and information. Thus there is a limit to the number of such relationships that any person can sustain at any one time. For example, in Kappa, the global R&D company researched by Orlikowski (see Chapter 11), the amount of travelling done by staff to sustain effective social relations contributed to the problem of burn-out. Thus as organizational size increases, so does the potential problems and difficulties of sustaining relationships with all the people who may have relevant knowledge and experience (see Figure 13.4 for a graphical representation of this process).

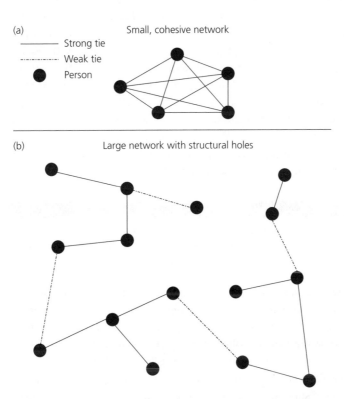

Fig. 13.4. Typical social relations within networks of different size

Table 13.1. Knowledge-related benefits and disadvantages of cohesive networks and networks with structural holes

	Cohesive networks	**Network with structural holes**
Characteristics	Tightly knit networks, where long-established social relations exist, strong norms have developed, and high levels of interpersonal trust exist	Networks where interpersonal connections are loose, limited norms exist, and interpersonal trust is limited
Advantages	Creates an environment conducive to knowledge sharing and cooperation within the network	Provides people with access to a wide range of knowledge and information which makes people open to change and a diversity of viewpoints
Disadvantages	Creates a potential rigidity, due to the effort required to sustain network (sustain norms, reciprocate where expected), which may hinder people's ability to adapt through limiting the range of knowledge and information they utilize	Knowledge-sharing and social interaction inhibited and slowed down by a lack of cohesiveness and established social norms

Becker (2001) referred to this as the problem of 'large numbers'. Becker argues that the typically dispersed character of an organization's knowledge base creates three fundamental problems/issues for organizational management, one of which is the problem of large numbers. This problem stems to two factors. Firstly, there is the issue of opaqueness, or intransparency, which refers to the difficulties of developing an overview when knowledge is fragmented and dispersed, which is a problem that increases as the level of dispersal or number of fragments increases. Secondly, is the issue of resource requirements involved in bringing together the fragments of a dispersed knowledge base, which is a problem that again increases proportionally with organizational size. Thus, for Becker, there is a direct relationship between organizational size and the difficulty of managing and integrating an organization's knowledge base.

Stop and think

Due to the amount of work involved in sustaining them, is there a limit to the number of strong ties that people can have? If so, what is the approximate size of this limit—5, 10, 20, 50, more?

Connecting these insights to the work of Gargiulo and Benassi (2000) it can be argued that the type of network relations that people can have will vary with organizational size. Gargiulo and Benassi contrast the advantages and disadvantages in terms of knowledge searching and acquisition of cohesive networks compared to networks with structural holes (see Table 13.1). In Gargiulo and Benassi's analysis the type of network that any individual possesses is determined by personal choice. However, the difficulties outlined above of trying to support a large number of strong, close social relationships means that the larger an organization becomes, the more difficult it will be for people to sustain cohesive networks with all relevant people, and the more people's social networks will become filled with structural holes (see Figure 13.4).

Thus the larger an organization, the more people's social networks will have structural holes, and the smaller an organization, the more easy it will be for people to develop, possess, and sustain cohesive networks. As a consequence, the knowledge dynamics within large and small companies are likely to be quite different. As suggested by Table 13.1 and Figure 13.4, this does not mean that large multinationals are less effective at sharing, searching for, or integrating knowledge than in small companies, simply that their knowledge dynamics will be different.

ILLUSTRATING THE ISSUES

Pharma-co: organizational size and cohesive networks

Pharma-co, as already discussed in previous examples in Chapters 3 and 8 is a UK-based pharmaceutical company, which in the late 1990s began attempting to implement an information management system that would improve intra-organizational communication and cooperation. However, at the same time, it was involved in two mergers which trebled its turnover, and doubled its number of employees (employing approximately 10,000 staff worldwide by the end of the 1990s). Within Pharma-co there had traditionally been little communication and knowledge-sharing across business units. Instead, staff in each of Pharma-co's business units had relatively cohesive localized networks, and each unit was narrowly focused on producing their own products for their own customers. This lack of communication and interaction was summed up by one manager as follows: 'the thing that is perceived to have impeded integration of the European operation is an absence of any connectivity between the manufacturing groups. . . . There is no dialogue between them at any level in Europe . . . there is no exchange of any experience or information or knowledge at all.'

Following the merger, this pattern of business unit autonomy continued. While the mergers significantly increased the size of the company, they also increased the potential benefits from inter-unit interaction, due to the increased overlap between the different business units. But, the culture of compartmentalism and isolation which facilitated the creation of local and cohesive networks that had existed prior to the mergers, became intensified following the mergers due to fears of rationalization and job losses, and acted to prevent such interactions occurring. Thus, paradoxically, while mergers improved the potential benefits of knowledge-sharing, the increased size of the organization, combined with the culture of autonomy and climate of anxiety and mistrust which emerged following the merger, combined to make the possibility of such collaboration occurring unlikely, through entrenching people even further than had been traditional within their local networks.

Stop and think

Wider evidence suggests that the post-merger situation of fear and mistrust that occurred in Pharma-co is not untypical (see Empson 2001). What can management do in such situations to develop trust, reduce fears, and facilitate knowledge-sharing processes?

In conclusion, this section has shown how organizational/network size can significantly affect the dynamics of knowledge processes. In general, as organizational size increases, not only does the complexity of managing knowledge processes increase, but the character of the network of social relations between people, which crucially underpin knowledge processes, will also change.

Knowledge sharing across sociocultural boundaries and business systems

Chapter 6 examined in detail the dynamics and complexities of knowledge processes that involve interactions between people from different communities. The specific focus here is on the dynamics of knowledge processes that involve the spanning of sociocultural boundaries as well as distinctive and quite different business systems. As has been shown already in this chapter, one characteristic of multinational corporations is the need for workers from different countries to cooperate. Thus the dynamics of such interactions are an important aspect of knowledge processes within multinationals. What are *not* examined here are the methods by which such boundaries can be surmounted to make processes of knowledge processes more effective. Such issues are dealt with in Chapter 6. The focus here is on what impact sociocultural and institutional systems have on processes of knowledge-sharing, integration, and knowledge production.

The sociocultural values that people possess, and the character of the business systems that exist, are closely interrelated, as business systems are created and reproduced by people in possession of particular sociocultural values, while simultaneously the sociocultural values people have are shaped by the character of the business systems they work in. For analytical clarity, however, these topics are examined separately here. In general, as with the issues of organizational size, neither topic has received much attention in the knowledge management literature. Thus, the illustrative examples utilized are not taken from the knowledge management literature. Nevertheless, both examples presented usefully illustrate the relationship between sociocultural values and business systems, to the dynamics of knowledge processes.

Organizational knowledge processes and bridging sociocultural differences

Sociocultural values and beliefs refer to the systems of values, knowledge, and beliefs that individual people possess. Such values are shaped by an enormous diversity of social and cultural factors including social class, the countries in which people are born and live, educational experience, family and parental influences, religion, experiences of work, professional codes of behaviour and ethics, etc. Some, most notably Hofstede (1980, 2001), argue that distinctively national cultural characteristics can be identified in different countries. But, while this perspective has been highly influential, it has simultaneously been subject to significant criticism (McSweeney 2002; Soderberg and Holden 2002).

Having said that, numerous examples can be given of differences in sociocultural values that exist, and their impact on organizational processes. In the knowledge management literature the greatest, if not sole focus, is on differences between Japan and Europe and the USA. Nonaka and Takeuchi (1995) suggest that there are quite distinctive differences between Japan and the Western world (Europe and the Americas) with regard to the way knowledge is conceptualized and used in organizations. While this could be criticized as crude cultural stereotyping, there is some evidence that there are distinctive differences between Asian and European values and attitudes. For example, Pauleen and Yoong (2001) found there to be a greater degree of respect for authority and a higher degree of formality in business relations in Japanese and Chinese cultures than in European and Australian cultures. Such differences were also shown to make misinterpretation and distortion possible in communication processes.

One explanation for the existence of the differences in sociocultural values that people across the globe possess is that they are shaped by the system of cultural values that people are born, educated, socialized, and work within. The most well-known advocate of such a perspective is Hofstede, whose influence is visible in the work of some of those who write about multinational companies, thus, Macharzina et al. (2001) talk about how knowledge is deeply culturally bound, while Van Maanen and Laurent (1993, 275) talk about how values and behaviour are shaped by 'underlying codes of meaning'.

Such differences have been shown to have a profound influence on knowledge processes. Firstly, such differences, as was discussed in Chapter 6, make the sharing and integration of knowledge between people with different systems of sociocultural values extremely complex and difficult. The lack of common knowledge, shared system of values, or overlapping sense of identity that can exist in such situations is the primary explanations for these difficulties. Secondly, the sociocultural values that people possess importantly shape the way knowledge is produced, meaning is made, and, using the language of the practice-based perspective on knowledge, how processes of perspective making and taking occur. Thus people actively use their sociocultural values to produce meaning and create knowledge, and two people may construct quite different meanings from the same events, based on their different value systems.

The example immediately below provides an illustration of such a process. Further, an acknowledgement of the role played by sociocultural values in shaping the way people create meaning and produce knowledge challenges the idea embedded in the transmitter–receiver model of knowledge-sharing utilized by the objectivist perspective on knowledge (see Chapter 2). Thus, knowledge cannot simply be diffused and transferred, unaltered, between people with different cultural values.

ILLUSTRATING THE ISSUES

Disneyland in Japan and the USA: sociocultural influences on processes of perspective making

Van Maanen and Laurent (1993) provide an analysis of how sociocultural values affect the way visitors make sense of the Disneyland Adventure parks in Tokyo and the USA. At first glance, Disneyland Tokyo looks to be a perfect replica of Disney's American theme parks. Thus it appears to contain the same cultural codes and messages, which are interpreted and received in a similar way by equally enthusiastic Japanese and American visitors. Thus, since Disneyland Tokyo opened it proved to be just as, if not more successful than the American Disneyland parks, and has been visited by enormous numbers. However, in subtle ways Disneyland Tokyo has been modified to account for different sociocultural values. Thus Disneyland Tokyo has fewer outdoor food retailers and has more sit-down restaurants than the American parks. There are some new, specific rides that describe and defend Japanese ways of life. It has picnic areas close to the park that go against Disney's values of not allowing food to be brought to its parks. Finally, in Disneyland Tokyo, but not in the American parks, white gloves are worn by vehicle drivers, while second names rather than first names are used on worker's name badges.

Van Maanen and Laurent also argue that while the same values exist in the Japanese and American parks, the way they are interpreted, and made sense of by their different audiences is fundamentally different. The dominant values in Disney's theme parks in both the USA and Japan are of order, safety, and cleanliness. However, while this is argued to appeal to the American visitors for the contrast and escape it provides to their typical life experiences, the same values appeal to its Japanese visitors because they reinforce and reflect, rather than contrast with, their dominant cultural values and life experiences. Thus Japanese visitors are recontextualizing the values of Disneyland's parks through the lens of their own sociocultural value systems, and the perspectives they make are thus totally different from those of American visitors to similar parks a continent away.

Stop and think

This case suggests that cultural values in Japan and the USA are significantly different. Do such significant differences exist between other countries?

Organizational knowledge processes and the spanning of different business systems

Lam (1997), as discussed in Chapters 6 and 11 (see, p. 78 and p. 162), identified significant differences between the UK and Japanese companies she researched both in terms of the character of their knowledge base and the dynamics of their innovation processes. Other studies by Lam (1994, 1996) also show significant differences between Japan and the UK in terms of how technical and knowledge-based work is organized. Lam (1997) suggested that the differences between the Japanese and UK companies she examined could be explained primarily by the different business systems that exist and operate in Japan and the UK.

Lam's findings fit within a broader stream of analysis that considers how the character-istics of business systems, which vary significantly across the globe, shape the work practices and strategies utilized by the companies that operate within them (Hall and Soskice 2002; Whitley 1990, 1999). As was discussed in Chapter 11, one specific subtheme within this area focuses on the existence and character of national systems of innovation. Another broad strand within this broad perspective examines how the character of business systems affects the character and role of HRM functions in organizations (Ferner 1997; Ferner et al. 2001; Varul and Ferner 2000).

Table 13.2. Key institutional dimensions shaping the character of business systems

Institutional dimensions of business systems	Examples
The degree and character of market regulation	In the USA, labour markets have much weaker legislation protecting workers' rights than in other countries
The extent of government ownership in industry	In France, compared to other Western European countries such as the UK, the government still has significant levels of ownership in a number of business sectors
The role of trade unions in business decision-making and their relations with business management	In Germany trade unions have a significant role in business decision-making through being given significant bargaining power enshrined in law
The role of banks and financial institutions in industry	In Japan banks have a powerful role at the head of large industrial groups, and have close links with large business organizations
The type of financial system and the economic performance demands they place on organizations	In the UK the financial system places pressure on businesses to focus on relatively short-term economic goals such as share price

The term 'business system', as utilized by these writers, refers to the structure of social, political, and economic institutions that constitute and shape the environment within which business organizations operate. Key institutions in these structures include governments and financial institutions. Research shows that these institutional structures vary significantly between different countries and regions, with Whitley (1999) developing a typology of six distinctive types of business systems made up from significantly different institutional structures. Some of the key aspects of the institutional structure that characterize business systems are outlined in Table 13.2, and include the nature and degree of legal regulation, as well as the character of the financial system.

ILLUSTRATING THE ISSUES

The 'Japanization' of UK industry: the role of institutional factors

Following the global diffusion of Japanese business practices and philosophies such as lean production, there have been debates regarding the extent to which such practices have been customized to local conditions. Much evidence suggests that in the UK these Japanese working practices have been significantly customized. For example, Taylor et al. (1994) refer to the 'selective and uneven' adoption of Japanese practices in a detailed study of two UK organizations. Morris et al. (2000) in a study examining twenty-three companies in the UK found there to be 'considerable divergence' from the ideal of Japanese practices. They found for example that compatibility existed in terms of the care applied to selection, recruitment, and socialization, but that the investment in training and 'high trust' cultures typical of Japanese practices were absent.

This customization of Japanese working practices can be explained by the characteristics of the UK's business system. Thus, Morris et al. (2000) argue that the differences they found could largely be explained by institutional factors. Elger and Smith (1994, 121) also suggest that the economic short-termism prevalent in the UK and the general underfunding of training this produces, has been a significant contextual factor, constraining the ability of UK managers to fully implement Japanese methods unaltered. Finally, Scarbrough and Terry (1998), in a study of two car plants in the UK Midlands, found that trade unions had a significant role following the implementation of Japanese working practices, which was anomalous with their general philosophy, which could be explained by the different historical roles played by trade unions in Japanese and UK business systems.

Thus overall, due to the constraints and pressures imposed by the specific institutional characteristics of the UK's business system, Japanese working practice and knowledge have not been implemented and transferred unaltered, but instead have been significantly customized.

Knowledge processes that span different business systems, as shown by Lam, can prove complex, due to the effect they have on the character and structuring of organizational knowledge. As the above example also shows, the sharing of knowledge across such boundaries can also result in it being changed and reconfigured. However, the general lack of attention to such issues in the contemporary knowledge literature means that the relationship between business systems and organizational knowledge processes is relatively uncharted.

Conclusion

The fragmented and dispersed character of the knowledge base within multinationals means that there are potentially significant benefits from effectively managing it. Thus the potential synergy that could be created from bringing together elements of this dispersed knowledge is enormous. This helps to explain why multinationals corporations have been some of the most enthusiastic adopters of knowledge management initiatives. However, paradoxically, these same characteristics of the knowledge base make its management an extremely complex and difficult task. This is due to both the size of the knowledge base in these organizations, which means the knowledge base is highly fragmented, combined with the fact that this knowledge is dispersed among communities which can have different sociocultural values and which operate within distinctive business systems.

One way in which multinationals can manage their knowledge base is through the way business is structured, with the chapter showing how hierarchical and network-based structures produce very different knowledge-sharing dynamics. However, Birkinshaw et al.'s (2002) contingency perspective suggests that the dominant logic that suggests that network structures are inherently better for knowledge-sharing compared to hierarchical structures, in all situations, was challenged.

The chapter also considered how organizational size, a relatively neglected topic, affects the character of knowledge processes. It was concluded that not only is organizational size directly related to the complexity of knowledge processes, but that organizational size can also fundamentally alter the character of knowledge dynamics, through shaping the type of networks that people can develop and sustain.

Finally, the chapter also considered the complexity of sharing knowledge between communities that are located in different and distinctive business systems and where people possess different sociocultural values. The sharing of knowledge across such boundaries is not a simple, direct transfer, as the sociocultural values that people possess shape the way they interpret and understand the knowledge of others. Thus knowledge-sharing in this context involves an active process of perspective-making whereby the knowledge of others is understood in relation to a person's existing values. Equally, the sharing of knowledge between people and communities who operate within different business systems was also not found to be straightforward, and typically involves the transformation and customization of any shared knowledge.

REVIEW QUESTIONS

1   Hofstede (1988, 2001) argues that distinct national cultures can be identified. To what extent does your own personal experience confirm or challenge this? Further, do such cultural differences significantly hinder processes of knowledge-sharing?

2   Ford and Chan (2003), in one of the few studies to examine the effect of cultural differences on organizational knowledge processes, found that language competences significantly affected such processes. In general, informal knowledge flows were most likely within cultural groups, while formal business-related communication was more likely between cultural groups. What do such findings say about the importance of providing language training as a way of dealing with the difficulties of cross-cultural knowledge processes?

3   The illustrative example of Dell (see p. 200) showed that it had a centralized hierarchical structure, and utilized a codification-based knowledge management strategy. To what extent are such knowledge management strategies compatible with hierarchical structures? Further, would such a knowledge management strategy be compatible with a network-based structure?

FURTHER READING

- M. Becker (2001). 'Managing Dispersed Knowledge: Organizational Problems, Managerial Strategies and their Effectiveness', *Journal of Management Studies*, 38/7: 1037–51.
  Examines how organizational size affects the character of organizational knowledge bases, as well as the most appropriate strategies for managing knowledge.

- J. Birkinshaw, R. Nobel, and J. Ridderstale (2002). 'Knowledge as a Contingency Variable: Do the Characteristics of Knowledge Predict Organizational Structure?' *Organization Science*, 13/3: 274–89.
  Provides an analysis which suggests that organizational structure needs to be sensitive to the character of an organization's knowledge base.

- A. Gupta and V. Govindarajan (2000). 'Knowledge flows within Multinational Corporations', *Strategic Management Journal*, 21: 473–96.

  Presents an objectivist perspective on the complexities of knowledge sharing in multinational corporations.

- A-M. Soderberg and N. Holden (2002). 'Rethinking Cross Cultural Management in a Globalizing Business World', *International Journal of Cross Cultural Management*, 2/1: 103–21.

  Discusses the challenges for multinational corporations of managing their knowledge bases in the contemporary business environment.

14

Knowledge-intensive firms and knowledge workers

Introduction

As was discussed in Chapter 1, many commentators and writers characterize contemporary society as being a knowledge society, with the importance of knowledge to work and economic activity having grown enormously in the last quarter of the twentieth century. The growing importance of knowledge to the world of work is also argued to have transformed both the character of the work activities people undertake, as well as the nature of organizations. Key to these transformations has been the growing importance of knowledge workers and knowledge-intensive firms. In fact, if contemporary society is a knowledge society, then almost by definition knowledge-intensive firms and knowledge workers represent constituent elements of it (Neef 1999).

This chapter examines the dynamics and characteristics of the knowledge processes within knowledge-intensive firms, which, as will be seen, are many and varied. What is regarded as, arguably, the key characteristic of both knowledge workers and knowledge-intensive firms is their distinctiveness. Thus, knowledge-intensive firms are regarded as qualitatively and fundamentally different from other types of organization. Therefore, the character and dynamics of knowledge processes in this organizational context are consequently also argued to be distinctive. For example, the importance of the knowledge possessed by knowledge workers is typically argued to make the issue of retention and organizational loyalty of greater importance than it is for other types of worker.

However, as will be seen as the chapter progresses, the topics of knowledge workers and knowledge-intensive firms are subjects that have been and continue to be extensively debated. Thus, for example, debate rages over definitions of knowledge workers and knowledge-intensive firms, the extent to which there has been an increase in the knowledge intensiveness of work, and whether knowledge workers are distinctive and require to be managed differently from other types of worker.

The chapter begins by looking at how writing on knowledge workers and knowledge-intensive firms is typically embedded in the knowledge society rhetoric. Following this, an extended section examines the debate over definitions of knowledge work and knowledge-intensive firms. The third section then considers the character of knowledge processes within knowledge-intensive firms. The fourth section of the chapter examines the topic of what facilitates and inhibits knowledge workers to participate in organizational knowledge processes. As will be seen, an interesting conclusion that emerges from much of the research on knowledge workers, is how willing they appear to be to work and use their knowledge. Sections 5 and 6 then conclude the chapter by considering the issues of retention, which is argued to be quite particular to knowledge workers, and how to manage and support knowledge work.

The rise of the knowledge worker

In the last quarter of the twentieth century, as discussed in Chapter 1, the character of work changed enormously. The dominant perspective on the analysis of these changes suggests that they have increased the knowledge intensity of work through creating a greater need for intellectual skills, and the manipulation of abstract symbols. Thus, these changes are argued to have produced an enormous expansion in the number of knowledge workers and knowledge-intensive firms. Such analyses typically utilize the post-industrial/knowledge society rhetoric and argue that not only has the number of knowledge workers increased, and the knowledge intensity of work gone up, but that knowledge is now the most significant source of competitive advantage, and that abstract and theoretical knowledge has taken on a heightened level of importance. However, such analyses have not gone unchallenged.

One writer who was among the first to popularize such analyses was Robert Reich (Blackler 1995; Rifkin 2000). Reich's analysis was focused largely on the USA, but his argument was relevant to all of the most industrialized economies (Reich 119). He argued that the shift towards high value-added, knowledge-intensive products and services in these economies gave rise to what he termed 'symbolic analysts'. These are workers who, firstly 'solve, identify and broker problems by manipulating symbols' (178), and secondly need to make frequent use of established bodies of codified knowledge (182). Thus, typical of symbolic analytical occupations are research and product design (problem solving), marketing and consultancy (problem identification), and finance/banking (problem brokering). According the Reich's analysis, by the late 1980s this category of work had grown to account for 20 per cent of employment in the USA, and was one of the USA's three key occupational categories. Statistical analysis from the UK suggests that the proportion of professional/knowledge-intensive workers in Britain was also 20 per cent in the early 1990s (Elias and Gregory 1994). Finally, even those who are critical of the knowledge work/society rhetoric acknowledge the trajectory of increasing knowledge intensiveness. Thus, Knights et al. (1993) suggest that knowledge work 'is less viable as an occupational classification than as a catch-phrase for signaling contemporary changes in the organization of work in the direction of knowledge intensiveness' (975).

Stop and think

If knowledge workers constitute approximately 20 per cent of the workers in the most industrialized nations, does this suggest that their importance to these economies has been exaggerated, or is their contribution to knowledge creation and wealth generation disproportional to their numbers?

While Chapter 1 presented a critique of the knowledge society rhetoric, the critique is revisited and extended here. Three elements to the critique are presented here, all of which question the way the rise of the knowledge worker has been conceptualized. Firstly, while there has been a growth in knowledge-intensive occupations, there has simultaneously been a growth in relatively low-skilled and routine work (Elias and Gregory 1994; NSTF 2000; Thompson et al. 2001). Thus, suggestions that the expansion of knowledge-intensive work is the only or main aspect in the contemporary restructuring of occupations are over-simplistic. Secondly, the suggested link between knowledge work and economic performance has also been questioned as being unproved. Thus, a major report by the OECD into the knowledge-based economy suggested that, 'the relation between knowledge creation and economic performance is still virtually unmapped' (1996, 29), and in the final paragraph of its introduction concludes that 'our understanding of what is happening in the knowledge-based economy is constrained by the extent and quality of the available *knowledge-related indicators*' (1996, 8, emphasis in original). Finally, another critique of the knowledge work/er rhetoric, drawing on Foucault's concept of power/knowledge (see Chapter 7) suggests that this rhetoric requires to be understood as less of an objective/scientific statement, and more of a truth claim which attempts to legitimate contemporary social change as positive and emancipatory (Knights et al. 1993).

Defining and characterizing knowledge workers and knowledge-intensive firms

While the growing importance of knowledge workers and knowledge-intensive firms has been widely articulated, and has to a large extent become a taken-for-granted truth, providing a precise definition of a knowledge worker or a knowledge-intensive firm, and describing their general characteristics has proved much more difficult. Further, a lot of ink has been spilled in the debate that has developed in this area. This section begins by presenting the mainstream definition of these terms, before introducing the critique of this perspective, which leads to another definition of the term knowledge worker.

 Knowledge worker

Someone whose work is primarily intellectual, creative, and non-routine in nature, and which involves both the utilization and creation of knowledge.

Fundamentally, the mainstream perspective conceptualizes knowledge workers as constituting an elite and quite distinctive element of the workforce in contemporary economies, who are required to be highly creative and make extensive use of knowledge (particularly abstract theoretical knowledge) in their day-to-day work. Thus, Reich's definition of symbolic analysts fits with such a conceptualization. Rifkin's (2000, 174) definition of knowledge workers as the, 'creators, manipulators and purveyors of the stream of information that makes up the postindustrial, post-service, global economy', also fits with such a conceptualization. From such definitions knowledge-intensive firms are defined as organizations that employ a significant proportion of such workers. Thus, one of the most widely used definitions of a knowledge-intensive firm is that provided by Alvesson (2000, 1101) as, 'companies where most work can be said to be of an intellectual nature and where well-qualified employees form the major part of the workforce.'

ILLUSTRATING THE ISSUES

Architects: the archetypal knowledge worker

Architects can be regarded as knowledge workers for a variety of reasons. Firstly, their work is creative and relatively non-routinized, involving the design of specific structures to meet the particular demands of their clients. Secondly, architecture requires the acquisition and utilization of an extensive body of abstract theoretical knowledge, such as of scientific and engineering principles regarding the properties of materials. Thirdly, architecture involves the integration and synthesis of different bodies of knowledge, for example combining aesthetic considerations with engineering principles. Finally, architects work at a high level of abstraction, and typically utilize and manipulate abstract symbols in the conduct of their work, for example in designing structures before building them.

Based on such definitions, an enormous range of occupations can be classified as knowledge work. Typical of the sort of occupations characterized as such are: lawyers (Hunter et al. 2002; Starbuck 1993), consultants (Robertson and Swan 2003; Empson 2001; Morris 2001), IT and software designers (Schulze 2000; Swart and Kinnie 2003), advertising executives (Alvesson, Beaumont, and Hunter 2002), accountants (Morris and Empson 1998), scientists and engineers (Beaumont and Hunter 2002; Lee et al. 1997), architects (Blackler, quoting from Sveiby and Lloyd 1987; Frenkel et al. 1995), and artists and art directors/producers (Beaumont and Hunter 2002). Definitions of knowledge workers therefore overlap with and include the classical professions (such as lawyers, architects, etc.), but also extend beyond them to include a wide variety of other occupations (such as consultants, advertising executives, IT developers, etc.). Scarbrough (1999) suggests that the main reason why knowledge workers do not represent a clear and distinct occupational category is that the knowledge intensification of work has been so widespread that it has affected a broad swathe of diverse occupations.

One problem with the definitions of knowledge workers outlined is that they are somewhat vague. In an attempt to overcome such problems, Frenkel et al. (1995) develop a more detailed definition, and conceptualize knowledge work in relation to three dimensions (see Table 14.1). The first dimension, creativity, is defined as a process of 'original problem solving', from which an original output is produced (779), with the level of creativity in work varying on a sliding scale from low to high. Thus work with a high level of creativity would include software design, where programmers design and produce new software to meet the specific requirements of their clients. The second dimension is the

Table 14.1. Frenkel et al.'s three dimensional conceptualization of work (from Frenkel et al. 1995)

Dimensions	Characteristics
Creativity	Measured on a sliding scale from low to high
Predominant Form of Knowledge Used	Characterizes work as involving the use of two predominant forms of knowledge: 1. contextual knowledge 2. theoretical knowledge
Type of Skills Involved	Characterizes work as involving three main categories of skill: 1. intellective skills 2. social skills 3. action-based skills

predominant form of knowledge used in work, with knowledge being characterized as being either theoretical or contextual. Theoretical knowledge represents codified concepts and principles, which have general relevance, whereas contextual knowledge is largely tacit and non-generalizible, being related to specific contexts of application. The third and final dimension is skill, with the skills involved in work being divided into three categories: intellective skills, social skills, and action-based skills. Action-based skills relate to physical dexterity, social skills to the ability to motivate and manage others, while intellective skills are defined as the ability to undertake abstract reasoning and synthesize different ideas.

Using these dimensions, as illustrated in Figure 14.1, Frenkel et al. (1995) define a knowledge worker as anyone who,

1. has a high level of creativity in their work,

2. requires to make extensive use of intellective skills, and

3. makes use of theoretical rather than contextual knowledge.

Thus, architects, as described previously, are classified as knowledge workers using this model. On the other hand, skilled production workers are less likely to be defined as knowledge workers, as such work involves modest levels of creativity, requires more extensive use of action-based rather than intellective skills, and where the predominant form of knowledge is contextual rather than theoretical.

A critique and a reformulation: all work as knowledge work and the concept of 'knowledge intensiveness'

Explicitly embedded in Frenkel et al.'s conceptualization of knowledge work is the privileging of theoretical knowledge over contextual knowledge. Thus occupations that

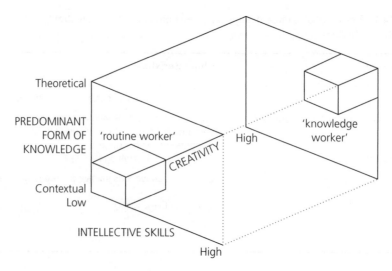

Fig. 14.1. Framework for conceptualizing work (from Frenkel et al. 1995)

involve the use of high levels of contextual knowledge, and low levels of theoretical knowledge, such as the highly skilled flute makers examined by Cook and Yanow (1993), are not classified as knowledge work by Frenkel et al. This privileging of abstract/theoretical knowledge is typical, either explicitly or implicitly, in the mainstream conceptualization of knowledge work, and provides the basis of one of the main critiques of such definitions.

Such a privileging of theoretical knowledge, and the use of the term 'knowledge worker' to refer to an exclusive group of workers, is a subjective and somewhat arbitrary definition. The main problem with such definitions is that they risk losing sight of the fact that all work is knowledge work to some extent (Allee 1997; Alvesson 2000; Grant 2000; Thompson et al. 2001). Knights et al. (1993), advance such an argument, drawing on Giddens's (1979) argument that all behaviour involves a process of self-reflexive monitoring and is thus knowledgeable. Such arguments lead to an awareness that most types of work involve the development and use of tacit knowledge (Kusterer 1978; Manwaring and Wood 1985). Further, Beaumont and Hunter (2000) report the findings of a study which concluded that knowledge generation/creation was not simply the domain of a small, elite group of workers, and that knowledge was created at all levels within organizations (Cutcher-Gershenfeld et al. 1998).

ILLUSTRATING THE ISSUES

Example: the knowledgeability of bus-driving

Bus-driving is not normally an occupation that is defined as knowledge work. However, when all types of knowledge are regarded as equal, the knowledgeability of bus-driving becomes more apparent. Firstly, bus-driving involves the acquisition of formal and codified knowledge about the rules and procedures of driving. Further, these principles have to be applied knowledgeably on a daily basis to the specific weather and road conditions that the driver encounters. Secondly, drivers require some level of knowledge regarding the mechanical working of their vehicles, for example knowing when a vehicle is not running properly and requires some form of maintenance. Thirdly, bus-drivers require significant social skills to be able to cope with the diversity of passengers they encounter. Finally, bus drivers-require to be able to understand and apply knowledge of organizational rules and procedures so that they can carry out their work to meet the performance targets they have been set.

Stop and think

Think of another occupation that is not typically classified as knowledge work. In what ways does it involve the use, application, and possibly even the creation of knowledge. Would it be inaccurate to describe this occupation as being knowledge work?

One way to take account of such insights, but maintain the idea that an elite category of knowledge workers exists has been the development and use of the term 'knowledge intensiveness'. Thus, while it can be accepted that all work is knowledge work, some work can be conceptualized as more knowledge-intensive than other work (for example, architecture compared to bus-driving). However, as Alvesson (2000) makes clear, knowledge intensiveness is a somewhat vague concept. Further, as Alvesson suggests in a later paper, 'any evaluation of "intensiveness" is likely to be contestable' (2001, 864), and there will thus always be room for debate on which occupations can be defined as knowledge-intensive.

Table 14.2. The ambiguities inherent to knowledge work (from Alvesson 2001)

Topic	Mainstream perspective	Area of ambiguity
Knowledge: what it is and what it is like?	Knowledge is codified, objective, scientific	Knowledge is subjective, socially constructed, context-specific, equivocal
The significance of knowledge as an element of knowledge work	Using institutionalized knowledge systematically and creating knowledge are the core activities of knowledge workers	The systematic utilization of formal bodies of knowledge, the need for high-level cognitive capabilities are not necessarily the most significant elements in knowledge work
The results of knowledge work	The contribution of the knowledge and intellectual effort of knowledge workers in the provision of client solutions, and in underpinning the economic performance of knowledge-intensive firms is regarded as transparent	The complexity of the work undertaken by knowledge workers makes the quality of their advice/solutions/products difficult to establish, and makes the unambiguous establishment of the contribution of the efforts of knowledge workers to such products/services problematic

Knowledge work and ambiguity

Thus far this chapter has shown the ambiguity that exists in defining knowledge workers and knowledge-intensive firms. Alvesson (2001), in an interesting critique of the mainstream perspective on knowledge workers/knowledge-intensive firms, argues that such ambiguity actually represents one of the defining characteristics of the work done in knowledge-intensive firms. The argument developed by Alvesson suggests that these mainstream conceptions are too closely wedded to objectivist perspectives on knowledge, and that greater account requires to be taken of the way knowledge is conceptualized from a practice-based perspective. Fundamentally, Alvesson suggests that doing so reveals three key areas of ambiguity that are irresolvable, and represent an intrinsic element of the work carried out by knowledge workers (see Table 14.2).

ILLUSTRATING THE ISSUES

Not 'just a consultant': the ambiguous culture in a scientific consultancy

Robertson and Swan (2003) describe and analyse the ambiguous character of the culture in a small, scientific consultancy, Universal consulting. Universal Consulting, which employed 180 people (140 of whom were consultants), developed scientific and technological innovations to solve client-generated problems. The central ambiguity of its culture was that while it had a strong culture, this culture celebrated and embraced diversity, heterogeneity, and a lack of standardization. Thus, paradoxically, a norm that was strongly defended was that there were no norms (for example, on dress code, work patterns, project management methods). This can be illustrated by looking at two of the subelements of the culture that Robertson and Swan examine: performance management and recruitment and selection. In terms of performance management, a balance between control and autonomy was achieved. The consultants had high levels of autonomy to decide their working patterns and the projects they worked on. However, this was counterbalanced by a financially focused system of annual revenue targets for each consultant. These revenue targets were important, as they were used to rank consultants annually, with the ranking determining the level of each consultant's merit-based pay rise. However, the precise way in which rankings were produced was an opaque process, not fully understood by most. The ambiguous nature of the culture was also visible in Universal Consulting's recruitment and selection procedures. Primarily, people were selected for their fit with the culture. However, paradoxically, selection for fit didn't mean the selection of clones who looked, acted, and thought the same. Selection for fit meant selecting people who had a strong sense of individuality. Thus Universal Consulting was full of different, quite idiosyncratic people, but who were all high achievers, and who all had a strong sense of individualism in them. This ambiguity wasn't regarded as a problem by the consultants. In fact it was highly valued. This was primarily because it allowed the consultants to balance different identities underpinned by different values. The consultants typically had a sense of identity as both consultants (where they accepted the logic and requirement for economic-based control), and as members of a community of elite scientists. Thus in interviews there were frequent statements by the consultant's that they were not 'just a consultant'. The cultural ambiguity in Universal Consulting acted as an effective control system as it allowed the consultants to maintain both aspects of their identity and mediate the potential tensions between the company's need for an element of control and the consultant's desire for high levels of autonomy. Thus the autonomy had sustained their sense of identity as elite scientific experts, while the control-based systems reinforced their identity as consultants.

Stop and think

What does the role of Arthur Andersen's auditors/accountants in the collapse of Enron, and the difficulty of apportioning blame in the collapse say about the ambiguity inherent in evaluating the quality of knowledge-intensive work? For ongoing information on the Enron situation look at either of the following websites: http://www.multinationalmonitor.org/enronindex.html, http://www.thedailyenron.com/

Knowledge and knowledge processes in knowledge-intensive firms

As the definitions section has made clear, the utilization of knowledge represents one of the defining aspects of the work undertaken in knowledge-intensive firms. Thus to understand the character of knowledge-intensive firms, and the knowledge management challenges which exist within them, it is necessary to develop a fuller understanding of both the type of knowledge and knowledge processes which knowledge workers typically utilize and are involved with.

Types of knowledge

In examining the types of knowledge of relevance to knowledge-intensive firms, the typology developed by Empson (2001) is useful (see Table 14.3). Empson, whose focus is on professional service firms (specifically consultants and accountants), suggests that there are two main types of knowledge that workers in knowledge-intensive firms require to utilize: technical knowledge and client knowledge. The requirement for knowledge-intensive firms to provide specific, customized products/services to meet the particular needs of their clients means that knowledge of the client, and the industry/sector they work in, is typically crucial and equally as important as technical knowledge. Thus, without a detailed knowledge of the client, a knowledge-intensive firm would not be able to provide an effectively customized product/service.

One specific type of client knowledge worth touching on is knowledge of specific individuals in client organizations (the last category in Table 14.3). Such knowledge represents social capital (see Chapter 7), resources obtained through the network relations that individuals possess. The typically interactive nature of the work carried out by knowledge workers means that they often develop good relations with specific client staff (Alvesson 2000; Fosstenlokken et al. 2003). This knowledge, or social capital, is a key resource to knowledge-intensive firms, but is something they risk losing when the knowledge workers who possess such knowledge/capital leave. As will be seen later, this is another reason why the retention of knowledge workers is a key issue for knowledge-intensive firms.

Table 14.3. Types of knowledge used by knowledge workers (from Empson 2001)

Type of knowledge	Sub-categories	Description
Technical Knowledge	Sectoral	Technical knowledge, commonly understood and shared at a sectoral level by staff from a range of companies.
	Organizational	Organization-specific knowledge, such of company products, processes, routines, and procedures.
	Individual	Personal knowledge acquired through formal education or work experience.
Client Knowledge	Industry Level	Knowledge of industry-level factors, such as the factors shaping the dynamics of competition.
	Company	Knowledge of specific organizations, such as having an understanding of and sensitivity to their cultures and ways of working.
	Individuals	Having a knowledge of and acquaintance with key individuals in specific organizations.

For example, in relation to engineering consultants working in the aerospace industry, industry-level technical knowledge could be knowledge of wing-vibration dynamics, which are well understood and shared across most companies operating in the industry. Organizational level knowledge in this context could be an understanding of an organizational specific system/process for testing wing-vibration dynamics. Finally, in the same context, individual technical knowledge would be the expertise that individual consultants had built up over time, for example conducting wing-vibration tests and analyses.

Considering the example of film directors/producers, industry-level client knowledge would be knowledge of the factors at industry level that affect the chances of having a film funded, such as the characteristics of a typical-Hollywood blockbuster. Organizational-level knowledge in this context would be an understanding of the specific tastes and preferences of particular film companies, such as Disney or United Artists. Finally, individual client knowledge would be having an acquaintance with and understanding of important key individuals within particular companies who are able to influence decisions on the commissioning of films.

Knowledge processes

The key knowledge processes within knowledge-intensive firms can be divided into three broad categories: knowledge creation/application, knowledge sharing/integration, and knowledge codification, each of which is briefly described.

Knowledge creation/application
One of the key aspects of the work in knowledge-intensive firms is that it is typically not routine, repetitive work. Instead knowledge-intensive firms provide customized,

specifically designed products/services, rather than off-the-shelf ones. For example, Robertson and Swan (2003, 833) suggest one of the key characteristics of knowledge-intensive firms is, 'their capacity to solve complex problems through the development of creative and innovative solutions'. The production/creation of such client-specific, customized solutions requires and involves both the application of existing bodies of knowledge and the creation of new knowledge (Morris 2001).

Knowledge-sharing/integration

The development of client-specific, customized solutions involves more than the application and creation of knowledge: it also involves the sharing and integration of different bodies of knowledge, both between workers in knowledge-intensive firms, and between the knowledge-intensive firms and staff from client organizations (Fosstenlokken et al. 2003). The importance of knowledge-sharing/integration processes exists at two levels. Firstly, much of the work done within knowledge-intensive firms is project based, and because of the typical complexity of the projects, such project teams are often multi-disciplinary. In such situations, there is thus a need for the sharing and integration of the different types of specialist knowledge. The second way in which knowledge-sharing is important, which is a context examined in the example of the software company researched by Swart and Kinnie (2003), is the sharing of knowledge *between* project teams. Fundamentally, because project teams create and develop specialist knowledge during the process of their work, there are advantages to knowledge-intensive firms if such knowledge can be shared with other, non-project staff.

Knowledge codification

Morris (2001) argues that, because of the advantages to knowledge-intensive firms of sharing project-specific knowledge and learning across the organization, this acts as an incentive to knowledge-intensive firms to attempt to codify such knowledge and learning. Thus the codification of knowledge provides one specific way of sharing it within an organization (Quinn et al. 1996). Werr and Stjernberg (2003) also argue that the codification of some knowledge helps with the communication and sharing of tacit knowledge. However, the difficulties of doing so are significant. Firstly, much of this knowledge is highly tacit, and is not amenable to codification. Secondly, much project knowledge is specialized and context-specific in nature, and has only limited general relevance. Finally, in an issue examined more fully in the following section, knowledge workers may not be willing to facilitate the codification of the specialist knowledge they possess.

The willingness of knowledge workers to participate in knowledge processes: conflicting interests?

As has been highlighted consistently throughout book, the effectiveness of organizational knowledge processes is predicated on the active and willing participation of workers in them. However, a worker's willingness to provide such efforts cannot be taken for granted. Theoretically, this is as true for knowledge workers as it is for other workers. However, as will be seen later, empirical evidence on knowledge workers shows them to be commonly prepared to work extremely hard for their employers, which suggests that motivation to work may be less of an issue for such workers. Whether this is the case, and the factors that affect the willingness (or otherwise) of knowledge workers to participate in knowledge processes, is the focus of this section, which begins by considering the factors that may inhibit the willingness of knowledge workers to participate in organizational knowledge processes.

Inhibiting factors

As was discussed in Chapter 4, the potential for conflict between workers and their employers in inextricably embedded in the employment relationship. Scarbrough (1999) argues that the employment relationship involves balancing contradictory tensions between the benefits to both worker and employer of cooperation, and potential conflicts between them over whether and how economic gains are derived from such efforts, and the way they are divided. Alvesson (2000) also argues that such potential conflicts also exist, but, for reasons discussed later, suggests than such conflicts are less pronounced than between other types of employee and their employers.

Another factor examined in Chapters 4 and 7, which can inhibit the willingness of knowledge workers to participate in knowledge processes, is the potential for intra-organizational conflict between workers or work groups which exists (Quinn et al. 1996). Also, Alvesson (2000) suggests that people may have multiple identities that may be in conflict (such as to a work group, and the employer, or to a profession and the employer). Further, such conflicts are as likely in knowledge-intensive firms as in other types of organization. Thus Starbuck (1993) described the knowledge-intensive company he examined as being, 'internally inconsistent, in conflict with itself. . . . An intricate house of cards'. Finally, Empson (2001) presented an example of a knowledge-intensive firm in a post-merger situation, where workers from the two pre-merger companies were unwilling to share their knowledge with each other.

ILLUSTRATING THE ISSUES

Conflict in an art gallery: commercial considerations versus a public-sector ethos

Beaumont and Hunter (2002) examined the management of a collection of art galleries, and found that following the implementation of more commercially orientated working practices and funding procedures conflict emerged between these new commercial values, and the more public sector ethos maintained by a number of the galleries' key knowledge workers. The publicly managed organization examined was responsible for four different art galleries, which employed a total of over 800 staff. While one third of this staff was low-paid warders and gallery assistants, most of the staff, consisting of collections and restoration staff, could be described as being knowledge workers. The introduction of commercially oriented management values and systems resulted in government funding for the galleries being reduced from 100 per cent to 50–60 per cent, with the rest to be raised through fundraising.

Simultaneously, galleries were set performance targets regarding the number of visitors they should have. Traditionally, under the historical system of full public funding, while pay levels had not been high, and promotion potential was limited, the collections and restoration staff had had a significant amount of professional autonomy. While many of the younger collection and restoration staff were happy to embrace the new, more commercially focused culture, most of the older staff were against it. This was for two main reasons. Firstly, they perceived that the performance targets and requirement to find commercial funding had diminished their autonomy. Secondly, they also felt that these values not only devalued their expertise, but also dumbed down art. Thus, the move towards a commercially focused culture challenged the professional values of the older collections and restoration staff.

Stop and think

Could this conflict have been avoided through better or different management? What could gallery management have done to minimize or avoid this conflict?

Knowledge workers: the ideal workers?

While the previous section considered the factors which can create an unwillingness among knowledge workers to participate in knowledge processes, other evidence suggests such workers are prepared to invest significant amounts of time and effort into their work, and that motivating them to do so is not difficult (Alvesson 1995; Deetz 1998; Kunda 1992; Robertson and Swan 2003). As these workers are prepared to make such efforts, with minimal levels of supervision, and without regarding such effort as being problematic, Alvesson suggests such workers represent the ideal subordinates (2000, 1104), and suggests four reasons why knowledge workers are prepared to make such efforts:

1. they find their work intrinsically interesting and fulfilling;
2. such working patterns represent the norms within the communities they are a part of;
3. a sense of reciprocity, whereby they provide the organization with their efforts in return for good pay and working conditions;
4. such behaviour reinforces and confirms their sense of identity as a knowledge worker, where hard work is regarded as a fundamental component.

Robertson and Swan (2003) provide a further explanation: the structure of the employment relationship is less clear than for other workers, and the potential for conflict on the basis of it thus becomes dissipated. Primarily they suggest that the employer–employee, manager–managed relationship is not as clear cut in knowledge-intensive firms as in other, more hierarchically based organizations. In knowledge-intensive firms such boundaries are fuzzy, and evolve over time, and therefore the interests of employers and employees are more likely to be in common.

Managing knowledge workers: balancing autonomy and control

Managing knowledge workers and motivating them to participate actively in organizational knowledge processes involves maintaining a delicate balance between control and autonomy. As will be seen in the following section, knowledge workers typically demand and expect high levels of autonomy in their working conditions and work patterns. Simultaneously, knowledge-intensive firms require to have some level of management control, to ensure that the efforts of their workforce are economically viable and sustainable (for example, providing the firm with regular profits). In Universal Consulting, the company examined by Robertson and Swan (2003) that was examined previously in this section, such a balance was managed through the use of a deliberately ambiguous culture. Overall however, managing the delicate balance between the simultaneous and potentially contradictory need for both control and autonomy, makes the management of knowledge workers a complex and difficult process.

Knowledge workers and the problem of retention

As illustrated, while some empirical evidence suggests that motivating knowledge workers to participate in organizational knowledge processes does not appear to be a problem, developing their organizational loyalty such that they remain working with their employers for extended periods, does appear to be more problematic. This is to a large extent because labour market conditions, where the skills and knowledge of knowledge workers are typically relatively scarce, creates conditions for knowledge workers which are favourable to mobility (Flood et al. 2001; Scarbrough 1999).

However, there is a general consensus in the literature on knowledge workers that having a high turnover rate is a potentially significant problem for knowledge-intensive firms (Alvesson 2000; Beaumont and Hunter 2002; Flood et al. 2000; Lee and Maurer 1997). Firstly, this is a potential problem because the knowledge possessed by knowledge workers is typically highly tacit. Therefore, when they leave an organization, they take their knowledge with them. For example, one key source of knowledge possessed by knowledge workers is social capital, their knowledge of key individuals (for example in client organizations). The need for knowledge workers to work closely with client organizations means that they often develop close relations with important client staff. Thus, when such workers leave, there is a risk for their employer that they will lose their clients as well. The second main reason why poor retention rates may be a problem for knowledge-intensive firms is that the knowledge, skills, and experience possessed by knowledge workers is often a crucial element in organizational performance.

Alvesson (2000) argues that one of the best ways to deal with the turnover problem is to create a sense of organizational loyalty in staff, particularly through developing their sense of organizational identity. Alvesson identifies two broad types of loyalty and four strategies for developing them (see Table 14.4). The weakest form of loyalty is instrumental-based loyalty, which is when workers remains loyal to their employer for as long as they

Table 14.4. Type of loyalty and strategies for developing them (based on Alvesson 2000)

Type of loyalty	Strategy for development	Means of development
Instrumental-based Loyalty	Financial Strategy	Providing employees with good pay and fringe benefits.
	Institutional-based Strategy	Developing a vision and set of values and encouraging employees to identify with them. Achieved through culture management, vision building, use of stories.
Identification-based Loyalty	Communitarian-based Strategy	Developing a sense of community and social bonding amongst workers. Achieved through use of social events and meetings which bring people together and allow them to develop strong relations with, and knowledge of each other.
	Socially Integrative Strategy	A combination of the institutional- and communitarian-based strategies.

receive specific personal benefits, with one of the most effective ways of developing such loyalty being through pay and working conditions. The second and stronger form of loyalty is identification-based loyalty, which is loyalty based on workers having a strong sense of identity as being members of the organization, and where they identify with the goals and objectives of their organization. The three strategies for developing identification-based loyalty are illustrated in Table 14.4. This type of loyalty is typically not developed through financial rewards, and is instead built through developing a culture that workers can buy into, creating a sense of community amongst staff, or both.

ILLUSTRATING THE ISSUES

A communitarian-based strategy for developing loyalty: an HR consultancy

Cheshire Consultants are an HR consultancy firm based in the North West of England, which specializes particularly in the area of recruitment and selection and employee development. Cheshire Consultants is a small company, employing only twelve consultants plus some supporting administrative and management staff. Its consultants could be described as mobile teleworkers, as for much of their working week they are out of the office, visiting and working at various client locations. Thus, these work patterns mean that during the course of their normal day-to-day work, there are limited opportunities for the consultants to interact with each other. However, to counteract this, what Alvesson (2000) labelled a communitarian-based strategy is utilized to reinforce social relations and sustain a sense of community identity amongst staff. This was done through two main mechanisms. Firstly, the owner/managing director of the company made efforts to maintain contact with all consultants on an almost daily basis, partly to support their work and provide advice, but also to simply sustain social contacts with them. These contacts were regarded as typically positive and helpful by most consultants. The second strategy was to have regular monthly meetings which were primarily social in purpose, and which were never cancelled or compromised by demands of work. Most consultants found that this strategy helped them to sustain a sense of identity as members of an organizational community, even though they spent most of their time out of the office.

Stop and think

Instrumental-based loyalty, derived through pay and financial rewards is argued to be a weak form of loyalty. Do you agree? How significant is pay and related financial reward in the development of organizational loyalty and commitment?

HRM policies to motivate knowledge workers

This final section examines the way organizations can motivate knowledge workers and facilitate their work through the specific HRM policies that they utilize. However, before doing this, the section begins by examining the debate regarding whether knowledge workers require to be managed differently from other types of worker.

Special treatment for knowledge workers?

The mainstream perspective on the management of knowledge workers is that they represent a distinctive and important part of the workforce and thus require a form of management different to that used for other workers (Alvesson 2000; Robertson and O'Malley-Hammersley 2000; Tampoe 1993). The factors that are typically argued to make knowledge workers a distinctive element in an organization's workforce are:

- they are typically very highly qualified, and also require to continually develop their knowledge;
- their knowledge and skills are particularly important to organizational performance;
- their knowledge and skills are difficult to codify and are typically highly tacit;
- their knowledge and skills are typically scarce and highly valued in labour markets, making it relatively straightforward for knowledge workers to change jobs; and
- their work tasks, focused as they are on the creation, utilization, and application of knowledge, are highly specialized in nature.

Stop and think

If knowledge workers do receive special treatment by their employers in terms of favourable levels of pay, good working conditions, and high levels of autonomy, is this likely to make workers who don't receive such treatment less likely to participate fully in organizational knowledge processes? Further, could such attitudes have a negative effect on organizational performance?

However, this perspective has been criticized by a growing number of writers, who typically base their analysis in the perspective that all workers should be regarded as knowledge workers (Allee 1997; Beaumont and Hunter 2002; Garvey and Williamson 2002). The general critique of the 'distinctiveness' argument is that such approaches neglect the fact that if all workers are knowledge workers, then the knowledge of all workers is important to organizational performance. Further, these writers argue that organizations that utilize such an approach and treat knowledge workers as special and distinctive, face a number of risks. Firstly, there is the risk that such divisive policies may lead to the development of a sense of resentment among the workforce that do not receive these favourable conditions. Secondly, and relatedly, there is the risk that as a consequence of such attitudes, these workers having a low level of loyalty and commitment to their organization, being less willing to share their knowledge, or generally being less willing to work as productively as possible.

Facilitating knowledge work via HRM

While much has been written about knowledge workers and knowledge-intensive firms, surprisingly there are still only a relatively small number of papers which examine in detail HRM issues related to the management of knowledge workers (Alvesson 2000; Beaumont and Hunter 2002; Quinn et al. 1996; Robertson and O'Malley-Hammersley 2000; Robertson and Swan 2003; Swart and Kinnie 2003; Tampoe 1993). However, from these few studies there is a general consensus regarding the most effective ways to facilitate the work of knowledge workers.

Recruitment and selection

Attention to recruitment and selection procedures is regarded as important. This is not only to ensure that people with appropriate skills and knowledge are recruited, but also that the people recruited have a willingness to share their knowledge appropriately, and that the attitudes and behaviours of new recruits are likely to be compatible with the existing organizational culture.

Providing rewarding and fulfilling work

Another factor identified as being important to knowledge workers is that the work they have should be intrinsically satisfying and stimulating, and provide them with constant challenges.

Autonomy

As well as work being intrinsically interesting, knowledge workers also typically regard having high levels of autonomy over their work tasks, and working patterns as important. As discussed previously however, managing the delicate balancing between providing autonomy and maintaining some level of control is likely to be one of the greatest challenges for those managing knowledge workers.

Opportunities for personal development

Finally, providing knowledge workers with constant opportunities to continue their personal development, for example through training and education, represents another way of motivating knowledge workers. While such a strategy is a potentially double-edged sword, as supporting such activities potentially makes it easier for staff to leave, without supporting continued development, staff may be likely to leave anyway.

ILLUSTRATING THE ISSUES

HR practices to facilitate organization-wide knowledge-sharing

Swart and Kinnie (2003) examined a small software company in the South East of England, and identified a number of HR practices that appeared to be effective at facilitating organization-wide knowledge-sharing. The company examined employed less than fifty staff, and provided bespoke software solutions to meet the particular needs of their clients. Staff typically worked within short-term project teams, being allocated to these teams on the relevance of their knowledge, and on the extent of their prior experience. It was recognized by company management that there were potential advantages to management if the knowledge and learning gained within each project team could be shared with others. To achieve and facilitate this, a number of mechanisms were utilized. Firstly, recruitment and selection procedures were used to try and identify staff that would be willing to share their knowledge. Secondly, a mentoring system was used. In the mentoring scheme senior staff were allocated two or three mentees each, with these relations being set up to ensure that mentors and mentees didn't work in the same project teams. Thus, through the mentoring scheme project-specific learning was shared more widely. Organization-wide knowledge-sharing was also encouraged via the company's performance management system. Part of the performance management system was used to determine individual merit-based pay rises. However, another aspect of it was developmental in focus, where staff were encouraged to reflect on learning and consider development needs. As with the mentoring scheme, these biannual development reviews spanned project boundaries, and helped share project-learning more widely. Finally, a number of communication mechanisms (such as electronic newsgroups), and regular social events spanned project boundaries, and were open to all staff, which helped staff to get to know each other and develop a sense of community.

Conclusion

The importance of knowledge workers and knowledge-intensive firms is closely tied to the rhetoric regarding the contemporary rise and emergence of the knowledge society, which has not gone unquestioned. In the debate over defining knowledge workers and knowledge-intensive firms, two perspectives were shown to exist. While the mainstream perspective suggests that knowledge workers are a distinctive and elite element in the contemporary workforce, others argue that this neglects accounting for the extent to which all work is knowledge work, and thus how all workers can be defined as knowledge workers. However, what appears to distinguish knowledge workers from other workers is the character of the work activities they undertake, which are focused on the intensive creation, application, and utilization of knowledge. On the topic of what motivates knowledge workers to effectively share and utilize their knowledge, knowledge workers appear to be almost the ideal subordinates/workers, as with minimal level of supervision they are quite often willing to work extremely hard, and don't regard this as being problematic. However, developing the organizational loyalty of knowledge workers is more problematic, with high levels of job mobility being common among knowledge workers. Finally, on the topic of managing knowledge workers, and facilitating their work, the provision of interesting work, high levels of autonomy, and continuous opportunities for personal development appear to be key. However, the demands/expectations of knowledge workers for high level of autonomy creates tensions with the need for managers in knowledge-intensive firms for some level of control. Managing this delicate balance represents one of the key challenges for those managing knowledge workers.

REVIEW QUESTIONS

1   In Frenkel et al.'s conceptualization of work, knowledge work is defined as work where the predominant form of knowledge is theoretical knowledge. However, does this underestimate the extent to which such work also involves the use of contextual knowledge? Think of a specific knowledge-intensive occupation, and consider the extent to which contextual knowledge is likely to be important.

2   Is knowledge intensiveness a useful concept for defining knowledge work, or does the term contain too much ambiguity to be useful?

FURTHER READING

- M. Alvesson (2001). 'Knowledge Work: Ambiguity, Image and Identity', *Human Relations*, 54/7: 863–86.
  Good discussion, analysis, and critique of the mainstream literature on knowledge workers and knowledge-intensive firms.

- M. Robertson and J. Swan (2003). 'Control—What Control?' Culture and Ambiguity within a Knowledge-Intensive Firm', *Journal of Management Studies*, 40/4: 831–58.
  Contains a detailed examination of the role of culture in knowledge intensive firms, based on an analysis of a case study company.

- M. Alvesson (2000). 'Social Identity and the Problem of Loyalty in Knowledge-Intensive Companies', *Journal of Management Studies*, 37/8: 1101–23.
  Interesting paper on how the management of identity can be used to address the problem of loyalty in knowledge-intensive firms.

- J. Kinnie (2003). 'Sharing Knowledge in Knowledge-Intensive Firms', *Human Resource Management Journal*, 13/2: 60–75.
  An analysis of a single case study focusing on how HRM practices can be used to facilitate intra-organizational knowledge-sharing.

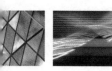

15

Conclusion

Introduction

The purpose of this concluding chapter is not to summarize the arguments stated in the book. Instead, it will focus on dealing with some general questions that hang over knowledge management like accusations (as both a practice and a body of writing) questioning its usefulness and even its viability. The objective of this chapter is therefore to examine and discuss these criticisms. These criticisms can be embodied into three questions, each of which is dealt with. Firstly, questions have been raised regarding the quality, intellectual coherence, and rigour of much of the writing on knowledge management. Secondly, perhaps the potentially most challenging criticism is that the term 'knowledge management' can be argued to be an oxymoron, raising questions regarding the viability of knowledge management as an organizational practice. Finally, knowledge management has been accused of being the latest in an apparently unending stream of management fashions, and that interest in the topic is thus likely to wane rapidly in the near future.

Section 1 of the conclusion therefore discusses the question of the quality of the writing on knowledge management. In doing so firstly it has to be acknowledged that it is hard to talk in general terms about this work as it is so diverse in character. However, this section concludes that, based on the evidence presented in the book, it cannot be said that all the writing on the topic is weakly conceptualized, as a significant proportion of it is robust in this respect.

Section 2 moves on to consider the second question, that of the viability of knowledge management as an organizational practice. However, it is first necessary to acknowledge the diversity of strategies and philosophies of knowledge management that exist. For example, Chapter 9 outlined the two knowledge management strategies of personalization and codification described by Hansen et al. (1999). Further, Alvesson and Karreman (2001) develop an even more detailed typology of knowledge management strategies (see Figure 15.1), each of which is related to a particular style of management. Thus questions regarding the viability of knowledge management require to take account of this diversity. However, such an enormous task is beyond the scope of this book and is not attempted here.

Instead, more general issues related to the viability of knowledge management are considered. In criticisms regarding knowledge management two specific issues emerge as potentially problematic. Firstly, does the nature of knowledge itself make it unmanageable? Secondly, to what extent are the interests of workers and organizations in such processes compatible?

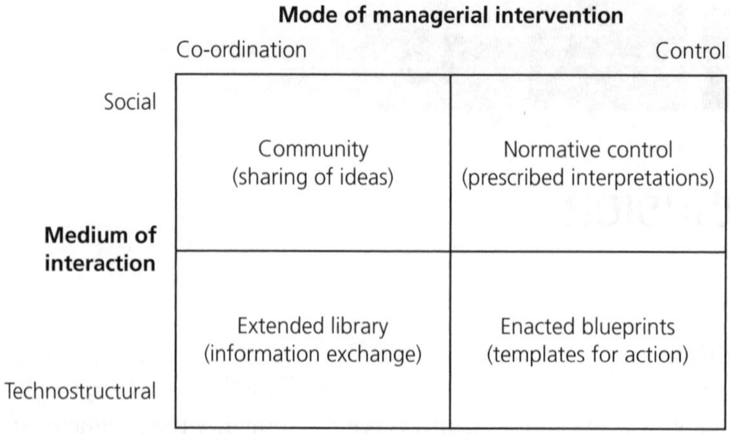

Mode of managerial intervention

Co-ordination   Control

	Co-ordination	Control
Social	Community (sharing of ideas)	Normative control (prescribed interpretations)
Medium of interaction Technostructural	Extended library (information exchange)	Enacted blueprints (templates for action)

Fig. 15.1. A typology of knowledge management strategies (from Alvesson and Karreman 2001)

The third and final section of the chapter goes beyond these debates and the general content of the book. This section begins by discussing the question of whether knowledge management can be characterized as an ephemeral, passing fashion of limited substance. After this the section broadens out to consider the context in which knowledge on knowledge management is produced and consumed. This is useful as it gives an insight into the specific agents and processes through which the ideas and practices of knowledge management examined in the book have emerged.

Reflections on the knowledge management literature

As has been seen throughout the book, a diversity of perspectives exists on virtually every aspect of knowledge management. From definitions of what knowledge is, through the role of IT systems in knowledge management initiatives, to the way communities of practice should be managed and supported, debates and disagreements exist. Thus, it is hard to make general statements regarding the quality of writing on the topic, as the knowledge management literature is not coherent in character. In fact, one of the defining characteristics of the literature on knowledge management is the plurality and diversity of perspectives that exist and continue to thrive. Nevertheless, this difficult task is attempted here, through discussing and commenting on two papers which have made generalizing statements about the character and quality of the literature on knowledge management (Swan and Scarbrough 2001; Alvesson and Karreman 2001).

Swan and Scarbrough (2001), in the editorial introduction to a special issue of the *Journal of Management Studies* on knowledge management, lament what they characterize as the uncritical and unreflexive nature of the mainstream literature on knowledge management. Such literature is typically based on an objectivist perspective on knowledge (see Chapter 2) and unproblematically characterizes knowledge as an economic commodity,

Table 15.1. Problems with conceptions of knowledge in the 'popular' knowledge management literature (from Alvesson and Karreman 2001)

Problem	Problem description
Ontological Incoherence	Blending together of incompatible constructivist and objectivist views of knowledge—for example Nonaka (1994)
Vagueness	Lack of distinctness regarding the content and character of knowledge in organizations
All-embracing and Empty View of Knowledge	All-encompassing definitions of knowledge have little clarity and make possibilities for conceptual insights difficult—for example Davenport and Prusak (1998)
Objectivity	Typically utilize objectivist definitions of knowledge unproblematically
Functionalism	Unproblematically assumes that having knowledge and managing knowledge is a good thing and neglects to deal with potential negative aspects of both having or managing knowledge: knowledge as simultaneously enabling and constraining

failing to discuss the socially constructed, political, subjective, context-dependent, and dynamic characteristics of knowledge (see Chapter 3). Further, such literature is strongly managerialist in tone, being typically quite prescriptive, concerning itself with questions of *how* knowledge can be managed, rather than questions of *can* or *should* it be managed.

Alvesson and Karreman (2001) are even more scathing regarding what they call the 'popular' knowledge management literature. However, one weakness with Alvesson and Karreman's analysis is that they are not very explicit about the types of work they are criticizing, giving only a few examples. The main focus of their criticism relates to the way, 'knowledge', 'management', and 'knowledge management' are conceptualized. While management as a concept is typically not defined or discussed in any detail in this literature, there are five specific problems with the way knowledge is conceptualized (see Table 15.2). Fundamentally, they argue that conceptualizations of knowledge in this literature are generally weak, sloppy, contradictory, and do not stand up to rigorous criticism. This general line of argument is agreed with by Edwards et al. (2003).

Stop and think

Pick an example of a popular, mainstream piece of writing on the topic of knowledge management. To what extent are the five problems of conceptualizing knowledge identified by Alvesson and Karreman (2001) relevant to it?

While the dominance of mainstream perspectives was true when Swan and Scarbrough and Alvesson and Karreman wrote their critiques, this has arguably become less true over time, as the debates on knowledge management have matured. Thus, as this book demonstrates, a strong and vibrant body of critical work on knowledge management exists and has usefully questioned and challenged the assumptions of mainstream, managerialist perspectives. However, this is not to say that the literature on knowledge management in its totality, encompassing both mainstream and critical perspectives, is not without its problems. One of the main weaknesses of this body of work is that even now the topics of power and conflict are still relatively neglected. Thus, the lead taken by those writers examined in Chapter 7 to account for such issues when examining knowledge management has typically not been followed by a significant number of writers.

Knowledge management: viable organizational practice or a contradiction in terms?

As was outlined earlier, organizational attempts to manage knowledge cannot be characterized as unitary. In fact, as illustrated (see Figure 15.1), there are a diversity of philosophies and strategies with regard to how organizations should manage their knowledge. This section does *not* attempt to compare and evaluate the effectiveness of these different strategies. Instead, this section considers the more general question of whether knowledge management is viable as an organizational practice. This question can be divided into two elements. Firstly, do the inherent characteristics of knowledge make it difficult to control and manage? Secondly, to what extent are the interests of business organizations and their employees with regard to the objectives and outcomes of organizational knowledge processes compatible? If answered in the negative, both factors bring into question the general viability of organizational attempts to manage their knowledge base.

Is knowledge manageable?

The vast majority of the knowledge management literature builds on the assumption that knowledge is a resource amenable to management control (Scarbrough 1999, 9). In fact this represents probably the most fundamental assumption underpinning the viability of knowledge management. Without this ability, the feasibility of knowledge management becomes questionable. However, a number of writers suggest that some of the intrinsic characteristics of knowledge make it difficult to control and manage in a direct and straightforward sense. These characteristics of knowledge include:

- its ambiguity and dynamism (Alvesson and Karreman 2001),
- its variety and diversity (McAdam and McCreedy 2000),
- its invisibility and immeasurability (Soo et al. 2002), and
- its inseparability from human beliefs and values (von Krogh et al. 2000).

However, while knowledge may not be amenable to direct control, these critics typically acknowledge that when the term 'management' is used in a looser sense, organizational management does have some ability to shape and influence knowledge processes. For example, while von Krogh et al. (2000) argue that knowledge cannot be directly managed, this is more a semantic critique of the term 'management' than a suggestion that all attempts by organizational management to shape knowledge processes are doomed to failure. Von Krogh et al. (2000) are in fact very positive that there is much organizational management can to enable knowledge processes. Rather than the term 'knowledge management', they prefer the term 'knowledge enablement'.

Von Krogh et al.'s (2000, 17) perspective is summed up in the following quote, 'while you may be able to manage related organizational processes like community building and knowledge exchange, you cannot manage knowledge itself.' Von Krogh et al. thus suggest that in an indirect way, through utilizing/shaping people-centred processes and polices (they use the term 'caring' for people) organizational management has the ability to persuade workers to manage their knowledge towards the achievement of organizational objectives. Therefore, rather than suggesting that knowledge management is totally unfeasible, von Krogh et al. are instead advocating something closer to a community-based approach to knowledge management (see Figure 15.1).

In general, such a perspective is reinforced by the material presented in the book, where the importance of human, social, and cultural factors to knowledge management processes has been highlighted. Therefore, while it is misguided to suggest that knowledge management is about the direct manipulation by organizational management of an easily controllable resource, this does not mean that organizational management is totally powerless to shape organizational knowledge processes at all.

Where the von Krogh et al. (2000) perspective is weak, is on issues of power, politics, and conflict. Thus they typically assume that with the right management strategy, organizational objectives and workers' interests can be aligned, making workers willing to use and share their knowledge in organizational knowledge processes. However, when the insights developed in Chapters 4 and 7 are taken account of (relating to the potential for conflict intrinsic to the employment relationship, as well as the embeddedness of power in the employment relationship), such an assumption can be questioned. These issues are examined in the following section.

Contradictory outcomes and objectives from organizational knowledge processes?

Fuller (2002, 2) argues that, 'the dark secret of this field [knowledge management] is that its name is an oxymoron, for as soon as business enters the picture, the interests of knowledge and management trade off against each other'. Ultimately he argues that the interests of business in making short-term economic gains from the use of knowledge clash with other objectives and outcomes from the use of knowledge. If this were true, it would represent another significant question regarding the viability of knowledge management as an organizational practice.

When considered in the broadest terms, there is an enormous variety of objectives and outcomes from organizational knowledge processes, for individuals, organizations, and society in general (see Table 15.2). Further, as discussed in Chapters 4 and 7, the *potential* for conflict between workers and their employers is embedded in the employment relationship, which typically involves a power imbalance that favours the interests of business managers/owners over workers. These factors combined therefore suggest that the potential for conflict between organizational and other objectives from knowledge

Table 15.2. Outcomes and objectives of organizational knowledge processes

Level	Outcome/Objective
Individual	• Change/improvement in status and recognition • Material reward (for example improved pay, financial bonuses, holidays, working conditions) • Sense of fulfilment from the process itself, or the achievement of desired outcomes • Expression of commitment, or sense of obligation, to a group, profession, or organization
Organization	• Profit • Market share • Improve innovativeness • Cost reduction/control
Society	• The advancement of knowledge • Improve social conditions • Develop more effective public policies for local/national governments

processes is significant. Thus, as was illustrated in Chapter 4, a wide range of factors will shape the attitudes of workers towards participating in organizational knowledge processes.

This perspective, that the potential for conflict will inhibit the effectiveness of knowledge management initiatives, is undermined by the innumerable cases examined where workers have been willing to participate in organizational knowledge processes. The most extreme case of such willingness, discussed in Chapter 14, is of knowledge workers, many of who seem happy to work enormously hard for their organizations without regarding such behaviour as problematic. Thus, while the potential for conflict exists in the employment relationship, this does not mean that conflict between workers and their employers is inevitable, or that their interests are always divergent and incompatible. Scarbrough (1999, 7) argues that such behaviour on the part of knowledge workers can be explained by the relatively instrumental attitude to work of such workers, who are often primarily concerned with issues of equity and reward: ensuring that they are adequately and fairly rewarded for their efforts. Thus, if there is conflict between worker and employer it is most likely to be over the distribution of economic gains.

Stop and think

Based on your own, direct experience of knowledge management initiatives, and/or your reading of the literature on knowledge management, to what extent do you perceive the interests of workers and organizations to be in conflict?

However, the Scarbrough perspective, is challenged by evidence which supports the Fuller (2002) position, that the interests of knowledge and management can be incompatible, and that workers are concerned with more than their own or their employer's narrow economic interests. Such examples include:

- the art staff researched by Beaumont and Hunter (2002)—see Chapter 14,
- a significant proportion of the staff in the recently privatized UK Utility researched by Vince (2001)—see Chapter 10,
- the scientists examined by Breu and Hemingway (2001)—see Chapter 5,
- the Finnish academics researched by Hakala and Ylijoko (2001).

Common to all these cases was a concern by workers regarding the conflict they perceived to exist between the commercial interests of their employers with other aims and objectives.

Overall, therefore, whilst a willingness by workers to participate in organizational knowledge management initiatives is visible in innumerable cases, it still remains the case that such willingness cannot be taken for granted. Therefore, neither Fuller (2002) nor Scarbrough (2001) are correct, as while it cannot be assumed that workers are totally instrumental in their outlook, equally it is problematic to assume that that the interests of workers and their employers will always be diametrically opposed (Button et al. 2003).

Understanding the dynamics and agents in the diffusion of knowledge on knowledge management

This section begins by considering another general critique of knowledge management: that it represents the latest in an apparently endless succession of management fads (that includes BRP—Business Process Re-engineering, TQM—Total Quality Management, and culture-based management) and that interest in the topic is thus likely to wane rapidly. Following this, a broader focus is taken to look at how management knowledge in general, and knowledge on knowledge management specifically is commodified, produced, diffused, and consumed. This will allow a consideration of the type of people and organizations that are key in such processes, with a particular focus on the role of academics, business schools, and universities in such processes. Such a focus is warranted not only because the role of the university sector has been relatively neglected in such processes, but also because its role has been changing dramatically in recent years.

Knowledge management as a fashion?

Scarbrough and Swan (2001) have undertaken one of the most thorough analyses to determine whether the explosive growth of interest that has occurred in knowledge management can be understood as following fashion. Much of the evidence they present suggests that such an analysis is accurate. For example, the explosive growth of interest in the topic that occurred in the late 1990s (see Figure 1.1) followed by the inevitable bandwagon effects, provides support for such an analysis. Further, the growth of interest in the topic also appears to be taking the form of a normal distribution curve, which Abrahamson (1996) argues is characteristic of fashions. Another factor that makes knowledge management amenable to becoming a fashion is its ambiguity. This ambiguity means that, as illustrated in Figure 15.1 and Table 15.1, the term 'knowledge management' can mean quite different things to quite different people, and thus the concept can have a potentially broad appeal.

However, a weakness of such an analysis is that it implicitly assumes consumers are relatively passive, even naïve consumers, who are prey to the efforts of opportunistic consultants and suppliers. Scarbrough and Swan (2001) and Collins (2003) suggest that such a conception plays down the extent to which consumers play an active and positive role in the consumption of new management ideas. Thus for Scarbrough and Swan (2001) part of the reason for the growth of interest in knowledge management is that it provides potential solutions to deal with real organizational problems: how to cope with the growing importance of knowledge to organizational performance. Thus the general weakness of the fashion perspective is the light in which it portrays consumers.

The production and consumption of management knowledge

While fashion-based analyses are useful for describing and understanding the exponential growth of interest in knowledge management, such analyses are relatively broad brush and general in character. They thus have limited utility in shedding light on the particular character of the processes through which knowledge on knowledge management is produced and consumed, or the actors involved in such processes. Thus section fills in some of these details by making use of the cycle of knowledge production and consumption developed by Suddaby and Greenwood 2001). This cycle is relevant to the production of *all* management knowledge, and was not developed specifically in relation to knowledge management. However, this framework can be utilized to better describe and understand the context within which knowledge on knowledge management is both produced and consumed. Further, as a reader of this textbook, you are a consumer of knowledge on knowledge management, and can use the cycle more fully to understand the processes through which such knowledge is produced, as well as the diversity of processes through which you have acquired such knowledge (see the activity at the end of the chapter).

For Suddaby and Greenwood (2001, 933) the cycle they develop and describe represents a 'field level analysis of the process by which management knowledge is produced'. As can be seen in Figure 15.2, the production and consumption of management knowledge involve the complex interaction via a number of discrete, but interrelated processes of a diverse range of actors including consumers, business schools, individual academics, gurus, consulting companies, and large professional service firms. The cycle does not represent a simple stage model, with the production and consumption of knowledge occurring in neat, independent, sequential stages. Instead, all the processes typically occur simultaneously. However, Suddaby and Greenwood suggest the process of legitimation undertaken by gurus typically represents a starting point in the production of a new body of management knowledge. The description of the cycle presented here thus starts by examining this process. However, before doing this, the character and role of consumers, the centre of the cycle is examined.

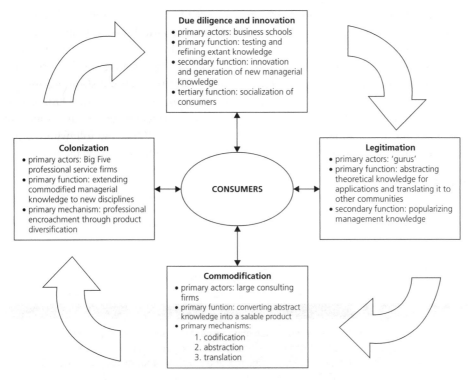

Fig. 15.2. Suddaby and Greenwood's cycle of knowledge production and consumption

Stop and think

Before looking at the cycle in detail, reflect upon your interest in knowledge management. When did it occur? What stimulated it? Further, through what mechanisms did/do you consume knowledge on knowledge management: newspapers, professional journals, 'airport books', management education?

While consumers are at the centre of the cycle, their character and role is often both poorly understood, and underconceptualized, as was discussed in the fashion debate just examined. However, Suddaby and Greenwood do little to develop such an understanding and spend little examining consumers in any detail. Further, they portray consumers in the way Scarbrough and Swan (2001) criticize them, as somewhat naïve (but sceptical) consumers of management knowledge, due to the way such knowledge is legitimated by gurus and academics. However, perhaps a more useful way of conceptualizing consumers is that portrayed by Scarbrough and Swan, where consumers, while being influenced by fashions in academic knowledge, are seen as actively seeking solutions to genuine organizational problems.

Gurus and the process of legitimation

The role of gurus in the production and consumption of knowledge can be conceptualized as the first stage in the cycle, as they play a role in popularizing and making legitimate a new body of knowledge and subject of study. For example, Peters and Waterman played such a role with the topic of culture in the 1980s through their book *In Search of Excellence* (Peters and Waterman 1983), and lecture tours which did much to popularize and legitimate the topic of organizational culture management. Gurus thus help transfer knowledge between different communities through transforming abstract theorization, or specific organizational practices, and making them generic. Gurus can be located both in the academic world and in the world of private enterprise. In a survey of academics and practitioners conducted by Edwards et al. (2003), the following writers were identified as being most influential in the area of knowledge management:

1. Nonaka

2. Nonaka and Takeuchi

3. Davenport and Prusak

4. Snowden

5. Brown and Duguid

Stop and think

Did you first come into contact with knowledge management as a subject through the work of a knowledge management guru? Is it one of the writers in the top five of the Edwards et al. survey? Who do *you* regard to be the gurus of knowledge management? Are they academics or do they work in the business sector, or both?

Consultants and the commodification of management knowledge

The commodification of management knowledge involves decontextualizing knowledge, and transforming it into a generic form, so that it can be sold as a product or service to other clients. Key agents in such processes are typically consultants, with the primary goal of economic gain acting as a significant incentive for these firms to attempt such processes of codification (Morris 2001). In relation to knowledge management, consultancies have played a key role in such processes (Scarbrough and Swan 2001), which perhaps helps to explain why a significant proportion of the knowledge management solutions being sold are generic tools and technologies, and why IT-based perspectives on knowledge management have been so popular.

The colonizing practices of large professional service firms

Colonization represents the attempts by organizations to expand the scope of their managerial knowledge products, with the key actors in such processes being large, global professional service companies such as PriceWaterhouseCoopers, Cap Gemini Ernst & Young, and Deloitte & Touche. Processes of colonization are closely related to processes of legitimation, as colonization ultimately involves specific actors struggling to be seen as more legitimate sources of management knowledge than other actors. One of the main themes in Suddaby and Greenwood's (2001) analysis relates to the importance of the not insignificant colonizing attempts by large professional service firms in transforming the cycle of knowledge production/consumption. Specific examples of what could be interpreted as colonizing attempts in the area of knowledge management are KPMG's efforts at publishing a series of Knowledge Management Surveys (for example KPMG 2000) and the publication of the book *Knowledge Unplugged*, by consultants from McKinsey's (Kluge et al. 2001). This process is looked at in more detail later due to its role in changing the nature of the context in which universities and business schools operate.

Due diligence, innovation, education, and the role of business schools

Suddaby and Greenwood characterize business schools as having three roles in the production and consumption of management knowledge. The role of business schools in such processes is examined in detail here, and in the following section. Such an examination is merited, to some extent due to the lack of attention paid to the nature of work in business schools (Willmott 1995).

The primary role of business schools is as quality controllers. Thus academic research typically follows rather than leads management practice, and plays a role in evaluating and refining management knowledge/practice (due diligence). However, this process of refinement can lead to production of new knowledge, through research-led innovation, which represents the second role of business schools.

The third role of business schools is the diffusion and dissemination of management knowledge via management education. The importance of this role should not be underestimated, due to the expansion in management education that has occurred in recent years (Sturdy and Gabriel 2000). For example, there are so many MBA programmes in existence globally that there are websites which can help students identify the most appropriate programme to their needs, with one site (http://www.mbainfo.com/)[9] having information on over 2500 different MBA programmes taught at over 1300 separate institutions. Sturdy and Gabriel (2000), based on reflections on their own experiences from teaching on an MBA programme in Malaysia, believe that MBA programmes can, to some extent, be characterized as a generic (knowledge-based) commodity, not unlike a car, and that extending the metaphor, lecturers on such programmes can be compared to car sales people. This part of the cycle links to the production and consumption of knowledge on knowledge management as specific modules on learning and knowledge management are increasingly becoming a key part of a significant number of MScs and MBA programmes. Thus, this represents an important, though often underemphasized mechanism through which people consume knowledge on knowledge management.

Stop and think

If you are a student on a management education course, to what extent can your course be considered to be a generic knowledge product/commodity? Further, to what extent, and in what ways do textbooks and books on knowledge management (such as this one) play a role in the commodification, legitimation, and diffusion of knowledge on knowledge management.

---

[9] Site accessed 18/09/03.

Changes in the cycle of knowledge production affecting business schools

As outlined earlier, it is worth looking in a little detail at the role of business schools in the cycle of knowledge production, as a number of different, external factors are impinging on them, which have implications for the cycle of knowledge production and the role of business schools in it. The three specific factors examined here are: (1) the colonizing activities of large professional service firms; (2) shifts from mode 1 to mode 2 knowledge production, and (3) the pernicious effects of neo-liberal/monetarist policies on the funding of universities. These pressures have a common effect on business schools, increasing the demands on them to commercialize their work, and develop closer links with business organizations (Fuller 2002, 5; Rynes et al. 2001; Stevens and Bagby 2001). The extent of these pressures is visible in the development of terms such as 'academic capitalism' (Slaughter and Leslie 1997), and in his presidential address to the Academy of Management Michael Hitt (1997) talked about the demands on business schools to become more entrepreneurial.

The colonizing activities of professional service firms
One key change in the cycle of knowledge production/consumption is that the largest, global professional service firms are attempting to extend their influence beyond their traditional boundaries (Suddaby and Greenwood 2001). Specifically, they seem to be attempting to develop a role in the creation as well as commodification and dissemination of knowledge and are thus turning their colonizing efforts to the internalization of traditional university functions (Huff 1999). Further, consultants are emerging as key competitors with universities in the production of research (Rynes et al. 2001).

Shifts from Mode 1- to Mode 2-based knowledge production
Gibbons et al. (1994), in a highly influential book, argue that fundamental changes in the nature of knowledge production processes occurred in the second half of the twentieth century. Fundamentally, they suggest that there has been a shift from what they label, inelegantly, a mode 1-based system, where knowledge production is discipline-based, university centred, individualistic, largely cognitive and based on a process of peer review, to a mode 2-based system, where knowledge production is, by contrast, transdisciplinary, team-rather than individual-based, and where knowledge is produced and validated through use rather than through abstract reflection. Thus, a mode 2-based system of knowledge production is highly problem oriented, and requires close collaboration with industrial/business partners. A number of writers suggest that there are pressures on business schools to undertake such a transition, and develop management knowledge through linking with relevant business partners (Hakala and Ylijoki 2001; Huff 1999). Thus this represents another external pressure, pushing business schools and private industry together.

Neo-liberal government policies and the funding of universities
The third and final factor acting to push business schools and private industry into a closer relationship has been a change in the way that governments fund universities. In general terms governments globally have moved towards the adoption of neo-liberal, monetarist policies. Such moves involve government attempts to tightly control, if not minimize/reduce, state expenditure. In relation to universities generally and business schools specifically, central government funding has been capped and increasingly tied to

performance-based measures, with encouragement provided to business schools and universities to seek higher levels of private sector funding (Fuller 2002; Hakala and Ylijoko 2001; Rynes et al. 2001; Trowler 2001; Wilmott 1995).

Conclusion

This chapter has therefore examined three key questions that hang over the topic of knowledge management, questioning both its quality and viability. The general conclusions reached were as follows. Firstly, while the analytical and theoretical rigour of some of the knowledge management literature is weak, there is a growing body of work in the area that is theoretically robust. Secondly, on the question of whether knowledge management is actually viable, the answer was a qualified yes. While the ability of organizations to directly manage and control knowledge was questioned, it was acknowledged that knowledge can be managed more indirectly by persuading workers to share and use their knowledge in particular ways. Thirdly, existing evidence does suggest that knowledge management is a contemporary management fashion. However, whether it is a passing fashion or not, two benefits from the explosion of interest in the topic that has occurred are that, firstly, it has raised awareness about the importance of knowledge in organizations and, secondly, the best of the work on the subject has contributed generally to an improved understanding of what knowledge and knowledge processes in organizations are like, as well as revealing the importance of human/social/cultural factors in such processes.

The second object of the paper was to understand the broad context within which knowledge on knowledge management is produced and consumed, which showed the range of actors and their roles in these processes.

REVIEW ACTIVITY

Name the players in the knowledge management production/consumption 'game'

Rather than provide a list of discrete questions, the book closes with an invitation to play the 'game' of naming the players and their roles in the production and consumption of knowledge on knowledge management? To do this, look in detail as Suddaby and Greenwood's cycle, and fill in the blanks.

Questions which may help you do this include:

- Where (if anywhere) is the start of the cycle?
- Who (if anyone) are the gurus of knowledge management?
  - Are they consultants? Academics? Both?
  - Through what mechanisms have their arguments been diffused (books, lectures, teaching, consultancy, . . .)
- Can you fill in more details for the unexplored category consumers?
  - Are consumers passive victims of passing fads?
  - Can you develop subcategories of different types of consumer?

- Are there organizations which represent collections of consumers which have been important in the knowledge management cycle? (trade associations, professional bodies?)
- What about the role of academia, business schools, and individual academics?
  - Is their role primarily the testing/refinement and legitimation of existing knowledge?
  - Are there particular universities, academics, or departments (business schools, IS/IT departments) that have played a particularly key role?
  - What role do university departments play in the diffusion of knowledge on knowledge management? Is this through providing education, the publication of books (such as this one)?
  - Is there evidence that academia is under pressure to commercialize its activities and outputs?
  - Is there evidence of (growing) linkages between academia and business organizations?
- What role have large professional service firms played in the production and consumption of knowledge on knowledge management?
  - Do particular organizations have a more important role than others?
  - Is there evidence of colonizing activity?
- Are there any missing actors from the cycle?
  - What about the role of the mass media? National newspapers, television? Has it had any role in the diffusion of knowledge on knowledge management?
  - Is this cycle useful in understanding the processes and agents involved in the production and consumption of knowledge on knowledge management?

FURTHER READING

- M. Alvesson and D. Karreman (2001). 'Odd Couple: Making Sense of the Curious Concept of Knowledge Management', *Journal of Management Studies*, 38/7: 995–1018.

  Provides a critical review of the early knowledge management literature, as well as developing a typology of knowledge management strategies.

- R. Suddaby and R. Greenwood (2001). 'Colonizing Knowledge: Commodification as a Dynamic of Jurisdictional Expansion in Professional Service Firms', *Human Relations*, 54/7: 933–53.

  Develop a generic model for understanding the dynamics of the production and consumption of management knowledge.

- A. Sturdy and Y. Gabriel (2000). 'Missionaries, Mercenaries or Car Salesmen? MBA Teaching in Malaysia', *Journal of Management Studies*, 37/7: 979–1002.

  Interesting personal reflections on the importance of MBA teaching for the diffusion of knowledge, and whether such teaching can be understood in commodity terms.

- G. Von Krogh, K. Ichijo, and I. Nonaka (2000). *Enabling Knowledge Creation: How to Unlock the Mystery of Tacit Knowledge and Release the Power of Innovation.* Oxford: Oxford University Press (especially Ch.1).

  Argues that knowledge is not something that can be directly managed, but that it can be managed more indirectly, via people management.

■ BIBLIOGRAPHY

Abrahamson, E. (1996). 'Management Fashion', *Academy of Management Review*, 21/1: 254–85.

Adler, P., and Kwon, S. (2002). 'Social Capital: Prospects for a New Concept', *Academy of Management Review*, 27/1: 17–40.

Ahuja, M., and Carley, K. (1999). 'Network Structure in Virtual Organizations', *Organization Science*, 10/6: 741–57.

Allee, V. (1997). *The Knowledge Evolution: Expanding Organizational Intelligence*. Oxford: Butterworth-Heinemann.

Alter, C., and Hage, J (1993). *Organisations Working Together*. Newbury Park: Sage.

Alvesson, M. (1995). *Management of Knowledge Intensive Firms*. London: De Gruyter.

—— (2000). 'Social Identity and the Problem of Loyalty in Knowledge-Intensive Companies', *Journal of Management Studies*, 37/8: 1101–123.

—— (2001). 'Knowledge Work: Ambiguity, Image and Identity', *Human Relations*, 54/7: 863–86.

—— and Karreman, D. (2001). 'Odd Couple: Making Sense of the Curious Concept of Knowledge Management', *Journal of Management Studies*, 38/7: 995–1018.

Amidon, D. (1998). 'The Evolving Community of Knowledge Practice: The Ken Awakening', *International Journal of Technology Management*, 16/1–3: 45–63.

Andrews, K., and Delahaye, B. (2000). 'Influences on Knowledge Processes in Organizational Learning: The Psychosocial Filter', *Journal of Management Studies*, 37/6: 797–810.

Antonelli, C. (2000). 'Collective Knowledge Communication and Innovation: The Evidence of Technological Districts', *Regional Studies*, 34/6: 535–47.

Ardichvili, A., Page, V., and Wentling, T. (2003). 'Motivation and Barriers to Participation in Virtual Knowledge-Sharing Communities of Practice', *Journal of Knowledge Management*, 7/1: 64–77.

Argyris, C. (1990). *Overcoming Organizational Defences*. Needham Heights, Mass: Allyn & Bacon.

Armstrong, H. (2000). 'The Learning Organization: Changed Means to an Unchanged End', *Organization*, 7/2: 355–61.

Atkinson, C. (2002). 'Career Management and the Changing Psychological Contract', *Career Development International*, 7/1: 14–23.

Badham, R., Couchman, P., and McLoughlin, I. (1997). 'Implementing Vulnerable Socio-Technical Change Projects', in I. McLoughlin and M. Harris (eds.), *Innovation, Organizational Change and Technology*. London: International Thomson Business Press, 146–69.

Bain, P., and Taylor, P. (2000). 'Entrapped by the 'Electronic Panoptican'? Worker Resistance in the Call Centre', *New Technology, Work and Employment*, 15/1: 2–18.

Ball, K., and Wilson, D. (2000). 'Power, Control and Computer-Based Performance monitoring: Repertoires, Resistance and Subjectivities', *Organization Studies*, 21/3: 539–66.

Barnes, B. (1977). *Interests and the Growth of Knowledge*. London: Routledge & Kegan Paul (Routledge Direct Editions).

Bartlett, C., and Ghoshal, S. (1993). 'Beyond the M-Form: Towards a Managerial Theory of the firm', *Strategic Management Journal*, 14 (Winter Special Issue): 23–46.

Bate, S., and Robert, G. (2002). 'Knowledge Management and Communities of Practice in the Private Sector: Lessons for Modernizing the Health Service in England and Wales', *Public Administration*, 80/4: 643–63.

Baumard, P. (1999). *Tacit Knowledge in Organizations*. London, Sage.

Beaumont, P., and Harris, R. (2002). 'Examining White Collar Downsizing as a Cause of Change in the Psychological Contract', *Employee Relations*, 24/4: 378–88.

—— and Hunter, L. (2002). *Managing Knowledge Workers*. London: CIPD.

Bechky, B. (2003). 'Sharing Meaning across Occupational Communities: The Transformation of Understanding on a Production Floor', *Organization Science*, 14/3: 312–30.

Becker, M. (2001). 'Managing Dispersed Knowledge: Organizational Problems, Managerial Strategies and their Effectiveness', *Journal of Management Studies*, 38/7: 1037–51.

Bell, D. (1973). *The Coming of Post-Industrial Society*. Harmondsworth: Penguin.

Bertoin Antal, A., Dierkes, M., Child, J., and Nonaka, I. (2001). 'Organizational Learning and Knowledge: Reflections on the Dynamics of the Field and Challenges for the Future', in M. Dierkes, A. Bertoin Antal, J. Child, I. Nonaka (eds.), *Handbook of Organizational Learning and Knowledge*. Oxford: Oxford University Press, 921–40.

Bettis, R., and Prahalad, C. (1995). 'The Dominant Logic: Retrospective and Extension', *Strategic Management Journal*, 16: 5–14.

Bhagat, R., Kedia, B., Harveston, P., and Triandis, H. (2002). 'Cultural Variations in the Cross-Border Transfer of Organizational Knowledge: An Integrative Framework', *Academy of Management Review*, 27/2: 204–21.

Birkinshaw, J., Nobel, R., and Ridderstale, J. (2002). 'Knowledge as a Contingency Variable: Do the Characteristics of Knowledge Predict Organizational Structure?' *Organization Science*, 13/3: 274–89.

Black, J., and Edwards, S. (2000). 'Emergence of Virtual or Network Organizations: Fad or Feature', *Journal of Organizational Change Management*, 13/6: 567–76.

Blackler, F. (1995). 'Knowledge, Knowledge Work and Organizations: An Overview and Interpretation', *Organization Studies*, 16/6: 1021–46.

—— Crump, N., and McDonald, S. (2000). 'Organizing Processes in Complex Activity Systems', *Organization*, 7/2: 277–300.

—— Reed, M., and Whitaker, A. (1993). 'Editorial Introduction: Knowledge Workers and Contemporary Organizations', *Journal of Management Studies*, 30/6: 851–62.

Boeker, W. (1992). 'Power and Managerial Dismissal: Scapegoating at the Top', *Administrative Science Quarterly*, 37: 400–21.

Boland, R., and Tenkasi, R. (1995). 'Perspective Making and Perspective Taking in Communities of Knowing', *Organization Science*, 6/4: 350–72.

—— —— and Te'eni, D. (1994). 'Designing Information Technology to Support Distributed Cognition', *Organization Science*, 5/3: 456–75.

Bolisani, E., and Scarso, E. (2000). 'Electronic Communication and Knowledge Transfer', *International Journal of Technology Management*, 20/1–2: 116–33.

Breu, K., and Hemingway, C. (2002). '*The Power of Communities of Practice for Subverting Organisational Change*'. Paper presented at 3rd European Conference on Organizational Knowledge, Learning and Capabilities, Athens, Greece, 5–6 April.

Brown, J., and Duguid, P, (1991). 'Organization Learning and Communities of Practice: Towards a Unified View of Working, Learning and Innovation', *Organization Science*, 2/1: 40–57.

—— —— (1998). 'Organizing Knowledge', *California Management Review*, 40/3: 90–111.

—— —— (2001). 'Knowledge and Organization: A Social Practice Perspective', *Organization Science*, 12/2: 198–213.

Bryman, A. (1992). *Charisma and the Leadership of Organizations*. London: Sage.

Buck, J., and Watson, J. (2002). 'Retaining Staff Employees: The Relationship between Human Resource Management Strategies and Organizational Commitment', *Innovative Higher Education*, 26/3: 175–93.

Burrell, G., and Morgan, G. (1979). *Sociological Paradigms and Organisational Analysis: Elements of the Sociology of Corporate Life*. London: Heinemann Educational.

Burton-Jones, A. (1999). *Knowledge Capitalism*. Oxford: Oxford University Press.

Button, G., Mason, D., and Sharrock, W. (2003). 'Disempowerment and Resistance in the Print Industry? Reactions to Surveillance-Capable Technology', *New Technology, Work and Employment*, 18/1: 50–61.

Byrne, R. (2001). 'Employees: Capital or Commodity?' *Career Development International*, 6/6: 324–330.

Cabrera, A., and Cabrera, E. (2002). 'Knowledge Sharing Dilemmas', *Organization Studies*, 23/5: 687–710

Capelli, P. (1999). *The New Deal at Work: Managing the Market-Driven Economy*. Boston, Mass: Harvard Business School Press.

Carchedi, G. (1991). *Frontiers of Political Economy*. London: Verso.

Carrington, L. (2002). 'Oiling the Wheels', *People Management*, 27 June: 31–4.

Cascio, W. (1999). 'Virtual Workplaces: Implications for Organizational Behaviour', in

C. Cooper and D. Rousseau (eds.), *Trends in Organizational Behaviour: vol. 6, The Virtual Organization*. Chichester, UK: John Wiley & Sons, 1–14.

Castells, M. (1998). *The Rise of Network Society*. Oxford: Basil Blackwell.

Chen, Z., and Francesco, A. (2000). 'Employee Demography, Organizational Commitment, and Turnover Intentions in China: Do Cultural Differences Matter?' *Human Relations*, 53/6: 869–87.

Child, J. (2001). 'Learning Through Strategic Alliances', in M. Dierkes, A. Bertoin Antal, J. Child, I. Nonaka (eds.), *Handbook of Organizational Learning and Knowledge*. Oxford: Oxford University Press, 657–80.

Ciborra, C., and Patriotta, G. (1998). 'Groupware and Teamwork in R&D: Limits to Learning and Innovation', *R&D Management*, 28/1; 1–10.

Clark, P. (2000). *Organizations in Action: Competition Between Contexts*. London: Routledge.

Clegg, S. (1998). 'Foucault, Power and Organizations, in A. McKinlay and K. Starkey (eds.), *Foucault, Management and Organization Theory*. London: Sage, 29–48.

Cohen, W., and Levinthal, D. (1990). 'Absorptive Capacity: A New Perspective on Innovation and Learning', *Administrative Science Quarterly*, 35: 128–52.

Collins, D. (2003). 'The Branding of Management Knowledge: Rethinking Management "Fads" ', *Journal of Organizational Change Management*, 16/2: 186–204.

Contu, A., and Willmott, H (2000) Comment on Wenger and Yanow. Knowing in Practice: A 'Delicate Flower' in the Organizational Learning Field, *Organization*, 7/2: 269–76

—— —— (2003). 'Re-Embedding Situatedness: The Importance of Power Relations in Learning Theory', *Organization Science*, 14/3: 283–96.

Cook, S., and Brown, J. (1999). 'Bridging Epistemologies: The Generative Dance Between Organizational Knowledge and Organizational Knowing, *Organization Science*, 10/4: 381–400.

—— and Yanow, D. (1993). 'Culture and Organizational Learning', *Journal of Management Enquiry*, 2/4: 373–90.

Coopey, J. (1995). 'The Learning Organization, Power, Politics and Ideology', *Management Learning*, 26/2: 193–213.

—— (1998). 'Learning the Trust and Trusting to Learn: A Role for Radical Theatre', *Management Learning*, 29/3: 365–82.

—— and Burgoyne, J. (2000). 'Politics and Organizational Learning', *Journal of Management Studies*, 37/6: 869–85.

Coyle-Shapiro, J., and Kessler, I. (2000). 'Consequences of the Psychological Contract for the Employment Relationship: A Large Scale Survey', *Journal of Management Studies*, 37/7: 903–30.

Craib, I. (1997). *Classical Social Theory*. Oxford: Oxford University Press.

Cramton, C. (2001). 'The Mutual Knowledge Problem and Its Consequences for Dispersed Collaboration', *Organization Science*, 12/3: 346–71.

Cranfield Business School (1998). *Europe's State of the Art in Knowledge Management. Information Strategy*. London: The Economist Group.

Cravens, D., Piercey, N., and Shipp, S. (1996). 'New Organizational Forms for Competing in Highly Dynamic Environments: the Network Paradigm', *British Journal of Management*, 7/2: 203–18.

Crompton, R., and Reid, S. (1983). 'The Deskilling of Clerical Work', in S. Wood (ed.), *The Degradation of Work? Skill, Deskilling and the Labour Process*. London: Hutchinson, 163–78.

Crossan, M., Lane, H., and White, R. (1999). 'An Organizational Learning Framework: From Intuition to Institution', *Academy of Management Review*, 24/3: 522–37.

Cutcher-Gershenfeld, J. Nitta, M., and Barrett, B. (1998). *Knowledge-Driven Work*. Oxford: Oxford University Press.

Davenport, T., and Prusak, L. (1998). 'Working Knowledge: How Organizations Manage What they Know. Harvard Business School Press: Boston, Mass.

Davies, A., and Brady, T. (2000). 'Organisational Capabilities and Learning in Complex Product Systems: Towards Repeatable Solutions', *Research Policy*, 29: 931–53.

Deetz, S. (1998). 'Discursive Formations, Strategized Subordination and Self-Surveillance', in A. McKinlay and K. Starkey (eds.), Foucault, Management and Organization Theory. London: Sage, 151–72.

DeFillippi, R., and Arthur, M. (1998). 'Paradox in Project Based Enterprise: The Case of Filmmaking', *California Management Review*, 40/2: 125–39.

De Long, D., and Fahey, L. (2000). 'Diagnosing Cultural Barriers to Knowledge Management', *Academy of Management Executive*, 14/4: 113–27.

DeSanctis, G., and Monge, P. (1999). 'Introduction to the Special Issue: Communication Processes for Virtual Organizations', *Organization Science*, 10/6: 693–703.

Dougherty, D. (2001). 'Reimagining the Differentiation and Integration of Work for Sustained Product Innovation', *Organization Science*, 12/5: 612–31.

Dovey, K. (1997). 'The Learning Organization and the Organization of Learning: Learning, Power, Transformation and the Search for Form in Learning Organizations', *Management Learning*, 28: 331–49.

Driver, M. (2002). 'The Learning Organization: Foucauldian Gloom or Utopian Sunshine?' *Human Relations*, 55/1: 33–53.

Drucker, P. (1993). *Post-Capitalist Society*. Oxford: Butterworth-Heinemann.

Duarte, D., and Snyder, N. (2001). *Mastering Virtual Teams: Strategies, Tools and Techniques that Succeed*. San Francisco: Jossey-Bass.

Dyer, J., and Nobeoka, K. (2000). 'Creating and Managing a High-Performance Knowledge-Sharing Network: The Toyota Case', *Strategic Management Journal*, 21: 345–67.

Easterby-Smith, M. (1997). 'Disciplines of Organizational Learning: Contributions and Critique', *Human Relations*, 50/9: 1085–113.

Easterby-Smith, M., Crossan, M., and Nicolini, D. (2000). 'Organizational Learning: Debates Past, Present and Future', *Journal of Management Studies*, 37/6: 783–96.

Edwards, J., Handzic, M., Carlsson, S., and Nissen, M. (2003). 'Knowledge Management Research and Practice: Visions and Directions', *Knowledge Management Research & Practice*, 1/1: 49–60.

Elger, T., and Smith, C (1994). 'Transplants, Transfer and Adaptation: Prologue', in T. Elger and C. Smith (eds.), *Global Japanization? The Transnational Transformation of the Labour Process*. London: Routledge, 115–22.

Elias, P., and Gregory, M. (1994). *The Changing Structure of Occupations and Earnings in Great Britain 1975–1990: An Analysis based on the New Earnings Survey Panel Dataset*. Warwick: Institute for Employment Research.

Empson, L. (2001). 'Fear of Exploitation and Fear of Contamination: Impediments to Knowledge Transfer in Mergers between Professional Service Firms', *Human Relations*, 54/7: 839–62.

Farr, K. (2000). 'Organizational Learning and Knowledge Managers', *Work Study*, 49/1: 14–17.

Felstead, A., Ashton, D., and Green, F. (2000). 'Are Britain's Workplace Skills Becoming More Unequal?' *Cambridge Journal of Economics*, 24/6: 709–27.

Fenton, E., and Pettigrew, A. (2000a). 'Theoretical Perspectives on New Forms of Organizing', in A. Pettigrew and E. Fenton (eds.), *The Innovating Organization*. London: Sage, 1–46.

—— —— (2000b). 'Integrating a Global Professional Service Organization: The Case of Ove Arup Partnership', in A. Pettigrew and E. Fenton (eds.), *The Innovating Organization*. London: Sage, 47–81.

Ferner, A. (1997). 'Country of Origin Effects and HRM in Multinational Companies', *Human Resource Management Journal*, 7/1: 19–37.

—— Qunitanilla, J., and Varul, M. (2001). 'Country of Origin Effects, Host Country Effects, and the Management of HR in Multinationals: German Companies in Britain and Spain', *Journal of World Business*, 36/2: 107–27.

—— and Varul, M. (2000). 'Internationalisation and the Personnel Function in German Multinationals', *Human Resource Management Journal*, 10/3: 79–96.

Flood, P., Turner, T., and Hannaway, C. (2000). *Attracting and Retaining Knowledge Employees: Irish Knowledge Employees and the Psychological Contract*. Dublin: Blackhall.

—— —— Ramamoorthy, N., and Pearson, J. (2001). 'Causes and Consequences of Psychological Contracts among Knowledge Workers in the High Technology and Financial Services Industry', *International Journal of Human Resource Management*, 12/7: 1152–1165.

Ford, D., and Chan, Y. (2003). 'Knowledge Sharing in a Multi-cultural Setting: A Case Study', *Knowledge Management Research & Practice*, 1/1: 11–27.

Fox, S. (2000). 'Practice, Foucault and Actor-Network Theory', *Journal of Management Studies*, 37/6: 853–68.

Foucault, M. (1980). *Power/Knowledge: Selected Interviews and Other Writings 1972–1977*. London: Harvester Wheatsheaf.

Forsgren, M. (1997). 'The Advantage Paradox of the Multinational Corporation', in I. Bjorkman and M. Forsgren (eds.), *The Nature of the*

International Firm. Copenhagen: Copenhagen Business School, 69–85.

Fosstenlokken, S., Lowendahl, B., and Revang, O. (2003). 'Knowledge Development through Client Interaction: A comparative Study', *Organization Studies,* 24/6: 859–80.

Frenkel, S., Korczynski, M., Donohue, L., and Shire, K. (1995). 'Re-constituting Work: Trends towards Knowledge Work and Info-normative Control', *Work, Employment and Society,* 9/4: 773–96

—— —— Shire, K., and Tam, M. (1999). *On the Front Line: Organization of Work in the Information Economy.* London: ILR Press.

Friedman, V., Lipshitz, R., and Overmeer, W. (2001). 'Creating Conditions for Organizational Learning' in M. Dierkes, A. Bertoin Antal, J. Child, and I. Nonaka (eds.), *Handbook of Organizational Learning and Knowledge.* Oxford: Oxford University Press, 757–74.

Fulk, J. (2001). 'Global Network Organizations: Emergence and Future Prospects', *Human Relations,* 51/1: 91–9.

Fuller, S. (2002). *Knowledge Management Foundations.* Oxford: Butterworth-Heinemann.

Gabriel, Y. (1991). 'Beyond Happy Families: A Critical Re-evaluation of the Control-Resistance-Identity Triangle', *Human Relations,* 52/2: 179–203.

Gallie, D., White, M., Cheng, Y., and Tomlinson, M. (1998). *Restructuring the Employment Relationship.* Oxford: Clarendon Press.

Gargiulo, M., and Benassi, M. (2000). 'Trapped in Your Own Net? Network Cohesion, Structural Holes, and the Adaptation of Social Capital', *Organization Science,* 11/2: 183–96.

Garvey, B., and Williamson, B. (2002). *Beyond Knowledge Management: Dialogue, Creativity and the Corporate Curriculum.* Harlow, UK: Financial Times/Prentice Hall.

Gherardi, S. (2000). 'Practice Based Theorizing on Learning and Knowing in Organizations', *Organization* 7/2: 211–33.

—— and Nicolini, D. (2002). 'Learning in a Constellation of Interconnected Practices: Canon or Dissonance?' *Journal of Management Studies,* 39/4: 419–36

—— —— and Odella, F. (1998). 'Towards a Social Understanding of How People Learn in Organizations: The Notion of Situated Curriculum', *Management Learning,* 29/3: 273–97.

Ghoshal, S., and Bartlett, C. (1990). 'The Multinational Corporation as an Interorganizational Network', *Academy of Management Review,* 15/4: 603–25.

Gibbons, M., Limoges, C., Nowotny, H., Schwartzman, S., and Scott, P., and Trow, M. (1994). *The New Production of Knowledge: The Dynamics of Science and Research in Contemporary Societies.* London: Sage.

Giddens, A. (1979). *Central Problems in Social Theory.* London: Macmillan.

—— (1991). *Modernity and Self-Identity: Self and Society in the Late Modern Age.* Cambridge: Polity Press.

—— (2000). *The Third Way and its Critics.* Cambridge: Polity Press.

Gittelman, M., and Kogut, B. (2003). 'Does good Science Lead to Valuable Knowledge? Biotechnology Firms and the Evolutionary Logic of Citation Patterns', *Management Science,* 49/4: 366–82.

Glazer, R. (1998). 'Measuring the Knower: Towards a Theory of Knowledge Equity', *California Management Review,* 40/3: 175–94.

Goodall, K., and Roberts, J. (2003). 'Repairing Managerial Knowledge-ability over Distance', *Organization Studies,* 24/7: 1153–76.

Grant, R. (1996). 'Towards a Knowledge Based Theory of the Firm', *Strategic Management Journal,* 17 (Winter Special Issue), 109–22.

—— (2000). 'Shifts in the World Economy: The Drivers of Knowledge Management', in C. Despres and D. Chauvel (eds.), *Knowledge Horizons: The Present and the Promise of Knowledge Management.* Oxford: Butterworth-Heinemann, 27–54.

Gray, P. (2001). 'The Impact of Knowledge Repositories on Power and Control in the Workplace', *Information Technology and People,* 14/4: 368–84.

Guest, D. (1998), 'Beyond HRM: Commitment and the Contract Culture', in P. Sparrow and Marchington (eds.), FT/Pitman, Human Resource Management: The New Agenda, 37–51.

—— and Conway, N. (1999), 'How Dissatisfied are British Workers? A Survey of Surveys'. IPD: London.

—— and Patch, A. (2000). 'The Employment Relationship, The Psychological Contract and Knowledge Management: Securing Employees Trust and Contribution.' Paper presented at Knowledge Management: Concepts and Controversies, University of Warwick, April.

Gupta, A., and Govindarajan, V. (2000). 'Knowledge Flows within Multinational Corporations', *Strategic Management Journal*, 21: 473–96.

Hakala, J., and Ylijoki, O-H. (2001). 'Research for Whom? Research Orientations in Three Academic Cultures', *Organization*, 8/2: 373–80.

Hales, C. (1993). *Managing Through Organization: The Management Process, Forms of Organisation and the Work of Managers*. London: Routledge.

—— (2002). ' 'Bureaucracy-lite' and continuities in managerial work', *British Journal of Management*, 13/1: 51–66

Hall, P., and Soskice, D. (2001). *Varieties of Capitalism*. Oxford: Oxford University Press.

Handy, C. (1984). *The Future of Work: A Guide to a Changing Society*. Oxford: Basil Blackwell.

Hansen, M. (1999). 'The Search-Transfer Problem: The Role of Weak Ties in Sharing Knowledge Across Organization Subunits', *Administrative Science Quarterly*, March: 82–111.

—— (2002). 'Knowledge Networks: Explaining Effective Knowledge Sharing in Multiunit Companies', *Organization Science*, 13/3: 232–48.

—— Nohria, N., and Tierney, T. (1999), 'What's Your Strategy for Managing Knowledge?' *Harvard Business Review*, 77/2: 106.

Hardy, C., Phillips, N., and Lawrence, T. (2003). 'Resources, Knowledge and Influence: The Organizational Effects on Interorganizational Collaboration', *Journal of Management Studies*, 40/2: 321–47.

Harris, L., and Ogbonna, E. (1998). 'Employee Responses to Culture Change Efforts', *Human Resource Management Journal*, 8/2: 78–92.

Harrison, R., and Leitch, C. (2000). 'Learning and Organization in the Knowledge-Based Information Economy: Initial Findings from a Participatory Action Research Study', *British Journal of Management*, 11: 103–19.

Hauschild, S., Licht, T., and Stein, W. (2001). *Creating a Knowledge Management Culture*. McKinseys.

Hayes, N., and Walsham, G. (2000). 'Safe Enclaves, Political Enclaves and Knowledge Working', in C. Prichard, R. Hull, M. Chumer, and H. Willmott (eds.), *Managing Knowledge: Critical Investigations of Work and Learning*. London: Macmillan, 69–87.

Hedberg, B. (1981). 'How Organizations Learn and Unlearn', in P. Nystrom and W. Starbuck (eds.), *Handbook of Organizational Design*. New York: Oxford University Press, 3–27.

—— Wolff, R. (2001). 'Organizing, Learning, and Strategizing: From Construction to Discovery', in M. Dierkes, A. Bertoin Antal, J. Child, and I. Nonaka (eds.), *Handbook of Organizational Learning and Knowledge*. Oxford: Oxford University Press, 535–56.

Hendriks, P. (2001). 'Many Rivers to Cross: From ICT to Knowledge Management Systems', *Journal of Information Technology*, 16: 57–72.

Hedlund, G. (1986). 'The Hypermodern MNC: A Heterarchy?' *Human Resource Management*, 25/1: 9–35.

—— (1994). 'A Model of Knowledge Management and the N-Form Corporation', *Strategic Management Journal*, 15 (Summer Special Issue), 73–90.

Hildreth, P., Kimble, C., and Wright, P. (2000). 'Communities of Practice in the Distributed International Environment', *Journal of Knowledge Management*, 4/1: 27–38.

Hirst, P., and Thompson, G. (1999). *Globalization in Question: The International Economy and the Possibilities of Governance*. Cambridge: Polity Press.

Hislop, D. (1999). 'The Movex Project: Knowledge Management at Brightco', in H. Scarbrough and J. Swan (eds.), Case Studies in Knowledge Management. London: Institute of Personnel and Development, 51–8.

—— (2000). 'Environmental Constraints and Sectoral Recipes: Strategic Change in Britain's Military Industrial Base', *Journal of Management Studies*, 37/5: 689–703.

—— (2002*a*). 'Linking Human Resource Management and Knowledge Management: A Review and Research Agenda', *Employee Relations*, 25/2: 182–202.

—— (2002*b*). 'Mission Impossible? Communicating and Sharing Knowledge via Information Technology', *Journal of Information Technology*, 17: 165–77.

—— Newell, S., Scarbrough, H., and Swan, J. (2000). 'Networks, Knowledge and Power: Decision-making, Politics and the Process of Innovation', *Technology Analysis and Strategic Management*, 12/3: 399–411.

Hitt, M. (1998). 'Twenty-First-Century Organizations: Business Firms, Business Schools, and the Academy', *Academy of Management Review*, 23/2: 218–24.

Hofstede, G. (1998). 'Identifying Organizational Subcultures: An Empirical Approach', *Journal of Management Studies*, 35/1: 1–12.

—— (2001). *Culture's consequences: Comparing Values, Behaviours, Institutions and Organizations across Nations*. Thousand Oaks, Calif.: Sage.

Hollingshead, A., Fulk, J., and Monge, P. (2002). 'Fostering Intranet Knowledge Sharing: An Integration of Transactive Memory and Public Goods Approaches', in P. Hinds and S. Kiesler (eds.), *Distributed Work*. London: MIT Press, 335–56.

Huczynski, Buchanan, D (2001). *Organizational Behaviour: An Introductory Text*. Harlow: Financial Times/Prentice Hall.

Huff, A. (2000). 'Changes in Organizational Knowledge Production', *Academy of Management Review*, 25/2: 288–93.

Hunter, L., Beaumont, P., and Lee, M. (2002). 'Knowledge Management Practice in Scottish Law Firms', *Human Resource Management Journal*, 12/2: 4–21.

Huzzard, T., and Ostergren, K. (2002). 'When Norms Collide: Learning Under Organizational Hypocrisy', *British Journal of Management*, 13: S47–59.

Iles, P. (1994). 'Developing Learning Environments: Challenges for Theory, Research and Practice', *Journal of European Industrial Training*, 18/3: 3–9.

Iverson, R., and Buttigieg, D. (1999). 'Affective, Normative, and Continuance Commitment: Can the 'Right Kind' of Commitment be Managed?' *Journal of Management Studies*, 36:3: 307–33.

Jackson, P. (1999). 'Introduction: From New Designs to New Dynamics', in P. Jackson (ed.), *Virtual Working: Social and Organisational Dynamics*. London: Routledge, 1–16.

Jacquier-Roux, V., and Bourgeois, B. (2002). 'New Networks of Technological Creation in Energy Industries: Reassessment of the Roles of Equipment Suppliers and Operators', *Technology Analysis and Strategic Management*, 14/4: 399–417.

Jarvenpaa, S., and Ives, B. (1994). 'The Global Network Organization of the Future: Information Management Opportunities and Challenges'. *Journal of Management Information Systems*, 10/4: 25–57.

—— and Leidner, D. (1999). 'Communication and Trust in Global Virtual Teams', *Organization Science*, 10/6: 791–815.

—— and Staples, D. (2000). 'The Use of Collaborative Electronic Media for Information Sharing: An Exploratory Study of Determinants', *Journal of Strategic Information Systems*, 9/1: 129–54.

Jones, O., and Beckinsale, M. (2001). 'Micropolitics and Network Mapping: Innovation Management in a Mature Firm', in O. Jones, S. Conway, and F. Steward (eds.), Social *Interaction and Organisational Change: Aston Perspectives on Innovation Networks*, London: Imperial College Press, 41–79.

—— Conway, S., and Steward, F. (2001). 'Introduction: Social Interaction and Organisational Change', in O. Jones, S. Conway, and F. Steward (eds.), Social *Interaction and Organisational Change: Aston Perspectives on Innovation Networks*. London: Imperial College Press, 1–40.

Kets de Vries, M. (1991). 'Whatever Happened to the Philosopher King? The Leaders Addiction to Power', *Journal of Management Studies*, 28/4: 339–51.

Kim, W., and Mauborgne, R. (1993). 'Procedural Justice, Attitudes, and Subsidiary Top Management Compliance with Multinationals' Corporate Strategic Decisions', *Academy of Management Journal*, 36: 502–28.

—— —— (1998). 'Procedural Justice, Strategic Decision-Making, and the Knowledge Economy', *Strategic Management Journal*, 19: 323–38.

Kluge, J., Stein, W., and Licht, T. (2001). *Knowledge Unplugged: The McKinsey Survey on Knowledge Management*. Basingstoke: Palgrave.

Knights, D., Murray, F., and Willmott, H. (1993). 'Networking as Knowledge Work: A Study of Strategic Interorganzational Development in the Financial Service Industry', *Journal of Management Studies*, 30/6: 975–95.

Kofman, F., and Senge, P. (1993). 'Communities of Commitment: The Heart of Learning Organizations', *Organizational Dynamics*, 22/2: 5–23.

Kogut, B., and Zander, U. (1992). 'Knowledge of the Firm, Combinative Capabilities, and the Replication of Technology', *Organization Science*, 3/3: 383–97.

Korten, D. (1995). *When Corporations Rule the World*. London: Earthscan.

KPMG (2000). *Knowledge Management Research Report*. KPMG Consulting.

Kumar, K (1995). *From Post-Industrial to Post-Modern Society: New Theories of the Contemporary World*. London: Blackwell.

Kunda, G. (1992). *Engineering Culture: Control and Commitment in a High-Tech Corporation*. Philadelphia: Temple University Press.

Kusterer, K. (1978). *Know-How on the Job. The Important Working Knowledge of 'Unskilled' Workers*. Boulder, Col.: Westview Press.

Lam, A. (1994). 'The Utilization of Human Resources: A Comparative Study of British and Japanese Engineers in Electronics Industries', *Human Resource Management Journal*, 4/3: 22–40.

—— (1996). 'Engineers, Management and Work Organisation: A Comparative Analysis of Engineers' Work Roles in British and Japanese Electronics Industries', *Journal of Management Studies*, 33/2: 183–212.

—— (1997). 'Embedded Firms, Embedded Knowledge: Problems in Collaboration and Knowledge Transfer in Global Cooperative Ventures', *Organization Studies*, 18/6: 973–96.

—— (2000). 'Tacit Knowledge, Organizational Learning and Societal Institutions: An Integrated Framework', *Organization Studies*, 21/3: 487–513.

Lane, C. (1998). 'Introduction: Theories and Issues in the Study of Trust', in C. Lane and R. Bachmann (eds.), *Trust Within and Between Organizations*. Oxford: Oxford University Press, 1–30.

LaPolombara, J. (2001). 'Power and Politics in Organizations: Public and Private Sector Comparisons', in M. Dierkes, A. Bertoin Antal, J. Child, and I. Nonaka (eds.), *Handbook of Organizational Learning and Knowledge*. Oxford: Oxford University Press, 557–81.

Lave, J., and Wenger, E. (1991). *Situated Learning: Legitimate Peripheral Participation*. Cambridge: Cambridge University Press.

Laurent, A. (1983). 'The Cultural Diversity of Conceptions of Management', *International Studies of Management and Organization*, 13: 75–96.

—— (1996). 'The Cross-Cultural Puzzle of International Human Resource Management', *Human Resource Management*, 25: 91–102.

Lazega, E. (1992), *Micropolitics of Knowledge: Communication and Indirect Control in Workgroups*. New York: De Gruyter.

Lee, T., and Maurer, S. (1997). 'The Retention of Knowledge Workers with the Unfolding Model of voluntary Turnover', *Human Resource Management Review*, 7/3: 247–75.

Leidner, D. (2000). 'Editorial', *Journal of Strategic Information Systems*, 9: 101–5.

Leonard-Barton, D. (1995) *Wellsprings of Knowledge: Building and Sustaining the Sources of Innovation*. Boston, Mass.: Harvard Business School Press.

Leonard, D., and Sensiper, S. (1998). 'The Role of Tacit Knowledge in Group Innovation', *California Management Review*, 40/3: 112–32.

Levinthal, D., and March, J. (1993). 'The Myopia of Learning', *Strategic Management Journal*, 14 (Special Issue): 95–113.

Levitt, B., and March, J. (1988). 'Organizational Learning', *Annual Review of Sociology*, 14: 319–340.

Liedtka, J. (1999). 'Linking Competitive Advantage with Communities of Practice', *Journal of Management Enquiry*, 8/1: 5–16

Lundvall, B-A. (1988). 'Innovation as an Interactive Process', in G. Dosi, C. Freeman, R. Nelson, G. Silverberg, and L. Soete (eds.), *Technical Change and Economic Theory*. London: Pinter, 45–67.

Lynn, D. (1998). 'New Product Team Learning: Developing and Profiting from Your Knowledge Capital', *California Management Review*, 40/4: 74–93.

Lyons, D. (1994). *The Electronic Eye: The Rise of Surveillance Society*. Cambridge, UK: Polity Press.

—— (2001). *Surveillance Society: Monitoring Everyday Life*. Buckingham: Open University Press.

McAdam, R., and McCreedy, S. (2000). 'A Critique of Knowledge Management: Using a Social Constructivist Model', *New Technology, Work and Employment*, 155–68.

—— and Reid, R. (2001). 'SME and Large Organisation Perceptions of Knowledge Management: Comparisons and Contrasts', *Journal of Knowledge Management*, 5/3: 231–41.

McClure Wasko, M., and Faraj, S. (2000). ' "It is What One does": Why People Participate and Help Others in Electronic Communities of Practice', *Journal of Strategic Information Systems*, 9/1: 155–73.

McDermott, R. (1999). 'Why Information Technology Inspired but Cannot Deliver Knowledge Management', *California Management Review*, 41/1: 103–117

—— and O'Dell, C. (2001). 'Overcoming Cultural Barriers to Knowledge Sharing', *Journal of Knowledge Management*, 5/1: 76–85.

McDonald, D., and Makin, P. (2000). 'The Psychological Contract, Organizational Commitment and Job Satisfaction of Temporary Staff', *Leadership and Organizational Development Journal*, 21/2: 84–91.

Macharzina, K., Oesterle, M-J., and Brodel, D. (2001). 'Learning in Multinationals', in M. Dierkes, A. Bertoin Antal, J. Child, and I. Nonaka (eds.), *Handbook of Organizational Learning and Knowledge*. Oxford: Oxford University Press, 631–56.

Machlup, F. (1962). The Production and Distribution of Knowledge in the US. Princeton, NJ: Princeton University Press.

McInerney, C., and LeFevre, D. (2000). 'Knowledge Managers: History and Challenges', in C. Prichard, R. Hull, M. Chumer, and H. Willmott (eds.), *Managing Knowledge: Critical Investigations of Work and Learning*. Macmillan: London, 1–19.

McKinlay, A. (1996). 'Philosophers in Overalls?: Craft and Class on Clydeside, *c.* 1900–1914', in W. Kenefick and A. McIvor (eds.), *Roots of Red Clydeside? Labour Unrest and Industrial Relations in West Scotland*. John Donald: Edinburgh, 86–106.

Management Review & AMA Research (1999). 'Survey on Knowledge Management', *Management Review*, April, 20–6.

Manwaring, T., and Wood, S. (1985). 'The Ghost in the Machine,' in D. Knights, H. Willmott, and D. Collinson (eds.), *Job Redesign: Critical Perspectives on the Labour Process*. London: Gower, 171–96.

Markus, L. (1994). 'Electronic Mail as the Medium of Managerial Choice', *Organization Science*, 5/4: 502–27.

Marshall, N., and Brady, T. (2001). 'Knowledge Management and the Politics of Knowledge: Illustrations from Complex Product Systems', *European Journal of Information Systems*, 10: 99–112.

Massey, A., Montoya-Weiss, M., and O'Driscoll, T. (2002). 'Knowledge Management in Pursuit of Performance: Insights from Nortel Networks', *MIS Quarterly*, 26/3: 269–89.

Maurice, M., Sorge, A., and Warner, M. (1980). 'Societal Differences in Organizing Manufacturing Units: A Comparison of France, West Germany and Great Britain', *Organization Studies*, 1/1: 59–86.

Maznevski, M., and Chudoba, K. (2000). 'Bridging Space over Time: Global Virtual Team Dynamics and Effectiveness', *Organization Science*, 11/5: 473–92.

—— (2000). 'The Bearable Lightness of Control: Organisational Reflexivity and the Politics of Knowledge Management', in C. Prichard, R. Hull, M. Chumer, and H. Willmott (eds.), *Managing Knowledge: Critical Investigations of Work and Learning*. London: Macmillan, 107–21.

—— (2002). 'The Limits of Knowledge Management', *New Technology, Work and Employment*, 17/ 2: 76–88.

—— and Starkey, K. (1998) *Foucault, Management and Organization Theory*. London: Sage.

McLoughlin, I. (1999). *Creative Technological Change: The Shaping of Technology and Organizations*. London: Routledge.

—— and Jackson, P. (1999). 'Organizational Learning and the Virtual Organisation', in P. Jackson (ed.), *Virtual Working: Social and Organisational Dynamics*. London: Routledge, 178–92.

Meeus, M., Oerlemans, L., and Hage, J. (2001). 'Patterns of Interactive Learning in a High-Tech Region', *Organization Studies*, 22/1: 145–72.

Meyer, J., and Allen, N. (1997). *Commitment in the Workplace: Theory Research and Application*. London: Sage.

—— —— and Smith, C. (1993). 'Commitment to Organizations and Occupations: Extension and Test of a Three Component Conceptualization', *Journal of Applied Psychology*, 78/4: 538–51.

Meyerson, D., Weick, K., and Kramer, R. (1996). 'Swift Trust and Temporary Groups', in R. Kramer and T. Tyler (eds.), *Trust in Organizations: Frontiers of Theory and Research*. London: Sage, 166–95.

Mintzberg, H., Ahlstrand, B., and Lampel, J. (1998) *Strategy Safari: The Complete Guide through the Wilds of Strategic Management*. Harlow: Financial Times Prentice-Hall.

Mirchandani, K. (1999). 'Re-Forming Organisations: Contributions of Teleworking Employees', in P. Jackson (ed.), *Virtual Working: Social and Organisational Dynamics*. London: Routledge, 61–75.

Mitchell, A., Sikka, P., and Willmott, H. (2001). 'Policing Knowledge by Invoking the Law: Critical Accounting and the Politics of Dissemination', *Critical Perspectives on Accounting*, 12: 527–55.

Mitsuru, K. (1999). 'Strategic Innovation in Large Companies through Strategic Community Management: an NTT Multimedia Revolution Case Study, *European Journal of Innovation Management*, 2/3: 95–108

Moon, J., and Sproull, L. (2002). 'Essence of Distributed Work: The Case of Linux Kernal', in P. Hinds and S. Kiesler (eds.), *Distributed Work*. London: MIT Press, 381–404.

Morris, J., Wilkinson, B., and Munday, M. (2000). 'Farewell to HRM? Personnel Practices in Japanese Manufacturing Plants in the UK', *International Journal of Human Resource Management*, 11/6: 1047–60.

Morris, T. (2001). 'Asserting Property Rights: Knowledge Codification in the Professional Service Firm', *Human Relations*, 54/7: 819–38.

—— and Empson, L. (1998), 'Organization and Expertise: An Exploration of Knowledge Bases and the Management of Accounting and Consulting Firms', *Accounting, Organizations and Society*, 23/5–6: 609–24.

Morrison, E., and Robinson, S. (1997). 'When Employees Feel Betrayed: A Model of How Psychological Contract Violation Develops', *Academy of Management Review*, 22: 226–56.

Mutch, A. (2003). 'Communities of Practice and Habitus: A Critique', *Organization Studies*, 24/3: 383–402.

Nadler, D., and Tushman, M. (1990). 'Beyond the Charismatic Leader: Leadership and Organizational Change', *California Management Review*, Winter: 77–97.

Nahapiet, J., and Ghoshal, S. (1998). 'Social Capital, Intellectual Capital and the Organizational Advantage', *Academy of Management Review*, 23/2: 242–66.

Nandhakumar, J. (1999). 'Virtual Teams and Lost Proximity: Consequences on Trust in Relationships', in P. Jackson (ed.), *Virtual Working: Social and Organisational Dynamics*. London: Routledge, 46–56.

Neef, D. (1999). 'Making the Case for Knowledge Management: the Bigger Picture', *Management Decision*, 37/1: 72–8.

Newell, S., Scarbrough, H., Swan, J., and Hislop, D. (2000), 'Intranets and Knowledge Management: De-Centred Technologies and the Limits of Technological Discourse', in C. Prichard, R. Hull, M. Chumer, and H. Willmott (eds.), *Managing Knowledge: Critical Investigations of Work and Learning*. London: Macmillan 88–106.

—— and Swan, J. (2000). 'Trust and Inter-Organizational Networking', *Human Relations*, 53/10: 1287–328.

Ngwenyama, O., and Lee, A. (1997). 'Communication Richness in Electronic Mail: Critical Social Theory and the Contextuality of Meaning', *MIS Quarterly*, 21/2: 145–67.

Nonaka, I. (1994). 'A Dynamic Theory of Organizational Knowledge Creation', *Organization Science*, 5/1: 14–37.

—— (1998). 'The Concept of "ba": Building a Foundation for Knowledge Creation', *California Management Review*, 40/3: 40–54.

—— and Takeuchi, H. (1995). *The Knowledge Creating Company*. Oxford: Oxford University Press.

—— Toyama, R., and Konno, N. (2000). 'SECI, Ba and Leadership: A Unified Model of Dynamic Knowledge Creation', *Long Range Planning*, 33/1: 5–34

—— —— and Byosiere, P (2001). 'A Theory of Organizational Knowledge Creation: Understanding the Dynamic Process of Creating Knowledge', in M. Dierkes, A. Bertoin Antal, J. Child, and I. Nonaka (eds.), *Handbook of Organizational Learning and Knowledge*. Oxford: Oxford University Press, 491–517.

NSTF (2000). *Skills for All: Research Report from the National Skills Task Force*. London: Department for Education and Employment.

OECD (1996). *The Knowledge-Based Economy*. Paris: Organisation for Economic Cooperation and Development.

Ogbonna, E., and Harris, L. (1998). 'Managing Organizational Culture: Compliance of Genuine Change', *British Journal of Management*, 9: 273–88.

Organ, D., and Ryan, K. (1995). 'A Meta Analytical Review of Attitudinal and Dispositional Predictors of Organizational Citizenship Behaviour', *Personnel Psychology*, 48: 775–802.

Orlikowski, W. (1992). 'The Duality of Technology: Rethinking the Concept of Technology in Organizations', *Organization Science*, 3/3: 398–427.

—— (2002). 'Knowing in Practice: Enacting a Collective Capability in Distributed Organizing', *Organization Science*, 13/3: 249–73.

—— Yates, J., Okamura, K., and Futimoto, M. (1995). 'Shaping Electronic Communication: The Metastructuring of Technology in the

Context of Use', *Organization Science*, 6/4: 423–44.

Orr, J. (1990). 'Sharing Knowledge, Celebrating Identity: War Stories and Community Memory in a Service Culture', in *Collective Remembering: Memory in a Society*, D. Middleton and D. Edwards (eds.). London: Sage, 169–89.

Pan, S., and Scarbrough, H. (1999). 'Knowledge Management in Practice: An Exploratory Case Study', *Technology Analysis and Strategic Management*, 11/3: 359–74.

Patriotta, G. (2003). 'Sensemaking on the Shopfloor: Narratives of Knowledge in Organizations', *Journal of Management Studies* 40/2: 449–75.

Pauline, D., and Mason, D. (2002). 2002 New Zealand Knowledge Management Survey: Barriers and Drivers of KM Uptake (downloaded from www.nzkm.net—4 December 2003).

—— and Yoong, P. (2001). 'Relationship Building and the Use of ICT in Boundary-Crossing Virtual Teams: A Facilitators Perspective', *Journal of Information Technology*, 16: 205–20.

Pavitt, K. (1984). 'Sectoral Patterns of Technical Change: Towards a Taxonomy and a Theory', *Research Policy*, 13: 343–73.

Pawlovsky, P. (2001). 'The Treatment of Organizational Learning in Management Science', in M. Dierkes, A. Bertoin Antal, J. Child, and I. Nonaka (eds.), *Handbook of Organizational Learning and Knowledge*. Oxford: Oxford University Press, 61–88.

Pedler, M., Burgoyne, J., and Boydell, T. (1997). *The Learning Company: A Strategy for Sustainable Development* (2nd ed.). London: McGraw-Hill.

Peters, T., and Waterman, R. (1983). *In Search of Excellence: Lessons from America's Best-Run Companies*. New York: Warner Books.

Polanyi, M. (1958). *Personal Knowledge*. London: Routledge & Kegan Paul.

—— (1983). *The Tacit Dimension*. Gloucester, Mass: Peter Smith.

—— (1969). *Knowing and Being*. London: Routledge & Kegan Paul.

Porter, M. (1995). *The Competitive Advantage of Nations*. London: Macmillan.

Powell, W. (1990). 'Neither Market nor Hierarchy: Network Forms of Organization', in B. Staw and L. Cummings (eds.), *Research in Organizational Behaviour*: vol. 12. JAI Press, 295–336.

—— (1998). 'Learning From Collaboration: Knowledge and Networks in Biotechnology and Pharmaceuticals Industries', *California Management Review*, 40/3: 228–40.

—— Koput, K., and SmithDoerr, L. (1996). 'Interorganizational Collaboration and the Locus of Innovation: Networks of Learning in Biotechnology', *Administrative Science Quarterly*, 41/1: 116–45.

Prencipe, A., and Tell, F. (2001). 'Inter-Project Learning: Processes and Outcomes of Knowledge Codification in Project-Based Firms', *Research Policy*, 30: 1373–94.

Prichard, C. (2000). 'Know, Learn and Share! The Knowledge Phenomenon and the Construction of a Consumptive-Communicative Body', in C. Prichard, R. Hull, M. Chumer, and H. Willmott (eds.), *Managing Knowledge: Critical Investigations of Work and Learning*. London: Macmillan, 176–98.

Quinn, B., Anderson, P., and Finkelstein, S. (1996). 'Managing Professional intellect: Making the Most of the Best', *Harvard Business Review*, April–May: 71–80.

Rabinow, P. (1991). *The Foucault Reader*. London: Penguin Books.

Raelin, J. (1997). 'A Model of Work-Based Learning', *Organization Science*, 8/6: 563–78.

Reed, M. (2000). 'In Praise of Duality and Dualism: Rethinking Agency and Structure in Organisation Theory', in S. Ackroyd and S. Fleetwood (eds.), *Realist Perspectives on Management and Organisations*. London: Routledge, 45–65.

Reich, R. (1991). *The Work of Nations: Preparing Ourselves for 21st-Century Capitalism*. London: Simon & Schuster.

Ribiere, V. (2001). *Assessing Knowledge Management Initiative Success as a Function of Organizational Culture*, PhD Dissertation, George Washington University (downloaded from www.km.gwu.edu—August 2002).

—— and Sitar, A. (2003). 'Critical Role of Leadership in Nurturing a Knowledge-Supporting Culture', *Knowledge Management Research & Practice*, 1/1: 39–48.

Rifkin, J. (2000). *The End of Work: The Decline of the Global Workforce and the Dawn of the Post-Market Era*. London: Penguin.

Roberts, J. (2000). 'From Know-How to Show-How? Questioning the Role of Information and Communication Technologies in Knowledge Transfer', *Technology Analysis and Strategic Management*, 12/4: 429–43.

Robertson, M., and O'Malley Hammersley, G. (2000). 'Knowledge Management Practices within a Knowledge-Intensive Firm: The Significance of the People Management Dimension', *Journal of European Industrial Training*, 24/2–4: 241–53.

—— Sorensen, C., and Swan, J. (2001). 'Survival of the Leanest: Intensive Knowledge Work and Groupware Adaptation', *Information Technology & People*, 14/4: 334–52.

—— and Swan, J. (2003). ' "Control—What control?" Culture and Ambiguity within a Knowledge Intensive Firm', *Journal of Management Studies*, 40/4: 831–58.

Robertson, S. (2002). 'A Tale of Two Knowledge-Sharing Systems', *Journal of Knowledge Management*, 6/3: 295–308.

Rousseau, D. (1990). 'New Hire Perceptions of their Own and their Employer's Obligations: A Study of Psychological Contracts', *Journal of Organizational Behaviour*, 11: 389–400.

Ruggles, R. (1998). 'The State of the Notion: Knowledge Management in Practice', *California Management Review*, 40/3: 80–9.

Rugman, A. (2000). *The End of Globalization*: London: Random House.

Rynes, S., Bartunek, J., and Daft, R. (2001). 'Across the Great Divide: Knowledge Creation and Transfer Between Practitioners and Academics', *Academy of Management Journal*, 44/2: 340–55.

Sackmann, S. (1992). 'Culture and Subculture: An Analysis of Organizational Knowledge', *Administrative Science Quarterly*, 34/March: 140–61.

Sadler, P. (2001). 'Leadership and Organizational Learning', in M. Dierkes, A. Bertoin Antal, J. Child, and I. Nonaka (eds.), *Handbook of Organizational Learning and Knowledge*. Oxford: Oxford University Press, 415–27.

Sakakibara, M., and Dodgson, M. (2003). 'Strategic Research Partnerships: Empirical Evidence from Asia', *Technology Analysis and Strategic Management*, 15/2: 227–45.

Salaman, G. (1974). *Community and Occupation: An Exploration of Work/Leisure Relationships*. Cambridge: Cambridge University Press.

—— (2001). 'A Response to Snell: The Learning Organization: Fact or Fiction?' *Human Relations*, 54/3: 343–60.

Sayer, A. (1992). *Method in Social Science*. London: Routledge.

Scarbrough, H. (1999). 'Knowledge as Work: Conflicts in the Management of Knowledge Workers', *Technology Analysis and Strategic Management*, 11/1: 5–16.

—— and Carter, C. (2000). Investigating Knowledge Management. London: CIPD.

—— Swan, J., and Preston, J. (1999). *Knowledge Management: A Literature Review*, London: Institute of Personnel and Development.

—— —— (2001). 'Explaining the Diffusion of Knowledge Management', *British Journal of Management*, 12: 3–12.

—— and Terry, M. (1998). 'Forget Japan: The Very British Response to Lean Production', *Employee Relations*, 20/3: 224–36.

Scase, R. (2001). 'Why We're so Clock Wise', *Observer*, 26 August, business section.

Schein, D. (1985). *Organizational Culture and Leadership*. London: Jossey-Bass.

Scherer, K., and Tran, V. (2001). 'Effects of Emotion on the Process of Organizational Learning', in M. Dierkes, A. Bertoin Antal, J. Child, and I. Nonaka (eds.), *Handbook of Organizational Learning and Knowledge*. Oxford: Oxford University Press, 369–94.

Schultze, U. (2000). 'A Confessional Account of an Ethnography about Knowledge Work', *MIS Quarterly*, 24/1: 3–41.

—— and Boland, R. (2000). 'Knowledge Management Technology and the Reproduction of Knowledge Work Practices', *Journal of Strategic Information Systems*, 9: 193–212.

—— and Leidner, D. (2002). 'Studying Knowledge Management in Information Systems Research: Discourses and Theoretical Assumptions', *MIS Quarterly*, 26/3: 213–42.

Senge, P. (1990). *The Fifth Discipline*. New York: Doubleday.

Senker, J., and Faulkner, W. (1996). 'Networks, Tacit Knowledge and Innovation', in R. Coombs et al. (eds.), *Technological Collaboration: The Dynamics of Co-operation in Industrial Innovation*. Cheltenham, UK: Edward Elgar, 76–97.

Shrivastava, P. (1983). 'A Typology of Organizational Learning Systems', *Journal of Management Studies*, 20: 7–28.

Skyrme, D., and Amidon, D. (1997). 'The Knowledge Agenda', *Journal of Knowledge Management*, 1/1: 27–37.

Slappendel, C. (1996). 'Perspectives on Innovation in Organizations', *Organization Studies*, 17/1: 107–29.

Slaughter, S., and Leslie, L. (1997). *Academic Capitalism*. Baltimore: John Hopkins University.

Smithson, J., and Lewis, S. (2000). 'Is Job Security Changing the Psychological Contract?' *Personnel Review*, 29/6: 680–702.

Snell, R. (2001). 'Moral Foundations of the Learning Organization', *Human Relations*, 54/3: 319–42.

Soderberg, A-M., and Holden, N. (2002). 'Rethinking Cross-Cultural Management in a Globalizing Business World', *International Journal of Cross Cultural Management*, 2/1: 103–21.

Sole, D., and Edmondson, A. (2002). 'Situated Knowledge and Learning in Dispersed Teams', *British Journal of Management*, 13: S17–34.

Somers, M. (1995). 'Organizational Commitment, Turnover and Absenteeism: An Examination of Direct and Interaction Effects', *Journal of Organizational Behaviour*, 16: 49–58.

Soo, C., Devinney, T., Midgely, D., and Deering, A. (2002). 'Knowledge Management: Philosophy, Processes, and Pitfalls', *California Management Review*, 44/4: 129–50.

Sorge, A. (1991). 'Strategic Fit and Societal Effects: Interpreting Cross-National Comparisons of Technology', *Organization Studies*, 12/2: 161–90.

Spender, J-C. (1996). 'Organizational Knowledge, Learning and Memory: Three Concepts in Search of a Theory', *Journal of Organizational Change Management*, 9/1: 63–78.

Stamps, D. (2000). 'Communities of Practice: Learning is Social, Training is Irrelevant?', in E. Lesser, M. Fontaine, and J. Slusher (eds.), *Knowledge and Communities*. Oxford: Butterworth-Heinemann, 53–64.

Stanworth, C. (1997). 'Telework and the Information Age', *New Technology, Work and Employment*, 13/1: 51–62.

Staples, D., Hulland, J., and Higgins, C. (1999). 'A Self-Efficacy Theory Explanation for the Management of Remote Workers in Virtual Organizations', *Organization Science*, 10/6: 758–76.

Starbuck, W. (1993). 'Keeping a Butterfly and an Elephant in a House of Cards: the Elements of Exceptional Success', *Journal of Management Studies*, 30/6: 885–921.

—— and Milliken, F. (1988). 'Challenger: Fine Tuning the Odds until Something Breaks', *Journal of Management Studies*, 25/4: 319–40

Steinmueller, W. (2000). 'Will New Information and Communication Technologies Improve the Codification of Knowledge?' *Industrial and Corporate Change*, 9/2: 361–76.

Sternberg, R. (1999). 'Innovation Linkages and Proximity: Empirical Results from Recent Surveys of Small and Medium Sized Firms in German Regions', *Regional Studies*, 33/6: 529–40.

Stevens, J., and Bagby, J. (2001). 'Knowledge Transfer from Universities to Business: Returns for All Stakeholders?' *Organization*, 8/2: 259–68.

Storey, J., and Barnett, E. (2000). 'Knowledge Management Initiatives: Learning from Failure', *Journal of Knowledge Management*, 4/2: 145–56.

—— and Quintas, P. (2001). 'Knowledge Management and HRM', in J. Storey (ed.), *Human Resource Management: A Critical Text*, London: Thomson Learning 339–63.

Sturdy, A., and Gabriel, Y. (2000). 'Missionaries, Mercenaries or Car Salesmen? MBA Teaching in Malaysia', *Journal of Management Studies*, 37/7: 979–1002.

Sturges, J., and Guest, D. (2001). 'Don't Leave Me This Way! A Qualitative Study of Influences on Organizational Commitment and Turnover Intentions of Graduates Early in their Career', *British Journal of Guidance and Counselling*, 29/4: 447–62.

Subramaniam, M., and Venkatraman, N. (2001). 'Determinants of Transnational New Product Development Capability: Testing the Influence of Transferring and Deploying Tacit Overseas Knowledge', *Strategic Management Journal*, 22: 359–78.

—— Rosenthal, S., and Hatten, K. (1998). 'Global New Product Development: Preliminary Findings and Research Propositions', *Journal of Management Studies*, 35/6: 773–96.

Suchman, L. (2003). 'Organizing Alignment: The Case of Bridge-Building', in D. Nicolini, S. Gherardi, and D. Yanow (eds.), *Knowing in Organizations: A Practice-Based Approach*. London: M. E. Sharpe.

Suddaby, R., and Greenwood, R. (2001). 'Colonizing Knowledge: Commodification as a Dynamic of Jurisdictional Expansion in Professional Service Firms', *Human Relations*, 54/7: 933–53.

Swan, J., and Scarbrough, H. (2001). 'Editorial: Knowledge Management: Concepts and Controversies', *Journal of Management Studies*, 38/7: 913–21.

Swan, J., Newell, S., Scarborough, H., and Hislop, D. (1999). 'Knowledge Management and Innovations: Networks and Networking', *Journal of Knowledge Management*, 3/4: 262–75.

Swart, J., and Kinnie, N. (2003). 'Sharing Knowledge in Knowledge-Intensive Firms', *Human Resource Management Journal*, 13/2: 60–75.

Symon, G. (2000). 'Information and Communication Technologies and the Network Organization: A Critical Analysis', *Journal of Occupational and Organizational Psychology*, 73: 389–414.

Szulanski, G. (1996). 'Exploring Internal Stickiness: Impediments to the Transfer of Best Practice within the Firm', *Strategic Management Journal*, 17 (Winter Special Issue), 27–43.

Tampoe, M. (1993). 'Motivating Knowledge Workers: The Challenge for the 1990s', *Long Range Planning*, 26/3: 49–55.

Taylor, B., Elger, T., and Fairbrother, P. (1994). 'Transplants and Emulators: The Fate of the Japanese Model in British Electronics, in T. Elger and C. Smith (eds.), *Global Japanization? The Transnational Transformation of the Labour Process*. London: Routledge, 196–225.

Taylor, P., and Bain, P. (1999). ' "An Assembly Line in the Head": Work and Employee Relations in a Call Centre', *Industrial Relations Journal*, 30/2: 101–17.

Taylor, S. (1998). 'Emotional Labour and the New Workplace', in Thompson, P., and Warhurst, C. (ed.) *Workplaces of the Future*. London: Macmillan, 84–103.

Tell, J. (2000). 'Learning Networks: A Metaphors for Inter-Organizational Development in SME's', *Enterprise and Innovation Management Studies*, 1/3: 281–302.

Tenkasi, R., and Boland, R. (1996). 'Exploring Knowledge Diversity in Knowledge Intensive Firms: A New Role for Information Systems', *Journal of Organizational Change Management*, 9/1: 79–91.

Thomas, J., Sussman, S., and Henderson, J. (2003). 'Understanding "Strategic Learning": Linking Organizational Learning, Knowledge Management and Sensemaking', *Organization Science*, 1/3: 331–45.

Thompson, P., Warhurst, C., and Callaghan, G. (2001). 'Ignorant Theory and Knowledgeable Workers: Interrogating the Connections Between Knowledge, Skills and Services', *Journal of Management Studies*, 38/7: 923–42.

Tidd, J., Bessant, J., and Pavitt, K. (2001). *Managing Innovation: Integrating Technological, Market and Organizational Change*, (2nd edn.). Chichester: John Wiley.

Tregaskis, O. (2003). 'Learning Networks, Power and Legitimacy in Multinational Subsidiaries', *International Journal of Human Resource Management*, 14/3: 431–47.

Trist, E., and Bamforth, K. (1951). 'Some Social and Psychological Consequences of the Longwall Methods of Coal-Getting', *Human Relations*, 4: 3–38.

Trowler, P. (2001). 'Captured by the Discourse? The Socially Constitutive Power of New Higher Education Discourse in the UK', *Organization*, 8/2: 183–201.

—— and Turner, G. (2002). 'Exploring the Hermeneutic Foundation of University Life: Deaf Academics in a Hybrid "Community of Practice" ', *Higher Education*, 43: 227–56.

Tsai, W. (2001). 'Knowledge Transfer in Intraorganizational Networks: Effects of Network Position and Absorptive Capacity on Business Unit Innovation and Performance', *Academy of Management Journal*, 44/5: 996–1004.

Tsang, E. (1997). 'Organizational Learning and the Learning Organization: A Dichotomy between Prescriptive and Descriptive Research', *Human Relations*, 50/1: 73–89.

Tsoukas, H. (1996). 'The Firm as a Distributed Knowledge System: A Constructionist Approach', *Strategic Management Journal*, 17 (Winter Special Issue), 11–25.

—— (2000). 'What is Management? An Outline of a Metatheory', in S. Ackroyd and S. Fleetwood (eds.), *Realist Perspectives on Management and Organisations*. London: Routledge, 26–44.

Van der Velden, M. (2002). 'Knowledge Facts, Knowledge Fiction: The Role of ICTs in Knowledge Management for Development', *Journal of International Development*, 14: 25–37.

Van Maanen, J., and Barley, S. (1984). 'Occupational Communities: Culture and Control in Organizations', in Straw, B., and Cummings, L. (eds.), *Research in Organizational Behaviour*. London: JAI Press, 287–365.

—— and Laurent, A. (1993). 'The Flow of Culture: Some Notes on Globalization and the Multinational Corporation', in S. Ghoshal and E. Westney (eds.), *Organization Theory and the Multinational Corporation*. New York: St Martins Press, 275–312.

Van Wijk, R., and van den Bosch, F. (2000). 'The Emergence and Development of Internal Networks and their Impact on Knowledge Flows: The Case of Rabobank Group', in A. Pettigrew and E. Fenton (eds.), *The Innovating Organization*. London: Sage, 144–77.

Vince, R. (2001). 'Power and Emotion in Organizational Learning', *Human Relations*, 54/10: 1325–51.

—— Sutcliffe, K., and Olivera, F. (2002). 'Organizational Learning: New Direction', *British Journal of Management*, 13: S1–6.

Von Hippel, E. (1976). 'The Dominant Role of Users in the Scientific Instrument Innovation Process', *Research Policy*, 5: 212–39.

—— (1988). *The Sources of Innovation*. Oxford: Oxford University Press.

Von Krogh, G., and Roos, J. (1996). *Managing Knowledge: Perspectives on Cooperation and Competition*. London: Sage.

—— Ichijo, K., and Nonaka, I. (2000). *Enabling Knowledge Creation: How to Unlock the Mystery of Tacit Knowledge and Release the Power of Innovation*. Oxford: Oxford University Press.

Walsham, G. (2001). 'Knowledge Management: The Benefits and Limitations of Computer Systems', *European Management Journal*, 19/6: 599–608.

Ward, A. (2000). 'Getting Strategic Value from Constellations of Communities', *Strategy and Leadership*, 28/2: 4–9.

Webster, F. (1996). *Theories of the Information Society*. London: Routledge.

Weick, K., and Westley, F. (1996). 'Organizational Learning: Affirming an Oxymoron', in S. Clegg, C. Nord, and W. Nord (eds.), *Handbook of Organization Studies*. London: Sage, 440–58.

Wenger, E. (1998). *Communities of Practice: Learning, Meaning and Identity*. Cambridge: Cambridge University Press.

—— and Snyder, W. (2000). 'Communities of Practice: the Organizational Frontier', *Harvard Business Review*, 78/1: 139–45.

—— McDermott, R., and Snyder, W. (2002). *Cultivating Communities of Practice*. Boston, Mass: Harvard Business School Press.

Werr, A., and Stjernberg, T. (2003). 'Exploring Management Consulting Firms as Knowledge Systems', *Organization Studies*, 24/6: 881–908.

Whitley, R. (1987). 'Taking Firms Seriously as Economic Actors: Towards a Sociology of Firm Behaviour', *Organization Studies*, 8/2: 125–47.

—— (1990). 'East Asian Enterprise Structures and the Comparative Analysis of Business Organization', *Organization Studies*, 11/1: 47–74.

—— (1999). *Divergent Capitalisms: The Social Structuring and Change of Business Systems*. Oxford: Oxford University Press.

Willman, P., Fenton O'Creevy, M., Nicholson, N., and Soane, E. (2001). 'Knowing the Risks: Theory and Practice in Financial Market Trading', *Human Relations*, 54/7: 887–910.

Willmott, H. (1995). 'Managing the Academics: Commodification and Control in the Development of University Education in the U.K.', *Human Relations*, 48/9: 993–1027.

WIR (1999). *World Investment Report 1999: Foreign Direct Investment and the Challenge of Development*. New York: United Nations Conference on Trade and Development (UNCTAD), United Nations.

Wolfe, R. (1994). 'Organizational Innovation: Review, Critique and Suggested Research Directions', *Journal of Management Studies*, 31/3: 405–31.

Woolgar, S. 'Five Rules of Virtuality', in S. Woolgar (ed.), *Virtual Society? Technology, Cyberbole, Reality*. Oxford: Oxford University Press, 1–22.

Yahya, S., and Goh, W-K. (2002). 'Managing Human Resources towards Achieving Knowledge Management', *Journal of Knowledge Management*, 6/5: 457–68.

YliRenko, H., Autio, E., and Sapienza, H. (2001). 'Social Capital, Knowledge Acquisition, and Knowledge Exploitation in Young Technology Based Firms', *Strategic Management Journal*, 22: 587–614.

Zack, M. (1999). 'Developing a Knowledge Strategy', *California Management Review*, 41/3: 125–45.

Zietsma, C., Winn, M., Branzei, O., and Vertinsky, I. (2002). 'The War of the Woods: Facilitators and Impediments of Organizational learning Processes', *British Journal of Management*, 13: S61–74.

Zuboff, S. (1998). *In the Age of the Smart Machine: The Future of Work and Power*. Oxford: Heinemann Professional.

Zucker, L. (1986). 'Production of Trust: Institutional Sources of Economic Structure, 1840–1920', in B. Staw and L. Cummings (eds.), *Research in Organisational Behaviour*, Greenwich, Conn.: JAI, 53–111.

■ INDEX

A

Absorptive capacity, innovation
168–70
Assets, knowledge 164
Autonomy
knowledge workers 228,231
practice-based perspectives
35–6

B

Boundary objects, communities of
practice 82–3
Business schools 246–7
Business strategies 124–7

C

Call centers, conflated knowledge
work 6–7
Codification
knowledge-intensive
firms 225
objectivist perspectives 23–5
Collective knowledge. *see* Group
knowledge
Commitment,
employee retention 130–3
learning 150–1
Communities of practice
benefits *64*
central premisses 59–62
characteristics 58–9
conclusions 70, 84
disadvantages 67–70
formal work groups
distinguished *58*
importance 57–8
intra-community knowledge
63–5
management difficulties 65–7
organizational bases 62–3
processes 81–3
effective underpinning, *65*
Conduit model of sharing
illustration *22*
practice-based perspectives 37
Conflicting interests

communities of practice 67–70
employee relationships 88–90
knowledge-intensive firms
225–7
learning
emotional component 154–5
linking power and politics
151–3
motivation and sharing
groups and individuals
49–50
organizations 48–9
politics 90–3
power and politics linked, *92*
Consumption and production
cycle *243*
Contestibility, practice-based
perspectives 34–5
Contextual knowledge 219–21
Control. *see* Autonomy
Cross-boundary knowledge
82–3
Crossan-Zeitsma learning
model *144*

D

Databases, objectivist perspectives
15–16, 23–5
Dispersed knowledge, N-V
organizations 183–5

E

Embeddedness
learning 143–6, 152
multinationals *203*
practice-based perspectives
28–30
socio-cultural factors 33
Embodiment
communities of practice 60
practice-based perspectives 31
Emotional component of learning
154–5
Employees
capitalism *90*
conflicts 48–9
fairness 50–1

knowledge-intensive firms
226–7
knowledge workers
conclusions 232–3
cultural ambiguities 222–3
definition and characteristics 217–19
employment growth 7–8
HRM policies 231–2
management 228
processes 224–7
relevance of power and conflict 89–90
retention of employees
228–9
rise in importance 216–17
scope 215–16
theoretical and contextual
knowledge 219–21
types of knowledge 223–4
willingness to participate
227
learning 150–1
motivation and sharing 46–8
N-V organizations 187–92
power, status and expertise
53–4
relevance of power and conflict
88–90
retention
commitment and psycho-
logical contract 130–3
HRM 130–3
knowledge workers 228–9
strategies *229*
trust 51–2
visibility of interactions 53
Employment growth, knowledge
workers 7
Epistemologies
generally 13–14
knowledge 223–4
learning *142*
objectivist perspectives 16–18
practice-based perspectives
27–8
Expertise, motivation for sharing
53–4
Explicit knowledge
conceptual assets 164

Explicit knowledge (*cont.*)
objectivist perspectives 18–19
practice-based perspectives
30–1
sharing 21–3
systemic assets 164

F

Facilitation. *see* Processes

G

Group knowledge
communities of practice 59–62
individual knowledge
distinguished 19–21
motivation and sharing 49–50
socio-cultural factors 33

H

Human resource management
(HRM)
attitudes to knowledge and
learning 133–6
conclusions 136
employee relationships 130–3
knowledge workers 231–2
linking strategies 124–7
motivation for sharing 52–3
scope 123–4
shared cultures 127–30

I

Identity
communities of practice 61, 69
intercommunity knowledge
76–7, 80–1
N-V organizations 190–2
Indeterminacy of practice 31
Individual knowledge, group
knowledge distinguished
19–21
Information and communication
technologies (ICT)
alternative design philosophy
119
conclusions 119–20
dispersed knowledge *184*
evolution of power 99–101
implementation, early methods
117–19
innovation 160

media richness 112–14
N-V organizations 192–3
objectivist perspectives 15–16,
23–5, 106–9
practice-based perspectives
109–17
processes *107*
roles *108*
scope 105–6
trust 114–17
Innovation
boundaries *172*
characteristics 158–60
characteristics of knowledge
165–7
communities of practice
63–5
conclusions 173–4
interactive process 160–3
knowledge creation 163–5
knowledge-intensive firms
224–5
network dynamics 167–74
obstacles to success *42*
politics 91
power and networks 173
processes 167–74
characteristics of knowledge
165–7
network dynamics 168–70
scope 157–8
typical components *159, 160*
Intercommunity knowledge
characteristics 75–80
importance 73–5
socio-cultural factors 80–1
Intra-community knowledge,
communities of practice
63–5

K

Knowledge
creation 163–5
epistemology 13–14
explicit knowledge
conceptual assets 164
objectivist perspectives
18–19
practice-based perspectives
30–1
sharing 21–3
systemic assets 164
group knowledge
communities of practice
59–62

individual knowledge distinguished 19–21
motivation and sharing
49–50
socio-cultural factors 33
HRM attitudes to knowledge
and learning 133–6
innovation 165–7
intensiveness 221
intercommunity knowledge
characteristics 75–80
importance 73–5
socio-cultural factors 80–1
intra-community knowledge
63–5
knowledge-intensive firms
223–4
objectivist perspectives
conclusions 25–6, 39
epistemology 16–18
individual and group knowledge distinguished 19–21
interrelation with data and
information 15–16
processes 23–5
sharing 21–3
tacit and explicit knowledge
distinguished 18–19
as power 94–9
practice-based perspectives
conclusions 39
contestability 34–5
embeddedness 28–30
embodiment 31
epistemology 27–8
management and sharing
36–9
multidimensionality 33
organizational bases 35–6
socio-cultural factors 32–3
tacit knowledge
conversion to explicit
knowledge 23–5
experiential assets 164
innovation 165–7
objectivist perspectives 18,
18–19
practice-based perspectives
30–1
privileging 7
sharing 21–3
theoretical knowledge 7,
219–21
Knowledge-intensive firms. *see*
Knowledge workers
Knowledge management
business schools 246–7

communities of practice 65–7, 81–3
conclusions 247–8
contradiction in terms 238–41
critical perspectives 8–9
criticisms of analytical frameworks 7–8
fashionable growth of interest 240–1
importance 1–3
intensification in post-industrial societies 3–6
key themes 9–10
knowledge workers 228
linking strategies 124–7
practice-based perspectives 36–9
production and consumption 242–5
reflections on literature 236–8
service industries 6–7
Knowledge workers
conclusions 232–3
cultural ambiguities 222–3
definition and characteristics 217–19
employment growth 7–8
HRM policies 231–2
management 228
processes
categories 224–5
conflicting interests 225–7
relevance of power and conflict 89–90
retention of employees 228–9
rise in importance 216–17
scope 215–16
theoretical and contextual knowledge 219–21
types of knowledge 223–4
willingness to participate 227

L

'Language game' models 37
Learning
alternative perspectives 146–55
characteristics 142–3
communities of practice 61–2, 63–5
company framework 148
conclusions 155
dynamics 143–6
HRM 133–6
linking power and politics 152
practice-based perspectives 38

processes 145
relevant factors 156
scope 141–2
typologies 142
Literature
growth 3
neglect of socio-cultural factors 44–5
quality and diversity 236–8

M

Media richness 112–14
Motivation for sharing
conclusions 54–5
conflicts within groups and individuals 49–50
employee relationships 46–8
fairness 50–1
HRM 125
human resource management (HRM) 52–3
intra-organizational conflicts 48–9
neglect of socio-cultural factors 44–5
organizational knowledge 46
power, status and expertise 53–4
trust 51–2
visibility of interactions 53
Multidimensionality, practice-based perspectives 33
Multinationals
centralized hierarchy 200
conclusions 212–13
decentralized hierarchy 201
importance 197–8
size 203–8
socio-cultural factors 208–10
structuring and dynamics 198–203

N

Network/virtual (N-V) organizations
conclusions 194
cross-boundary processes 186–92
definition and characteristics 180–3
dispersed knowledge 183–5
examples 179
hierarchical structures compared 181

ICT processes 192–3
innovation 167–74, 173

O

Objectivist perspectives
conclusions 25–6, 39
epistemology 16–18
ICT 106–9
individual and group knowledge distinguished 19–21
interrelation of knowledge and information 15–16
processes 23–5
sharing 21–3
tacit and explicit knowledge distinguished 18–19
Organizations
conflicts 48–9
global multinationals
conclusions 212–13
importance 197–8
size 203–8
socio-cultural factors 208–10
structuring and dynamics 198–203
HRM
attitudes to knowledge and learning 133–6
conclusions 136
retention, commitment and psychological contract 130–6
scope 123–4
shared cultures 127–30
innovation
characteristics 158–60
characteristics of knowledge 165–7
conclusions 173–4
interactive process 160–3
knowledge creation 163–5
network dynamics 167–74
power and networks 173
processes 167–74
scope 157–8
knowledge-intensive firms
conclusions 232–3
cultural ambiguities 222–3
definition and characteristics 217–19
HRM policies 231–2
management 228
processes 224–7

Organizations (*cont.*)
  retention of employees
    228–9
  rise of knowledge workers
    216–17
  scope 215–16
  theoretical and contextual
    knowledge 219–21
  types of knowledge 223–4
  willingness to participate
    227
learning
  alternative perspectives
    146–55
  characteristics 142–3
  conclusions 155
  dynamics 143–6
  relevant factors *156*
  scope 141–2
linking strategies 124–7
motivation for sharing 46–55
network/virtual (N-V)
  conclusions 194
  cross-boundary processes
    186–92
  definition and characteris-
    tics 180–3
  dispersed knowledge 183–5
  examples 179
  ICT processes 192–3
practice-based perspectives
  communities of practice
    62–3
  knowledge 35–6
  management and sharing
    36–9
types *178*

P

Pay, HRM attitudes to knowledge
    and learning 133–6
Personal resources *95*
Policies
  employee retention 130–3
  HRM
    attitudes to knowledge and
      learning 133–6
    conclusions 136
    employee relationships
      130–3
    knowledge workers 231–2
    linking strategies 124–7
    motivation for sharing 52–3
    scope 123–4
    shared cultures 127–30

knowledge-intensive firms
    231–2
strategies
  HRM 124–7
  learning company frame-
    work *148*
  resources 126
  retention of employees *229*
Politics
  learning 151–3
  linking learning and power
    152
  power and conflict linked *92*
  relevance of power and conflict
    90–3
Positional resources *95*
Positivism 17
Post-industrial societies
  changing characteristics 5
  characteristics *4*
  intensification of knowledge
    3–6
Power
  communities of practice 67–70
  conceptualization and
    importance 93–4
  conclusions 101–2
  cyclical relationship *94*
  defined
    evolution of social relations
      99–101
    as resource 94–9
  employee relationships 88–90
  importance 87–8
  innovation 173
  learning 151–3
  linking learning and politics
    152
  motivation for sharing 53–4
  politics 90–3
  politics and conflict linked *92*
Practice-based perspectives
  communities of practice
    59–62
  conclusions 39
  contestability 34–5
  dispersed knowledge 183–5
  embeddedness 28–30
  embodiment 31
  epistemology 27–8
  ICT 109–17
  management and sharing 36–9
  multidimensionality 33
  organizational bases 35–6
  socio-cultural factors 32–3
  tacit and explicit knowledge
    30–1

Processes
  communities of practice 63–5,
    65, 81–3
  contradiction in terms 238–41
  cyclical relationship of power
    94
  global multinationals
    conclusions 212–13
    importance 194
    size 203–8
    socio-cultural factors 208–10
    structuring and dynamics
      198–203
  HRM for knowledge workers
    231–2
  ICT
    objectivist perspectives
      106–9
    practice-based perspectives
      109–17
    scope 105–6
    trust 114–17
  innovation
    characteristics of knowledge
      165–7
    interaction 160–3
    network dynamics 168–70
  intercommunity knowledge
    sharing
    characteristics 75–80
    importance 73–5
  knowledge-intensive firms
    categories 224–5
    conflicting interests 225–7
    willingness to participate 227
  learning *145*
  N-V organizations 186–92
  outcomes and objectives *240*
  relevance of power and conflict
    defining power 93–101
    employee relationships
      88–90
    politics 90–3
Production and consumption
    cycle *243*
Psychological contract, employee
    retention 130–3

R

Realism, power and conflict 89
Recruitment, knowledge workers
    231
Relationship management,
    communities of
    practice 82

Research and development (R & D), interaction with innovation 161–2
Resources
　knowledge as power *95*
　linking strategies 126
Retention of employees
　HRM 130–3
　knowledge workers 228–9
　strategies *229*
Rewards
　HRM attitudes to knowledge and learning 133–6
　knowledge workers 231

S

Service industries, conflated knowledge work 6–7
Sharing
　communities of practice
　　central premisses 59–62
　　characteristics 58–9
　　conclusions 70, 84
　　disadvantages 67–70
　　importance 57–8
　　intra-community knowledge 63–5
　　management difficulties 65–7
　　organizational bases 62–3
　　processes 81–3
　conduit model *22*, 37
　global multinationals 208–10
　group knowledge
　　communities of practice 59–62
　　individual knowledge distinguished 19–21
　　motivation and sharing 49–50
　　socio-cultural factors 33
　ICT 117–19
　innovation
　　boundaries *172*
　　tacit knowledge 165–7
　intercommunity knowledge

characteristics 75–80
　importance 73–5
　socio-cultural factors 80–1
knowledge-intensive firms 225
motivation
　conflicts within groups and individuals 49–50
　employee relationships 46–8
　fairness 50–1
　human resource management (HRM), 52–3
　intra-organizational conflicts 48–9
　neglect of socio-cultural factors 44–5
　organizational bases 46
　power, status and expertise 53–4
　trust 51–2
　visibility of interactions 53
N-V organizations 186–92
objectivist perspectives 21–3
practice-based perspectives 36–9
Size
　multinational processes 203–8
　social relations *205*
Socio-cultural factors
　communities of practice 62
　evolution of power 99–101
　global multinationals
　　sharing 208–10
　　size *205*
　group knowledge 21
　HRM 127–30
　ICT
　　media richness 112–14
　　trust 114–17
　intercommunity knowledge 80–1
　motivation for sharing 52–3
　N-V organizations 190–2
　neglect by first-generation literature 44–5
　practice-based perspectives 32–3, 38–9

Stage model theory, innovation 159, 160–1
Status, motivation for sharing 53–4
Strategies
　HRM 124–7
　learning company framework *148*
　resources 126
　retention of employees *229*

T

Tacit knowledge
　conversion to explicit knowledge 23–5
　experiential assets 164
　innovation 165–7
　objectivist perspectives 18, 18–19
　practice-based perspectives 30–1
　privileging 7
　sharing 21–3
Theoretical knowledge, privileging 7, 219–21
Training, HRM attitudes to knowledge and learning 133–6
Trust
　ICT 114–17
　intercommunity knowledge 80–1
　learning 150–1
　motivation for sharing 51–2
　N-V organizations 190–2
Typologies. *see* Epistemologies

W

Work groups
　.*see also* Group knowledge
　communities of practice distinguished *58*